A CREDIT TO THEIR COMMUNITY

A CREDIT TO THEIR COMMUNITY

Jewish Loan Societies

in the United States

1880-1945

SHELLY TENENBAUM

Wayne State University Press Detroit

Library of Congress Cataloging-in-Publication Data

Tenenbaum, Shelly.

A credit to their community : Jewish loan societies in the United
States, 1880–1945 / Shelly Tenenbaum.

p.   cm. — (American Jewish civilization series)

Includes bibliographical references and index.

ISBN 0-8143-2287-5 (alk. paper)

1. Credit unions—United States—History.   2. Jews—United States—
Societies, etc.—History.   I. Title.   II. Series.

HG2037.T46   1993

334′.22′089924073--dc20   92-47377

❦

DESIGNER: S.R. TENENBAUM

COVER ART: ILLUSTRATION COURTESY OF THE ARTIST,
© 1987 BY ILENE WINN-LEDERER.

To my parents

Lola and Henry Tenenbaum

American Jewish Civilization Series

Editors

Moses Rischin
San Francisco State University

Jonathan D. Sarna
Brandeis University

Books in this series

Contents

♦

Illustrations

9

Tables

11

Abbreviations

AHFL	Association of Hebrew Free Loans
AHMF	Abraham Haas Memorial Fund
BAC	Business Advisory Committee
BHBLA	Bachelors' Hebrew Benevolent Loan Association
CUNA	Credit Union National Association
FLA	Federated Loan Association
HFLA	Hebrew Free Loan Association
HFLS	Hebrew Free Loan Society
IWLA	Independent Workmen's Loan Association
JAIAS	Jewish Agricultural and Industrial Aid Society
JFLA	Jewish Free Loan Association
JLF	Jewish Loan Fund
JLHA	Jewish Loan and Housing Association
JTS	Jewish Theological Seminary
JWS	Jewish Welfare Society
MCU	Massachusetts Credit Union
MCUA	Massachusetts Credit Union Association
MLA	Mutual Loan Association
MLS	Mastbaum Loan System
NCJC	National Conference of Jewish Charities
OWLA	Omaha Workmen's Loan Association
YIVO	Yiddish Scientific Institute

Acknowledgments

One of the most heartening aspects of working on this book was the encountering of so many generous individuals. I was touched by the interest that people exhibited in my work and by all the help that was extended to me. Months after meeting or interviewing someone, I would often receive a letter or a phone call with additional information. These gestures contributed to the substance of this work and maintained my enthusiasm for the project.

Marshall Sklare, of blessed memory, supervised my research when it began as a dissertation. His dedication to the sociological inquiry of American Jewish life has been a constant source of inspiration. I am particularly grateful to Calvin Goldscheider, who stimulated my thinking on ethnicity and contributed to the theoretical framework of the book. Ivan Light's pioneering research on ethnic enterprise shaped my interest in immigrant credit networks. His enthusiasm for my work encouraged me to transform the dissertation into a book. I thank Jonathan Sarna for being so generous with his time and knowledge. With his usual thoroughness, he suggested several helpful research avenues to explore and commented on previous drafts of the book.

Moses Rischin and Alice Friedman read drafts of the manuscript. I appreciate their comments. Arthur Evans, Director of Wayne State University Press, and Kathryn Wildfong, Managing Editor, patiently addressed my many queries and carefully supervised this book's production. Over the years I have also benefitted from the advice of Frank Adler, Asoka Bandarage, Edna Bonacich, Steven M. Cohen, Gordon Fellman, Marvin Fox, Lawrence Fuchs, Leon Jick, Stanley Lieberson, Jacob Marcus, Deborah Dash Moore, Abraham Peck, David Reimers, the late Joshua Rothenberg, Jeffrey Sammons, Michael Steinlauf, and Irving Zola. Archivists Nancy Becker (Western Reserve Historical Society), Eleanor Horvitz (Rhode Island Jewish Historical Society), Gina Hsin (American Jewish Historical Society), Gabriel Kirkpatrick (Credit Union National Association), the late Nathan Kaganoff (American Jewish Historical Society), Marsha Lotstein (Hartford Jewish Historical Society), Kevin Profitt (American Jewish Archives), Ruth Raphael (Western Jewish History Center), Lily Schwartz (Philadelphia Jewish Archives), and Norma Spungen (Chicago Jewish Archives) generously answered all my requests for aid. Oliver Pollack and Paul Levenson helped locate photographs. My research was also aided by the very able assistance of Peter Aladjem, Stephanie Fine, Justine Kalas, Debbie Katz, and Jamie Rosenthal. I thank Dan Perlman for his photographic expertise and Marilyn Halter for inventing the title of this book.

I am indebted to the staff and officers of several Hebrew free loan associations. Julius Blackman (San Francisco), Jules Feldman (Pittsburgh), Judah Gribetz (New York), Mark Meltzer (Los Angeles), Arnold Teitelbaum (New York) and Norma Williamson (Pittsburgh) welcomed me into their busy offices, provided me with photocopying facilities, and fed me valuable information. This book could not have been written without their cooperation. A personal connection with the Gribetz family was actually instrumental for the conception of this project. I first learned about Hebrew free loan societies some twenty years ago from Bruce and Arthur Gribetz, who told me about the activities of their grandfather Abraham Gribetz, long manager of the New York Hebrew Free Loan Society.

Several institutions provided me with critical support during various stages of the research process. I thank the American Jewish Archives, Clark University, Cohen Center for Modern Jewish Studies, Memorial Foundation for Jewish Culture, National Endowment for the Humanities, and National Foundation for Jewish Culture. The debt I owe these organizations is more than financial; the honor of receiving fellowships affirmed my own commitment to the project. During the academic year 1990–91, Radcliffe's Mary Ingraham Bunting Institute provided me with a peaceful place to work, as well as an opportunity to interact with an exciting group of scholars. My year at the Bunting Institute was a highlight of my academic career.

A close community of friends and family saw me through the various stages of writing this book. I thank you all for your love and friendship. Most of all, however, I am very grateful to Lynn Davidman, who was closely involved with this project from beginning to end. Lynn has been my intellectual partner since graduate school, and I am fortunate to be able to share my work with such a caring and wonderful person. Lynn graciously read successive drafts of the text and contributed to this book in many ways.

I cannot give enough thanks to my husband, Glenn Stevens, for his love, devotion, and ceaseless confidence in my work and abilities. I credit my son Jonathan for forcing me to complete the manuscript before his due date. His expected arrival was a far more effective deadline than any imposed by my editors. Finally, I thank my parents, to whom this book is dedicated with much love, for instilling in me a commitment to understand the world of Jews.

1

APPROACHES TO
ETHNICITY

"EVERY EVENING THE MARKET PEDDLERS
would stop in front of the office with their pushcarts or horse and
wagons to pay old debts and to make new loans, free of interest,"
reminisces Samuel Altman, a resident of Providence, Rhode Island.
Joseph Jagolizer, also from Providence, recollects how his father
borrowed regularly from the same Jewish loan association: "Was
that a busy place! Just like a bank. My father would go to Bazar's
Hall, where they were located, to borrow $50 every time, say if he
needed equipment in the blacksmith shop, or if he needed money
for something that would come up."[1] By supplying small entrepreneurs like the elder Jagolizer with necessary capital to start and
expand their businesses, Jewish loan societies facilitated the rise up
the economic ladder of late-nineteenth- and early-twentieth-century
Jews. Furthermore, these collective institutions were an important
feature of a cohesive ethnic economy in which Jewish factory owners
hired Jewish workers, Jewish retailers bought goods from Jewish
wholesalers, and Jewish shopkeepers relied on Jewish loan associations for funding.

Providence was only one of many communities that housed Jewish loan associations. They existed in the large urban centers of
New York, Chicago, Boston, and San Francisco, as well as in much
smaller communities such as Altoona, Pennsylvania; Lafayette, Indiana; Shreveport, Louisiana; and Elmira, New York. When the
masses of East European Jewish immigrants began to arrive in the

United States during the 1880s, they initially restricted their loan activity to recreating Hebrew free loan societies—institutions that loaned money without charging interest. Since at least the eighteenth century, Jews in Europe had established free loan associations that were based on biblical and talmudic injunctions to provide the Jewish poor with interest-free loans. By the early decades of the twentieth century, however, American Jews no longer limited themselves to traditional Hebrew free loan societies. They initiated new types of ethnic loan facilities that had no basis within Jewish culture and history: modern credit cooperatives, as well as remedial loan associations (philanthropic loan societies that charged interest fees).

Just as East European Jews had transported Hebrew free loan societies from their native homelands to the United States, other immigrant groups, such as Japanese and Chinese, included credit associations as part of their cultural baggage when they migrated to America.[2] Why did certain groups organize ethnic loan societies while others did not? And among groups that did form credit associations, why was there variation in the type of institution created? In order to answer these questions of differences in ethnic behavior, social scientists have developed two contrasting theoretical frameworks: cultural and contextual. A *cultural* interpretation stresses that groups' behaviors are based on traditions and values brought from their countries of origin; a *contextual* analysis explains ethnic conduct as immigrants' responses to conditions in their new societies.

In this book, I develop an analysis of Jewish immigrant loan activity that synthesizes these two theoretical perspectives. A cultural interpretation, with its assumption that American ethnic groups' behaviors are based on predisposing traits brought from their native homelands, is particularly helpful for understanding the emergence of Hebrew free loan societies, institutions that were unique to the Jewish community. This perspective, however, cannot account for the creation of new types of organizations for which there were no cultural antecedents. Contextual theory, with its emphasis on structural factors, can explain the formation of these ethnic institutions by relating the immigrants' behavior to the opportunities available in their new societies. This approach can help us understand how ethnic behavior changed during an immigrant group's transition between countries.

Ethnic Differences: Contrasting Perspectives

Ethnic differences abound in American society. Groups vary in terms of movement on the economic ladder, position on the political spectrum, and educational attainment. They also have a tendency to carve out their own economic niches. Contemporary Koreans in Los Angeles congregate in retail liquor shops; New England Greeks, in restaurants; and Chinese and Dominicans, in New York garment factories. Earlier in the century, a majority of gainfully employed Slavic and Hungarian men worked in the coal, iron and steel, metals, and slaughtering and meatpacking industries, while more than half of all Chinese earned their livelihood through restaurants and laundries. Jews in the United States, as well as in other regions of the world, were so well noted for their ethnic enterprises that when members of other ethnic groups succeeded in the business world, they, too became known as Jews. For example, Chinese immigrants in Southeast Asia were often called "the Jews of the East"; Asians in East Africa, "the Jews of Africa"; and Cubans, "the Jews of the Caribbean."[3] Explaining these and other ethnic differences poses a serious challenge to sociologists and historians of American ethnicity.

Most of the literature on ethnicity favors either a cultural interpretation or a contextual analysis. Until recently, advocates of cultural theory dominated the field. The most influential formulation of cultural theory was posited by Max Weber during the early years of the twentieth century in two essays that became *The Protestant Ethic and the Spirit of Capitalism*. Weber argued that religious values and orientations profoundly affected human behavior and thus institutional systems of society. He claimed that the predisposing values of Protestantism, particularly those of Puritanism, influenced the development of capitalism. Capitalism's motivating "spirit" of commitment and dedication to work, according to Weber, can be traced to the Protestant conviction that work is a means of glorifying God and that self-indulgence is a sin. Together, Weber reasons, these two tenets contributed to capital accumulation.[4]

Before Weber theorized about the connections between Protestant values and economic transformations, Werner Sombart had also attempted to identify the origins of the spirit of capitalism. For Sombart, however, Judaism, not Protestantism, exerted the important economic influence. According to his analysis, Puritanism was really a modified form of Judaism; hence, Judaism was the earlier source of the spirit of capitalism. Furthermore, Sombart saw many parallels between Jewish theology and capitalism. For example, both placed great emphasis on "the getting of money as a means to an end." In addition, Jewish law prescribed certain forms of rational economic conduct—self-control, circumspection, industry and thrift—which facilitated the development of capitalism.[5]

It is not my purpose to decide whether Protestantism or Judaism inspired the capitalist spirit. My concern is with Sombart's and Weber's use of religious orientations to understand human conduct. Sombart attributed Jewish business acumen to Jewish teachings, while Weber ascribed Protestant entrepreneurial success to Protestant values. While these early formulations of cultural theory were confined to analyzing the relationship between religious values and capitalist behavior, the application of this theoretical perspective was later extended by social scientists, who claimed that cultural characteristics of religious and national groups inclined members to behave in particular ways with respect to politics, family, education, and economics. During the early 1960s, sociologist Gerhard Lenski described how ethnic culture shaped group members' predispositions toward racial integration, freedom of speech, divorce, family solidarity, school attendance, college education, saving money, and belief in the American Dream.[6]

Contemporary sociologists and historians link the legacy of Irish political activity in America to their previous political experience in Ireland and the high incidence of Irish immigrant women domestics to a cultural sanction for this kind of work.[7] In contrast, an Italian cultural prohibition for women working in another family's home is correlated with the small number of female Italian servants: "No matter how poor, the Italian–American woman to this day does not work as a domestic. For to work in the house of another family (sometimes an absolute economic necessity in the old land) is seen as a usurpation of family loyalty by her family *and by her*" (emphasis original).[8]

A cultural analysis correlates varying degrees of ethnic success with ethnic values. Groups that arrive in the United States with values conducive to success move up the economic ladder, while those with a culture that does not embody "the capitalist spirit" lag behind. Mexican–Americans, some argue, lacked the cultural resources necessary for financial success. In their book on social stratification, authors Tamotsu Shibutani and Kian Kwan claim that Mexican culture discourages planning for the future and postponing gratification: "The Mexican milieu has long been overlaid with expectations of sudden injury, violence, or death; the history of Mexico is dotted with a succession of earthquakes, epidemics, and internal strife. Fatalism and indifference may appear irresponsible to outsiders; but when one cannot tell what tomorrow may bring, each person must live for the here and now."[9] In contrast to the experience of Mexicans, the economic success of Asian–Americans has been traced to their positive orientations toward hard work and education. Social scientists have argued that Japanese–Americans have inherited "an almost reverential attitude toward work," while Chinese–Americans' "respect for learning and for the scholar is a cultural heritage."[10]

Cultural approaches have been particularly common within discussions of Jewish economic mobility. Milton Gordon, one of this century's most esteemed sociologists of American ethnicity, utilized a cultural lens when he explained how Jews arrived in the United States with "the middle-class values of thrift, sobriety, ambition, desire for education, ability to postpone immediate gratifications for the sake of long-range goals, and aversion to violence already internalized."[11] Nathan Glazer argued, as did Sombart, that Judaism encouraged entrepreneurial attributes long before Protestantism. Hence, East European Jewish immigrants, according to Glazer, arrived in America with traits that facilitated a rapid economic climb:

> There is no question that Judaism emphasizes the traits that businessmen and intellectuals require, and has done so since at least 1,500 years before Calvinism. . . . The strong emphasis on learning and study can be traced that far back, too. The Jewish habits of foresight, care, moderation probably arose early during the two thousand years that Jews have lived primarily as strangers among other peoples.[12]

The popularity of the cultural perspective for understanding Jewish economic mobility is more than likely related to the lack of attention paid by academics to the existence of Jewish loan societies, as well as to other collectivist strategies. Since Jews worked so hard, practiced thrift, saved money, and postponed gratification, social historians and historical sociologists simply assumed that Jews relied exclusively on their own resources when they wanted to open their own businesses. This study of Jewish loan societies, however, suggests that collectivism was at least as important as individualism for Jewish economic development. Contextual analysis provides a helpful model for drawing attention away from individual motivations toward collective adaptations.[13]

Reacting against an often simplistic form of cultural determinism and an assumption that all members of an ethnic group behave monolithically, contextual theorists argue that economic and political structures are far more crucial than values for understanding ethnic differences.[14] For contextualists, American ethnicity "may have relatively little to do with Europe, Asia, or Africa, but much more to do with the exigencies of survival and the structure of opportunity in this country."[15] Within this framework, for example, Irish participation in urban politics is understood in terms of the expansion of city governments in the mid–nineteenth century and not as a reflection of a cultural aptitude for politics. According to contextual reasoning, even if Irish immigrants had arrived with a natural proclivity for politics but the political sector had not offered opportunity for occupational advancement, their cultural heritage would have counted for little. Similarly, the high concentration of Italians in construction, Poles in steel, and Jews in the garment trades can be understood in terms of the growth of these industries at the time that these groups arrived in the United States.

Ethnic differences in educational attainment have similarly been analyzed within a contextual model. In his sociohistorical study, *A Piece of the Pie: Blacks and White Immigrants Since 1880*, Stanley Lieberson highlights the importance of structural factors in his discussion of African–American educational levels. When educational opportunities were available to Southern blacks in the period immediately following the Civil War (an era labeled by historian C. Vann Woodward the period of "Forgotten Alternatives"), large numbers of blacks attended school. Over 60 percent of Southern black school children ages five through twelve were enrolled in school by 1865. It was not until a retrenchment in the commitment to equal education for blacks and whites set in during the last quarter of the nineteenth century that black educational advancement suffered enormously. When politicians cut the length of black school terms, the salaries of black teachers, and expenditures for black schools, black enrollments declined.[16] According to contextualists, it was not norms, values, or the legacy of slavery that should be correlated with low black educational rates; rather, it was an educational system based on inequality that was to blame. By the same contextual reasoning, a collective passion for learning was far less important to the high rates of Jewish college attendance than was the post–World War II need for an educated labor force. A maturing economy

> set in motion a long series of educational reforms leading to an expansion and overhaul of the nation's educational institutions. Especially in the northern industrial states where Jews were concentrated, there was a trend toward much heavier public investment in schools and colleges. The curricula were also changing away from their classical traditions toward science, vocational training, and professional education, and thus were more compatible with the talents and aspirations of children born outside the upper class.[17]

Advocates of structural analyses have recently challenged commonly held beliefs about the relationship between culture and family structure within the African–American community. For sociologist William Julius Wilson, the rise in single-parent families within the black community is "not a function of any inherent matriarchal tendency, but a rational, adaptational response to conditions of deprivation."[18] The sharp increase in black male unemployment rates, which are directly related to the flight of manufacturing jobs from urban centers, is the key to Wilson's analysis of why more black women are not marrying.

Rather than view ethnic solidarity as a cultural predisposition or as a primordial sentiment, contextual theorists argue that ethnic group solidarity will be maintained if two structural factors— residential and occupational concentration—are present. Ethnic neighborhoods, with their wide range of local institutions such as grocery stores, schools, churches, mutual aid societies, and newspapers, provide avenues for interpersonal networks. Similar occupational statuses foster similar life-styles, shared social and economic interests, and a high degree of interpersonal relationships. In his study of Chinese immigrants in the Caribbean, sociologist Orlando Patterson compares the rapid assimilation of Guyanese Chinese with the high rate of cultural exclusivity exhibited by Jamaican Chinese. Since both groups of Chinese came from the same region in China and therefore had identical cultural systems, Patterson discounted the role of values for understanding one group's assimilation pattern and the other's tendency toward solidarity. Instead, he attributed these differences to the varying opportunity structures found in the two countries. The wide range of occupational choices that were available in the Guyanese context facilitated "creolization and the abandonment of Chinese culture," while in Jamaica, the Chinese were concentrated in retail trade, which "allowed for, and reinforced, a choice of ethnic consolidation based on cultural distinctiveness."[19] Similarly, Edna Bonacich and John Modell found that Japanese–Americans exhibited strong degrees of solidarity as long as they were concentrated in small businesses. Once they spread throughout the corporate economy after World War II, however, their ethnic bonds weakened. In the conclusion to their book, *The Economic Basis of Ethnic Solidarity: Small Business in the Japanese American Community*, Bonacich and Modell write: "Ethnicity is not an eternal verity but a variable that is responsive to societal conditions, and that one very important condition is the economic position of the group in question. Ethnic affiliation is a resource that may be called upon to support certain economic interests. When those economic interests are no longer present, ethnicity is likely to subside in importance."[20]

The strength of the contextual perspective is its emphasis on change and variation. While cultural theorists view ethnicity as a constant, contextual theorists see ethnicity as an "emergent" phenomenon which varies depending on its interaction with social structural conditions. Sociologists William Yancey and Eugene Ericksen summarize the differences between their contextual approach and others' cultural interpretations.

> Rather than assume that the cultural heritage of all members of a particular group is transplanted from one social structure to another, we suggested that there is considerable evidence indicating that the impact of ethnic ancestry has varied over time, depending on the structural conditions which members of the group faced and the degree to which an ethnic group emerged as a social organization. It is precisely upon this point that we disagree with the approach to ethnicity which assumes that ethnic heritage is an ascribed monolith, the effects of which are the same for all immigrants, no matter what their positions were in the country of origin or destination . . . [A cultural approach] has ignored the dynamic and adaptive character of associations, interests, and identities, and thus has failed to consider the interdependence of these structures and the political economy which generates them.[21]

24

Since the mid-1970s the academic pendulum has shifted away from cultural interpretation and toward contextual analysis. The pendulum has swung so far, however, that culture has often been either neglected or completely discounted. When the role of culture is ignored, there is a tendency to view ethnics as passive agents who simply respond to the dictates of structural forces. Fortunately, there are several excellent studies that seriously discuss the interaction between values and structure and lead the way toward a balanced and comprehensive understanding of American ethnicity.[22] For example, in her analysis of predominately working-class East Central Europeans in Johnstown, Pennsylvania, historical sociologist Ewa Morawska pays attention to both limited regional economic opportunities and the immigrants' value system. Historian of education Joel Perlmann cautions us against trying to find "the single, consistently primary factor creating ethnic distinctiveness."[23] His comparative study of schooling among four ethnic groups in Providence, Rhode Island, serves as a model for understanding how a combination of factors such as culture, discrimination, and class shaped the respective educational experiences of Irish, Italians, Jews, and African–Americans between the late nineteenth century and the middle years of the Depression. This genre of scholarship, with its focus on both culture and context, has directly influenced my study of Jewish loan associations.

The interaction of culture—the values and traditions that East European Jews brought with them—with contextual factors (e.g., economic opportunities) shaped the emergence of Jewish loan societies in the United States. Although Hebrew free loan societies had clear cultural roots, they were not recreated simply because they had existed in the immigrants' countries of origin. In this volume, I argue that cultural patterns and institutions were transplanted only when they were appropriate in the American setting. Those that were incongruous with the new context were left behind. And when the American setting produced a need for new institutions and new types of behavior, immigrants were not restrained by their culture. American ethnics adapted their behavior to emerging social and economic circumstances.

The next chapter develops my analysis of the relative influences of culture and context on ethnic behavior by applying these two frameworks to an analysis of Jewish loan societies. How did Jewish tradition and history converge with American immigrant trends, business opportunities and banking practices to shape the emergence of these ethnic credit facilities? Chapters 3–6 focus on three different types of organizations: chapters 3–4 on Hebrew free loan societies; chapter 5 on philanthropic loan societies that charged small interest fees; and chapter 6 on credit cooperatives. Chapter 7 concludes the story of these ethnic institutions by analyzing their decline since the years of World War II and by providing a summary of the book's major findings.

A Note on Sources

Information on Jewish loan societies is scattered through a myriad of historical societies, libraries, and the offices of various credit organizations located throughout the country. Relevant records are housed at the American Jewish Archives (Cincinnati), the American Jewish Historical Society (Waltham, Massachusetts), the Credit Union National Association (Madison, Wisconsin), the Hartford Jewish Historical Society, Harvard University's Baker Library, the Jewish Federation of Saint Louis, the Jewish Theological Seminary, the Los Angeles Jewish Free Loan Association, the Massachusetts State House Library, the New York Hebrew Free Loan Society, the New York Public Library, the Philadelphia Jewish Archives Center, the Pittsburgh Hebrew Free Loan Association, the Rhode Island Jewish Historical Society, the Saint Louis Jewish Federation, the San Francsico Hebrew Free Loan Association, the University of Washington Library, the Washington Credit Union (West Roxbury, Massachusetts), the Western Jewish History Center (Berkeley), the Western Reserve Historical Society (Cleveland), and the Institute for Jewish Research of the Yiddish Scientific Institute, or YIVO (New York). Organizational records were supplemented by newspaper articles, Proceedings of the National Conference of Jewish Charities, interviews, and secondary sources.

The records varied in terms of quality and quantity. Some collections consisted of loose documents stacked in Hebrew free loan society file drawers, and others were comprised of well-catalogued materials housed in modern archives. My experiences ranged from sifting through unmarked boxes in the basement of one extant loan society with a flashlight as my only source of light, to borrowing fifty pounds of documents from another loan society (and carrying them through the length of a major airport), to working at archives and having staff persons deliver records to my table. The materials that were most helpful were correspondence, minute books, annual reports, and loan applications. Since some organizations, such as the New York Hebrew Free Loan Society, were in frequent contact with other loan societies, their records supply data on many institutions.

Correspondence files contained letters to borrowers, donors, federations, and officers of other loan societies. Surveys initiated by the manager of the Los Angeles Jewish Loan Fund in order to gather information on other organizations' policies on issues such as lending to non-Jews or on institutional experiences during periods of decline provided valuable comparative data. Minute books and annual reports supplied detail on the operations of loan organizations, portraits of individual applicants, and statistics about the loans distributed to borrowers. Furthermore, they gave me the opportunity to trace how institutions changed over time and how they responded to such pivotal events as the Great Depression and World War II. Their frequent references to the importance of Jewish loan societies for Jewish business development allowed me to explore the relationship between ethnic capital and ethnic enterprise. A collection of Pittsburgh Hebrew Free Loan Association loan applications also aided my examination of the role played by Jewish credit agencies in facilitating business expansion. By providing information on the reasons applicants requested loans, I was able to tabulate the percentages of men and women who borrowed for their businesses.

The organizational records that I relied on most heavily because of their rich detail were those of the Abraham Haas Memorial Fund (San Francisco), the Cleveland Hebrew Free Loan Association, the Los Angeles Hebrew Free Loan Association, the Los Angeles Jewish Loan Fund, the Mastbaum Loan System (Philadelphia), the New York Hebrew Free Loan Society, the Pittsburgh Hebrew Free Loan Association, and the San Francisco Hebrew Free Loan Association. Records of individual credit unions were particularly difficult to locate. My best primary sources on the role of Jews within the credit union movement were government reports that included sufficient information for identifying Jewish cooperatives, and materials housed in the library of the Credit Union National Association (CUNA) in Madison. The CUNA's Edward A. Filene collection includes valuable files on the movement's

Jewish leadership. In addition to examining these primary materials on Jewish philanthropic loan societies and credit cooperatives, I also relied on the data collected by Michael Freund for his 1932 study of Jewish loan societies; by Eleanor Horvitz, Marvin Pitterman, and Benton Rosen for their publications on Providence Hebrew free loan societies; by Oliver Pollack for his research on Omaha Jewish loan associations; by Chester Elsinger and Martin Light for their works on the Lafayette (Indiana) Orthodox Hebrew Free Loan Association; and by H. Joseph Hyman for his articles on the Indianapolis Jewish Community Credit Union.

2

TRADITIONAL CULTURE AND AMERICAN CONTEXT

NOT LONG AFTER THE MASSES OF EAST
European Jews began to arrive in the United States during the early 1880s, the new immigrants set to work recreating their traditional Hebrew free loan societies, philanthropic organizations based on a religious concept of providing the Jewish poor with interest-free loans. Beginning with the establishment of a free loan society in Pittsburgh in 1887, East European Jewish immigrants created hundreds of such credit facilities in diverse communities throughout the country. Boris Bogen's 1908 study on Jewish philanthropy recorded the existence of 157 Hebrew free loan societies; nineteen years later, according to an American Jewish Committee survey, the number of associations grew to 509.[1]

Independents, Affiliates, and Free Loan Services

Hebrew free loan societies can be divided into two broad categories: those that were independent of any organization and those that affiliated with synagogues. The former catered to a citywide clientele and generally had greater resources than those affiliated with synagogues. Affiliates operated under their own charters and administered their own treasuries but tended to loan funds only to members who belonged to the parent organization. In Boston, for example, the congregational Dorchester Hebrew Free Loan Association (HFLA), affiliated with Beth El Synagogue, loaned $1,015 during February 1924. By contrast, in that same year, the independent Boston Hebrew Free Loan Society (HFLS) disbursed, on a monthly average, nearly twenty times as much.[2]

Although affiliated free loan societies had relatively small treasuries, they were much more prevalent than independent ones. The 1927 nationwide study sponsored by the American Jewish Committee compared congregational and independent free loan societies and found that 85 were independent while 424 were connected to synagogues.[3] All but 7 of the 310 free loan associations located in New York City were synagogue affiliates.[4] Shortly before the turn of the century, Chicago had fourteen free loan associations: thirteen administered by local congregations and one independent.[5]

In addition to independent and affiliated Hebrew free loan societies, American Jews had access to free loan services offered by their ethnic institutions. The large Jewish relief agencies, such as United Hebrew Charities, as well as much smaller organizations, extended loans to their clients. For example, family clubs, organizations unique to the Jewish community, often provided their members with loans.[6] In his will dated June 25, 1932, Solomon Z. Balinky instructed his family, "Establish a family circle for your own convenience. Make each person pay twenty-five cents dues weekly. In time a substantial sum will be collected so that any member of the circle who finds himself in need may be able to borrow the sum he requires." His comments shed light on how a collective loan fund ensured that no one family member would shoulder the entire responsibility for lending funds or even endorsing notes:

> Such an arrangement will save you from heartless loan sharks and their exhorbitant interest charges. I believe that such an organizition is a good thing for every family. First, he who needs help will not be compelled to apply to strangers and secondly, it will be easier to render assistance this way; it is much better than having one person advance the entire amount of money from his own pocket or having him endorse a loan from some strange corporation, no matter how good it may be. Do as I advise and you will derive a great deal of benefit, for no one knows what the morrow may bring.[7]

At least two-fifths of the three thousand benevolent societies (e.g., fraternal orders and *landsmanschaften*)[8] surveyed in 1927 maintained free loan funds that collectively extended three million dollars annually. A decade earlier, two studies that focused on New York City also concluded that free loans were commonly offered by Jewish organizations. According to the the *Jewish Communal Register*, 34 percent of 632 mutual aid societies provided members with free loans while the Bureau of Jewish Social Research counted more than a thousand small Jewish organizations that operated some type of loan fund. The United Wilner Benevolent Association, a *landsmanschaft* founded in 1888, and the Jewish Sisters Mutual Aid Society, created by a group of Orthodox women in 1921, are just two of the many New York organizations that operated free loan funds. By paying an extra twenty-five cents quarterly, members of the United Wilner Benevolent Association could participate in a free loan fund. One year after it began, the Jewish Sisters Mutual Aid Society loaned a total of $5,548 without interest to 144 women and 15 men.[9]

In Kansas City, the Hebrew Ladies' Relief Association began granting loans within several years of its inception in 1890. The founding women, who were too busy with their existing work to take on this added loan responsibility, "decided it would be wise to enlist the aid of their husbands, brothers and fathers, in handling the Free Loan Department."[10] Only men who were related to members in good standing of the parent women's organization were allowed to serve within the organization.

For the sake of consistency and clarity, my analysis of Hebrew free loan societies will be limited to independent agencies. Their capital was raised from supporters' contributions and then loaned without interest to approved borrowers. To receive approval, an applicant had to provide the names of people who would endorse the loan. The endorsers, since they were ultimately responsible for the loan, served as security in case the borrower defaulted. After the endorsers were investigated and approved and their signatures obtained, the borrower received the funds. This endorser system proved so effective that most societies experienced annual default rates of under 1 percent. Although most organizations used religion as a criterion for approval, some opened their doors to borrowers of any religion or race.

Jews were not the only immigrant group to transfer their loan societies from their native countries to the new American context. Pre–World War II Japanese and Chinese organized rotating credit associations based on models from their respective countries of origin. In a simple rotating credit association of ten members, everyone agrees to pay a specific sum of money monthly into a common pool. If each member contributes ten dollars monthly, then every month a different person would be entitled to receive one hundred dollars. In reality, however, most rotating credit associations were more complex in organization. They varied in terms of interest policies, deductions from the pool, bidding for turns and transferability of funds. Regardless of these differences, the system provided immigrant Asian entrepreneurs with access to capital. The author of a 1939 study pointed out that the largest hotel enterprise ever attempted by Japanese–Americans, a transaction involving ninety thousand dollars, was financed by a rotating credit association.[11] Having cultural mechanisms in place for generating business capital undoubtedly facilitated the relative economic success of Jews and Asians.

The Cultural Basis of Free Loans

While the general concept of ethnic credit, then, was not unique to Jews, the particular model of free loans was ethnically distinct. Just as Asian immigrants turned to their culture and formed rotating credit associations, Jewish immigrants drew upon their own tradition and established free loan societies. The books of Exodus, Leviticus, and Deuteronomy explicitly state that one should not charge a Jewish poor person interest.[12] For example, Exodus 22:24 instructs, "If you lend money to My people, to the poor among you, do not act toward him as a creditor: exact no interest from them." According to a commentary on this biblical passage, Jews should not lend money with interest because

> all God's creations borrow from the other; day borrows from night and night from day. . . . The moon borrows from the stars and the stars from the moon. . . . The light borrows from the sun and the sun from the light. . . . Wisdom borrows from understanding, and understanding from wisdom. . . . The heavens borrow from earth, and earth from the heavens. . . . Lovingkindness borrows from righteousness, and righteousness from lovingkindness. . . . The Torah borrows from the commandments, and the commandments from the Torah.[13]

The Talmud, the compendium of Jewish law completed during the sixth century c.e., praises those who lend money to the poor. Ketuboth 67b specifies that if a poor person who refused charity is given a loan, then the loan should later be turned into a gift. If this person is reluctant to accept even a loan because of suspicions that it is really a gift, only then "he is told, 'Bring a pledge and you will receive [a loan]'." This practice is encouraged in order "to raise his [drooping] spirit."[14]

Jewish law is absolutely clear about its preference for loans over almsgiving. According to the Talmud, "He who lends [money] is greater than he who performs charity and he who puts in capital for partnership is greater than all" (Sabbath 63a). Rashi, the pre-eminent eleventh-century commentator on the Bible and Talmud, explains that lending is better than giving charity because there is no shame involved in the act of borrowing. Also, the wealthy may be inclined to lend higher amounts than they give away, so that the recipients are more likely to become financially independent from loans than from alms. Not until the twelfth century, however, when Moses Maimonides introduced his eight degrees of charity, did a "deliberately constructed scale of philanthropic values" develop.[15] Maimonides wrote in the Mishnah Torah:

> There are eight degrees in the giving of charity, one superior to the other. A high degree, than which there is no higher, is that of one who takes hold of an Israelite who has become impoverished and gives him a gift or a loan or goes into partnership with him or finds work for him, in order to strengthen his hand so that he be spared the necessity of appealing for help.[16]

In short, charitable lending has deep cultural roots within Judaism. It is a concept that originated in the Bible and was expanded upon in later years by both talmudic and medieval scholars. Talmudic laws were concerned with protecting the poor from the feeling of degradation associated with receiving charity. Medieval Jewish scholars like Rashi and Maimonides advocated loans as a preventive form of charity whereby the needy could obtain business resources to enable them to become self-sufficient.

When East European Jews established Hebrew free loan societies in the United States, they frequently referred to the religious tradition that inspired the formation of their institutions. Jewish texts were quoted at annual meetings and within organizational literature. At the fifth annual meeting in 1897, the president of the New York HFLS said that his organization was entitled to its name because "it pursues the true act of charity as is conveyed in the meaning of our Biblical ethics."[17] *The Poor Man's Bank,* a small book published in honor of the New York association's fiftieth anniversary, begins:

> This is the story of a Biblical precept faithfully followed for half a century by a group of devoted men. It is also the story of the institution they founded as the instrument to put into practice the ideal which they cherished. It is the story of the Hebrew Free Loan Society of New York which wears its heart on its sleeve where all may reach it, and its credo inscribed on its walls where all may see: *If thou loan money to my people, to the poor by thee, thou shalt not lay upon him interest.*[18]

Similarly, officers of the Boston HFLS claimed that Maimonides' eight degrees of charity inspired the organization's founders.[19]

In addition to being able to draw upon Jewish religious texts, East European Jewish immigrants also benefitted from their familiarity with actual Hebrew free loan societies that had existed in the European setting. During the eighteenth and nineteenth centuries, Hebrew free loan associations, known as *hevrot gemilut hasadim,* were a common feature of European Jewish communities.[20] Three different London organizations provided loans to the Jewish poor: the first was established in 1749; the second, in 1828; and the third, by a group of women, in 1847. The London Jewish Ladies' Loan Society is credited with having been "the means of keeping a home together, or of giving a hawker or small tradesman a fresh start in life, or of tiding over a time of exceptional sickness and distress."[21] During the mid–nineteenth century, free loan associations were founded in German cities (e.g., Frankfurt am Main, Cologne, Lubeck, and Memel) as well as in the Jewish communities of Antwerp and Amsterdam. In tsarist Russia, where Jews were prohibited from organizing separate loan societies, they secretly operated free loan associations in synagogues and houses of study. Between 1870 and 1895 hundreds of *hevrot gemilut hasadim* existed among specific occupational and religious groups (e.g., Hasidim) in Warsaw alone.[22] In 1828, a free loan association was established in Bialystock; in 1873, in Plock; in 1877, in Krasnopile; and in 1883, in Lomza.[23]

Free loan societies continued to be established in the twentieth century. During the first decade, Polish Jews created *hevrot gemilut hasadim* in Lublin (1903), Radom (1903), Wolkowysk (1906), and Stanislawow (1908/9). After World War I, the Joint Distribution Committee (organized by American Jews in 1914 to aid Jews in Eastern Europe) actively supported the creation of Jewish credit associations. In Poland, for example, 226 free loan societies existed in 1926; twelve years later the number increased to 826. In many small towns, over 90 percent of the Jewish working population used the organizations; and according to a survey from the late 1930s, 33 percent of all borrowers were artisans and 50 percent were small traders.[24] Samuel Kassow, a historian of Polish Jewish life, concludes that these artisans and traders used small loans "to buy wares for the market day and somewhat larger loans for the purchase of a horse or an artisan's license."[25] He reports the case of one typical borrower from the town of Wegrow:

> A woman enters with tears in her eyes. "Jews," she says, "you know that my husband is a scribe and makes 8 zlotys a week. Of course you know that one can't live on that wage. My children don't have any bread. . . . I would like to open a soda-water stand. . . . some soda water, some apples, and I'll be able to make do. But a license costs 28 zlotys. . . . Please, Jews, lend me 25 zlotys. I'll pay back one zloty a week.[26]

Free loans enabled individuals to enhance their earning ability, thus improving their own and their families' lives.

Unfortunately, we know little about the origin or early history of *hevrot gemilut hasadim*. It is possible that their development was influenced by European religious banks known as *monti di pieta*. Originally established by Franciscans in Italy during the mid–fifteenth century, these banks provided Catholic businessmen and poor people with low-interest loans. The desire to displace Jews from moneylending motivated the Franciscans to initiate Christian sources of credit. The first two *monti* were founded in Perugia and Orvieto around 1465. As the institution spread—by 1509, eighty-seven existed in Italy—protest arose among other sectors of the clergy over the practice of levying interest fees. Interest charges, opponents railed, "were contrary to all tradition, natural and Divine Law, and subversive of Christian brotherhood."[27] The issue was finally settled by Pope Leo X, who, at the Fifth Lateran Council of 1515, ruled in favor of the *monti* and threatened the banks' opponents with excommunication.

The papal decision further spurred the growth of these religious credit institutions.

The New World

Although distinct Hebrew free loan associations did not proliferate in America until the large-scale influx of East Europeans, American Jews had access to charitable loans since the colonial era. Synagogues, which had been the social welfare arms of the small colonial Jewish community, provided members with religious education, sick care, and burial benefits, as well as loan funds. In 1744 or 1745, Michael Judah borrowed five pounds from the New York synagogue, Shearith Israel, so that he could open a business in Norwalk, Connecticut. Judah generously repaid the synagogue when he bequeathed a share of his estate "to the sinagouge in Newyork."[28] Levi Michael petitioned the same congregation to grant him a loan so that he might return to Canada.[29] During the postrevolutionary era, Philadelphia's Congregation Mikveh Israel disbursed interest-free business loans that ranged from ten to twenty pounds.[30]

In the nineteenth century, however, philanthropy shifted away from the synagogue, and benevolent societies became the primary distributors of charity. At first, these mutual aid associations were connected to congregations, but by the late 1840s and the 1850s many had completely severed ties with their parent organizations. These withdrawals were facilitated by frequent synagogue secessions and a growing number of Jews who were unaffiliated with a synagogue but still wanted the privileges (e.g., burial) that an association offered. One of the many philanthropic functions fulfilled by benevolent societies was the provision of loans, sometimes to individual members and in other cases to communal institutions, particularly synagogues. Between 1855 and 1861, one Boston benevolent association granted Congregation Ohabei Shalom a series of four $150 loans, albeit with interest.[31]

Before the arrival of approximately two-and-a-half million East Europeans, mid-nineteenth-century Jews established only one Jewish loan association—the Bachelors' Hebrew Benevolent Loan Association (BHBLA). The origins of this first autonomous American free loan organization can be traced to 1847, when a group of men in New York City, mainly from the "the older synagogues or from the Native American or English groups" incorporated the BHBLA.[32] Any New York Jew who provided at least one endorser could borrow up to twenty-five dollars, to be repaid in monthly installments within one year. Those who were unable to obtain an endorser were allowed loans for a maximum of ten dollars. A semiannual treasurer's report from 1850 provides the only available account of the fund's finances: between January and June, borrowers received $370; and in June, $892 was due on past loans. Members (forty in 1848) provided capital, which was supplemented by an annual ball.[33] The BHBLA was last heard from in early 1857 when it transferred $800, a large proportion of its treasury, to the Jews' Hospital in New York under the condition that it "be reimbursed if ever called for by its members."[34] In all likelihood, the BHBLA dissolved at that time.

Leaders of the BHBLA strongly believed that their organization served the needs of the Jewish community better than traditional charitable societies did. Loans preserved the dignity of the poor while almsgiving, they felt, was degrading. In a letter to one of its supporters, officers of the BHBLA offered the following comparison:

> Our city can boast of several benevolent institutions, whose charities are devoted exclusively to Israelites; but there are none organized on the principles of the Bachelors' Hebrew Benevolent Loan Association . . . . Recipients of charity spend the small pittance which is meted out to them, and when their means are expended they are again compelled to seek assistance. The Bachelors' Hebrew Benevolent Loan Association intends to loan to industrious persons, whose means are scanty, the necessary funds wherewith to commence business, or purchase tools for any particular trade. Knowing the obligation they are under of returning the money loaned them, and feeling that upon their exertion depends the means of gaining a livelihood, it acts like a spur to their ambition, and eventually leads to independence, and often to the foundation of a fortune. . . . We have flung our banner to the winds, with the soul-inspiring words 'Never Despair' emblazoned on it; and fanned by the favouring breeze of prosperity, like the beacon-light to the shipwrecked mariner, it will guide the worthy and industrious poor the way to the harbour of safety.[35]

Isaac Leeser, prominent Jewish leader and editor of the *Occident*, a national Jewish newspaper, shared this preference for loans over alms. An 1848 editorial in his newspaper lauded the founding of the BHBLA. "This society," it declared, "will effect a greater good than any other yet existing in New York."[36] The newspaper continued to publish news of the BHBLA and encouraged other Jewish communities to establish similar organizations. It looked as if Leeser's encouragement might yield results when, in November 1856, a meeting was called to discuss the formation of a Philadelphia loan society.[37] The project died, however, when too few people attended the planning session. The *Occident* warned of the dangers inherent in continuing to give alms instead of loans:

> It appears that the greater part of the people think the present system of raising and distributing charity funds the only proper and the best mode; but they will be perhaps unpleasantly undeceived, when calls for aid are yet more augmented, and when they find that they have given to many undeserving, for want of means to distinguish the good from the bad.[38]

A decade later, when Philadelphia Jews established yet another benevolent society, the newspaper continued to press for a loan association.[39]

Isaac Leeser's call for the creation of many Jewish charitable loan associations went unanswered during his lifetime. The Central European immigrants who arrived between 1820 and 1870 had little need for loan societies, since they were able to meet their credit needs almost exclusively through their informal networks of individual borrowers. In Cincinnati, for example,

> Jewish peddlers relied upon Jewish retailers, and Jewish retailers in turn relied upon Jewish wholesalers and manufacturers to supply them with the goods and capital necessary to succeed. An informal banking system thus developed in which successful Jews lent money to new arrivals, but it was done within the framework of retail and wholesale establishments.[40]

Mid-nineteenth-century Jews were forced to rely on other Jews, since borrowing from Gentile merchants was usually not a viable option. In their respective studies of Cincinnati and Buffalo, historians Steven Mostov and David Gerber found that investigators for the credit information agency R. G. Dun and Company routinely portrayed Jewish businessmen as dishonest, thus exacerbating their difficulty in obtaining credit. Examples are "A Jew of the hardest mold; don't trust him"; "No more than Jewish honesty"; and "He is a Jew and although in point of fact he may now be perfectly responsible, yet Jews have a wonderful faculty of becoming at almost any moment they choose entirely irresponsible."[41]

But as the Jewish population expanded, informal intraethnic credit ties no longer sufficed. While the nation as a whole increased tenfold from 11 million in 1840 to 115 million in 1925, the American Jewish population increased more than three hundred times. In 1840 there were approximately 15,000 Jews living in the United States; in the early 1860s, 150,000 Jews; and in 1877, 280,000. From the 1880s on, the immigration of Jews from Eastern Europe led to an enormous population growth. One million Jews resided in the United States in 1900, 3 million in 1915, and 4½ million in 1925.[42]

A lack of mutual trust between German Jews and the East European newcomers exacerbated the difficulty of maintaining an informal credit system. The Cincinnati clothing firm of M & J Schradzki, for example, could not obtain credit from other Jews because, according to an R. G. Dun and Company investigator, "They are Poles and some are prejudiced against them on that account."[43] At the same time that German Jews were not comfortable lending money to the unfamiliar East Europeans, the new immigrants preferred not to depend on their German counterparts. Rather, the East Europeans made every effort to assist their own as soon as they were able by creating a plethora of institutions such as Hebrew free loan societies. They "were in a much better position to transplant and maintain their traditional communal institutions than were the German immigrants. Their numbers, density of settlement, common language, Yiddish, and their intensive religious culture enabled the devout and religiously minded among them to re-establish their traditional system in America."[44]

The Need for Credit

It was more than a combination of cultural factors and large-scale immigration that led East European Jews to transplant their Hebrew free loan societies to the United States. Their overrepresentation in business enterprises created an acute need for credit. Similarly, a large percentage of Japanese and

Chinese immigrants were self-employed in trade, influencing them to recreate their rotating credit associations. For example, by 1919 nearly half of all hotels and a quarter of all restaurants in Seattle were owned by Japanese.[45] Without access to capital, neither Jewish nor Asian businesses would have survived. Studies show that capital is "the decisive factor in determining the ability of business enterprises to survive."[46]

In 1900, one-fifth of all gainfully employed Jewish immigrants (23 percent of men and 10 percent of women) were in mercantile trade. In Los Angeles, at the turn of the century, East European Jews were peddlers, junk store owners, and traders of second-hand goods. Los Angeles Jews owned their own businesses at a rate almost three times greater than that of other city inhabitants. In Boston, in 1909, 45 percent of Jewish immigrant men were "engaged in business for profit," as opposed to only 5 percent of first-generation Irish and 22 percent of Italians. In nearby Worcester and Fall River, Massachusetts, 60 percent of Jewish immigrants were self-employed by World War I. By 1940, 41 percent of Jewish male immigrants in Providence had their own businesses, as compared to 11.5 percent of Italians. Even in predominately blue-collar Johnstown, Pennsylvania, three-quarters of immigrant Jews were self-employed in trade during the first four decades of the twentieth century.[47] In his comparative study of Jews and Italians in New York City, Thomas Kessner concludes that among the Jewish immigrants, "it was not medicine, law, or even their vaunted thirst for education that carried them forward. It was business."[48]

Peddling served immigrant Jews as an important steppingstone to larger retail ventures. In New York City,

> whole blocks of the East Side Jewry [were turned] into a bazaar with high-piled carts lining the curb, as few commodities failed to find a seller or buyer. Bandannas and tin cups at two cents, peaches at a cent a quart, damaged eggs for a song, hats for a quarter, and spectacles warranted to suit the eye for thirty-five cents. . . . Many an energetic pushcart peddler earned 15 to 20 dollars weekly and was able to advance to more settled types of commerce, leaving the itinerant trade to newcomers and to the less successful.[49]

Historian Judith Smith relates a story told by a daughter of a Jewish immigrant about her father's metamorphosis from a Hebrew teacher in Russia to a peddler in Providence. Wanting to continue working as a teacher, he had sought employment counsel from a local rabbi. Upon realizing that the newcomer planned to bring a wife and daughter to Providence, the rabbi advised him to forgo teaching and enter the world of business. The immigrant took the rabbi's advice and began peddling from house to house.[50]

The manufacture of clothing was an especially important avenue of entrepreneurship for East European Jewish immigrants. In 1900, one-third of Russian Jews employed in major cities earned their living in some branch of the apparel trade, an industry that was growing two to three times faster than the average of all industries. By 1905, it was a $306-million business with over two-thirds of the field concentrated in New York City, the entry point for the vast majority of immigrants. Eight years later, the industry's 16,552 factories were largely owned by Russian Jews and employed approximately 312,000 people, about three-quarters of whom were also Russian Jews.[51] Arthur Goren, a historian of American Jewish life, concluded that the clothing trade was "the backbone of the Jewish neighborhood economy in New York, Boston, Philadelphia, Baltimore, and Chicago."[52]

Furthermore, the skills of the East Europeans corresponded well with the expanding industry. Close to one-third of all gainfully employed Jewish immigrants arrived in the United States as tailors and seamstresses, and a full two-thirds possessed some urban industrial skills.[53] This fit between occupational skills and the needs of the American economy was crucial for the emerging Jewish concentration in the garment field.

Carving out an economic niche, however, does not necessarily ensure a group's entry into business. The steel industry, for example, with its very high capital requirements, did not provide Polish immigrants with possibilities of starting up their own firms. Only certain industries were conducive to individual enterprise; and the apparel trade, with its "sweatshop" structure, was particularly receptive to the multiplication of small shops. The industry's high degree of specialization prompted manufacturers to distribute work to contractors and subcontractors, who then employed a small number of immigrant workers in small shops. Called sweatshops for their poor working conditions, these small businesses offered many immigrants the opportunity to move from worker to entrepreneur: "The contractors were no longer passive middlemen but entrepreneurs, skilled tailors—or at least skilled organizers of labor—who supervised in their own homes or shops the operators, basters, pressers, finishers, fitters, fellers, buttonhole-makers, and basting-pullers."[54] In New York City, over sixteen thousand sweatshops existed in 1913.[55]

The apparel trade's high-risk character further prompted the development of immigrant Jewish businesses. Actually, the industry was split into both high- and low-risk sectors: immigrant entrepreneurs concentrated on manufacturing high-risk novelty goods, while Yankee manufacturers specialized in the production of low-risk staple products. The shoe industry in Massachusetts provides a clear example of this phenomenon. Prior to 1910, a Yankee elite dominated the shoe industry. During this period, both the women's shoe industry on the North Shore and the men's counterpart on the South Shore produced a sturdy staple shoe that was easy to manufacture and sell. Between 1910 and 1925, however, changing life-styles and changing functions of shoes brought about a styling revolution in the women's shoe industry. With advances in transportation and the transformation of dirt roads into paved ones, manufacturers could no longer sell the same functional women's walking shoe year after year. The sturdy walking shoe was replaced by the novelty fashion shoe, thus transforming the women's industry into one with a high-risk character. Subsequently, many of the native American manufacturers left the field of women's shoes; and room was made for Jewish immigrants to enter this world of entrepreneurship. The men's shoe industry, meanwhile, was not affected as much by the fluctuations of fashion and thus continued to be dominated by Yankees.[56]

As a result of their economic roles, enterprising groups such as Jews had a particularly strong need for capital. Their search for sources of credit, however, was shared by many Americans. The late nineteenth and early twentieth centuries brought about enormous changes in America's credit needs. A burgeoning population combined with the uprooting of millions of rural folk to urban settings meant that the usual forms of credit—reliance on family and friends—no longer fulfilled the nation's credit demands. Industrialization introduced a variety of consumer items—such as automobiles, refrigerators, and radios—on the market, necessitating new sources of funds to accommodate the material demands and appetites of American households.[57]

Banks were not an available source of funds for the vast majority of Americans. Before 1925, only one bank in all of New England and only one among the Middle Atlantic states operated personal loan departments.[58] An estimated 85 percent of the population was "beyond the pale of bank credit"; only those who furnished tangible security could obtain bank loans.[59] Massachusetts governor David I. Walsh reported in 1915 that "every banking door in the Commonwealth is barred to the man who wants to borrow $25 without security."[60] It was an era when local grocery stores and saloons served as "immigrant banks" to receive the savings of neighborhood residents and purchase steamship tickets for friends and relatives living abroad, often resulting in fraudulent activity. One South Chicago resident remembered "workers filing into their local drinking spots on payday in search of cash as well as libation."[61]

Due to a pattern of poor management and investment strategies, attempts to form ethnic banks proved largely unsuccessful.[62] In Chicago, "unsupervised by any government agency, [ethnic banks] failed at an alarming rate, leaving customers like Salvatore Cosentino penniless. He had saved $200 in a private bank owned by a West Side barber who ran it alongside his travel agency. When the barber–banker–steamship agent declared bankruptcy, Cosentino lost all his money."[63] Of 134 banks organized by blacks throughout the country between 1884 and 1935, only twenty-one existed in 1929; and another nine failed during the Great Depression. In California, Japanese and Chinese established ten state-chartered banks between 1900 and 1910, and only one survived until 1912. By the mid-1920s, all had closed their doors.[64] Similarly, Jewish banks in New York suffered from high failure rates. In 1914, the state superintendent of banks shut down three Jewish banks run by M. Yarmulowsky, Adolf Mandel, and Max Kobre. In response to losing their hard-earned savings,

> five hundred people gathered in front of M. Yarmulowsky's apartment, forcing him and his family to flee—they climbed up the roof and escaped from an adjoining house. The next day about a thousand demonstrators massed in front of Mandel's house, and the reserves had to be called out. . . . Mandel was convicted of having accepted a deposit after he knew the bank was insolvent; crowds of his victims stood in front of the courthouse and cheered the jury's verdict. As for Yarmulowsky and Kobre, the former received a suspended sentence and the latter committed suicide in 1916.[65]

The relatively large Public National Bank (which later became the Bank of the United States), founded by Joseph Marcus, survived the 1914 debacle but failed during the economic crisis of the 1930s.

In order to fill Americans' desperate need for credit, pawnshops and unlicensed lenders appeared in cities throughout the United States. Earning their reputation as loan sharks, it was not uncommon for small lenders to charge clients interest rates of 400 percent or more per year. In a 1914 article, the *New York Evening Post* publicized the story of one man, a clerk who earned $2,400 a year and borrowed $400 from moneylenders to help his son-in-law overcome serious legal difficulties. After a four-year period, the clerk paid back more than $2,000 and still owed $1,700 according to his lenders' calculations.[66]

Despite the exhorbitant fees, many Americans turned to loan sharks, testifying to the serious lack of other credit sources. Consequently, the unlicensed lending business mushroomed during the late nineteenth century. When staff workers of the Russell Sage Foundation monitored one daily newspaper, the *New York World*, they found that the number of lenders' notices increased dramatically between 1885 and 1900. While no more than two notices appeared in any one issue during January 1885, during a one-week period in October 1890, the number varied from fourteen to thirty-eight. During a week in 1900, twenty-four were inserted regularly; and for several days there were as many as twenty-seven.[67] Even though most states had legal rates of interest, it was relatively simple to get around the laws. Few states provided any penalty other than the loss of interest for charging more than the legal rate. Therefore, even in the rare case where a lender was prosecuted, he could always collect on the principal.

The publicity given to the unscrupulous practices of small lenders gave rise to calls for regulation. In 1916, a group of reputable lenders from the American Association of Small Loan Brokers met with members of the Russell Sage Foundation to formulate small loan legislation. The bill they drafted was applicable only for loans of three hundred dollars or less. The main provisions were that (1) all lenders charging more than the banking rate of interest were required to be licensed and frequently examined by the state banking department, (2) licensed lenders could charge a maximum interest rate of 3½ percent a month to be computed on unpaid balances without any additional fees, and (3) a supervising authority would have the power to enforce penalties in case of violations. By 1930, twenty-five states had passed this legislation, known as the Uniform Small Loan Law.

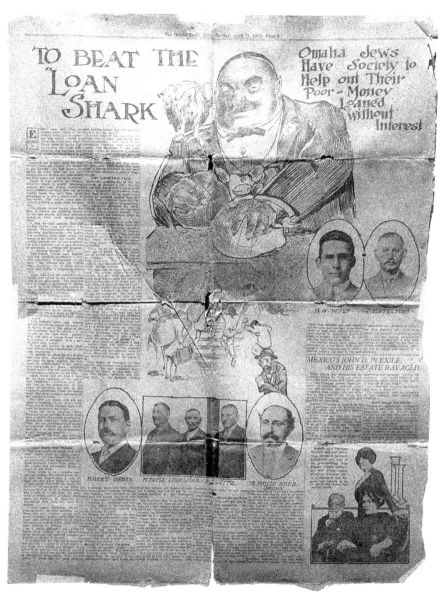

Article from the Omaha Daily News, April 21, 1912. Photograph from the collections of the Nebraska Jewish Historical Society.

A large group of lenders emerged under the authority of the Uniform Small Loan Law. By 1930, there were approximately three thousand licensed agencies advancing an estimated five million dollars a year. Included in these figures were several enormous chain-office concerns, known as personal finance companies, that made loans on household goods. The Household Finance Corporation, for example, founded in 1878 by Frank J. Mackey, is the oldest of these enterprises. In 1929 this one firm made close to 303,000 loans totaling more than fifty-six million dollars. The Beneficial Industrial Loan Corporation was organized in 1929 as a consolidation of a company of the same name with two other businesses. A year later, Beneficial's 263 subsidiaries located in 228 cities did an annual small loan business of over fifty million dollars.[68] Following the requirements of the Uniform Small Loan Law, personal finance companies were able to charge rates of 3½ percent per month, a figure that translates into a maximum of 42 percent per year.

At about the same time that these regulation efforts took place, Arthur J. Morris, an attorney from Norfolk, Virginia, devised a new plan to lend money to people who lacked the necessary security required by banks. In addition to requiring two endorsements, an investigation fee, and advanced discounted interest, borrowers had to purchase non-interest-bearing certificates. The required weekly repayments (fines were imposed in case of delinquency) were credited to the purchase of these certificates, and only when the purchase was completed were the certificates canceled and the loan liquidated. Critics charged that crediting payments to a non-interest-bearing certificate disguised the true rate of interest. Morris Plan Companies advertised themselves as "6 percent companies"; but in reality, they charged 18–20 percent a year.[69]

While these new finance organizations were a step in the right direction, their relatively high interest rates still militated against their ability to meet the credit needs of small borrowers adequately. Therefore, simultaneous with their efforts to pass legislation regulating unlicensed lending, reform-minded individuals also innovated two different types of loan agencies in order to fill the vacuum: remedial loan societies and credit unions.

Based on a philanthropic premise, remedial loan associations loaned money at relatively low interest rates, usually 6 percent. By purchasing shares of stock, wealthy individuals supplied the loan capital for a clientele that was generally working- and lower-middle-class. The collected interest was used to finance an organization's operational costs and not recycled back to the contributors. Credit unions, in contrast, were cooperative, rather than philanthropic, ventures and were savings, as well as loan, facilities. By pooling their funds together through deposits and purchased shares, members generated their own loan capital. They were able to borrow money at relatively low interest rates, earn interest on their savings, and receive dividends from surplus funds.

Because their economic roles generated a special need for capital, American Jews added credit unions—and to a lesser extent, remedial loan associations—to their ethnic loan repertoire. Like other Americans, Jews needed funds to purchase consumer items, meet expenses incurred during illness, and pay for coal. In addition, however, Jews sought credit outlets to sustain their businesses.[70] That they did not restrict their loan activity to traditional free loan associations points to the accommodating and dynamic nature of ethnicity. Collectively, Hebrew free loan societies, remedial institutions, and credit unions provided East European Jewish immigrants with crucial sources of entrepreneurial capital.

FREE LOANS AND ETHNIC ENTERPRISE

MAY BERMAN, SEPARATED FROM HER husband and the mother of five children, needed to borrow $100 to buy merchandise for her electrical supplies store in Pittsburgh. Seattle resident Morris Posner wanted $250 to buy goods for his poultry business. A manufacturer of nightgowns and bloomers, Charles Kaminer, sought a source of funds to run his New York shop.[1] All three of these early-twentieth-century Jewish entrepreneurs were successful in their quests for credit. With the help of local Hebrew free loan societies—philanthropic associations organized around a biblical and talmudic prohibition of charging interest to fellow Jews—they and many other Jewish small business owners throughout the United States were able to take advantage of available entrepreneurial possibilities.

A high percentage of free loan borrowers were in the fields of peddling and trade. In 1910, 29 percent of New York HFLS borrowers earned their livelihood as peddlers and merchants. Similarly, peddlers and merchants comprised 28 percent of San Francisco recipients of free loans in 1918. In Providence, peddlers, salesmen, and grocers were the three largest categories of borrowers. This pattern of occupational concentration was even more pronounced in Cleveland and Columbus. In Cleveland, where the Hebrew free loan association worked closely with the Jewish Peddlers' Association, peddlers and storekeepers received 70 percent of the loans in 1909. Almost half of the people who borrowed from the Columbus

HFLA in 1916 were peddlers who requested money to purchase merchandise.[2]

Leaders of free loan societies regularly stressed the importance of their organizations for entrepreneurial development. In 1903, the president of the New York HFLS reported that his organization assisted approximately six hundred people in starting businesses. As early as 1899 he stated, "We loan money for the purpose of some sort of business only, which may be expected to assist the borrower in his self-support; but we do not loan money to be directly eaten up."[3] Similarly, the Chicago Woman's Loan Association loaned money "purely for business purposes."[4] Minnie Low, founder of the Woman's Loan Association, attributed Jewish immigrant business development to the existence of local loan societies: "In the Chicago Ghetto, along the Jefferson Street market, as well as throughout the entire district, there are comparatively few of the peddlers, vendors, and keepers of small stands and shops, who have not been given a start in life or helped over rugged places by loans from local organizations."[5] The primary goal of the Pittsburgh HFLA was "to enable an individual to provide a living for himself and his family in business, trade or a profession."[6] According to one of the Boston HFLS's regular columns featured in the local paper, successful enterprise

> revolves around finance, and without the latter it is utterly impossible to carry out your business or professional intentions. The Hebrew Free Loan Society is a communal enterprise existing primarily to assist its fellow business man. It functions as a friend to a man or woman who passes through a period of temporary difficulties.[7]

Other observers of the free loan scene substantiated the relationship between free loans and Jewish businesses. A Providence newspaper reporter explained that the purpose of his city's free loan associations was "solely to provide means whereby the Jew can start in business for himself, or can meet the obligations of his business till it becomes established on a paying basis."[8] In Seattle, Bernice Greengard, a Hebrew Immigrant Aid Society staff worker during the 1920s, directed newcomers to the local Seattle Hebrew Ladies' Free Loan Society, who "could establish a little business."[9]

At least some of these pronouncements, however, were based on personal observations, rather than on any systematic data collected by the institutions. As a matter of policy, many Hebrew free loan societies did not inquire about their applicants' reasons for needing funds. Not wanting their clients to feel like recipients of relief who needed to justify their requests, the staff consciously limited their number of questions to a bare minimum. They usually collected more information on the endorsers—the ones ultimately responsible for the loans—than on the borrowers. In 1946, when a representative of the Cleveland HFLA wrote to Abraham Gribetz, executive director of the New York HFLS, that his organization was reevaluating its policy of not asking applicants to state their loan purposes, Gribetz responded:

> We wish to advise you that is has been our policy since the inception of our institution (in 1892) not to ask any questions of the borrower. We found this policy of real benefit and appreciation on the part of the borrower, in as much as it makes the applicant feel that he is not a recipient of charity, rather that he is negotiating an ordinary business loan. We on our part feel that any person entering our doors, knowing its philanthropic character, must be in need, or else would not come to us. Furthermore, it is basically certain, that the endorsers who know the applicant well, would not be willing to engage in their liability, unless they are reasonably sure the applicant is worthy and really in need.[10]

Fortunately, for the purposes of this study, extant documents from organizations that recorded the reasons their borrowers applied for loans provide us with the opportunity to verify the officers' impressions. Leaders of these loan associations believed it was their responsibility to query their applicants about their financial needs and business plans in order to ensure that loans would indeed be beneficial.[11]

Application cards from the Pittsburgh HFLA fully corroborate the assessments about the positive relationship between free loans and ethnic enterprise. Out of a sample of 1,038 loans granted between 1924 and 1950, over 60 percent were for entrepreneurial purposes. Four hundred and fifty-three people received these loans, and exactly two-thirds borrowed on at least one occasion for their businesses.[12] For example, Max Belkin and Morris Caplan each borrowed $100 in 1927. The former, the father of five, needed the loan to purchase a license and truck for his fruit store, while the latter, the father of two, applied for the funds in order to buy

Borrower making his monthly payment on a loan for his cleaning and tailoring shop. Photograph from the collection of the Los Angeles Jewish Free Loan Association.

vending machines for his confectionary store. Over an eight-year period, Albert Dubrowsky, the owner of a soap business, borrowed $1,100 to purchase fats, barrels, and manufacturing machinery. Louis Borowitz, who had three children, borrowed $150 in January 1929 to start a tailoring business. By 1932 he was established as a tailor and borrowed an additional $75. Mary Ackerman, a widow with two children, took out two loans in 1939 for a total of $170 to help her in her dressmaking business.

Women appeared regularly, although less frequently than men, in the annals of the Pittsburgh HFLA. One of every nine borrowers was female. Unlike male borrowers, however, most women did not request loans for business pursuits. Sixty percent of the women borrowed only for private needs, while the majority of men—70 percent—applied for business loans. Although a significant minority of women borrowed for their businesses, women received money mainly to pay for rent, household expenses, medical bills, insurance, home repairs, education for themselves and their children, moving expenses, holidays, and divorce costs. Typical portraits are provided by Clara Appelbaum and Ida Bender. Clara, a single woman and property owner, worked for the Department of Public Works. In 1941 she received two loans in order to pay taxes. Ida, a gasoline attendant who had three children, borrowed one hundred dollars in 1938 to pay personal bills, sixty dollars for coal in 1940, and one hundred dollars for dental work in 1942. The Pittsburgh data suggest a second important difference between male and female applicants. Women were far more likely than men to be single when they received a loan. Twenty-seven percent of women borrowers in Pittsburgh were widowed; and an additional 21 percent were either divorced, separated or never married. In contrast, almost all the male applicants were married.

On the West Coast, women were 11 percent of the San Francisco HFLA's borrowers and 10 percent of the people who received money from the Los Angeles Jewish Loan Fund during the 1930s.[13] The Jewish Loan Fund was an unusual organization, however. Until 1948, when the Jewish Loan Fund and the local HFLA combined their resources to become the Jewish Free Loan Association, it granted small free loans, as well as larger loans with interest. The interest-bearing loans—in 1936, they consisted of loans over $150—were intended for business investments.[14] Women who borrowed from the Jewish Loan Fund were four times as likely to be recipients of free loans than of interest loans, suggesting that women were less likely to borrow larger amounts intended for businesses.

By setting its loan maximum at twenty-five dollars during the early 1930s, leaders of the Providence Ladies' HFLA, an organization that limited its services to women, catered to a population that needed extra money for household and personal expenses. Although the low maximum amount rendered the organization inadequate for entrepreneurial purposes, it was beneficial to housewives who were otherwise totally dependent on their husbands for money. By not requiring husbands' signatures or permission, the Providence Ladies' HFLA provided Jewish women with at least some degree of autonomy. For most American women, pleading— and even stealing—from their husbands were their only options when they needed more than their husbands allowed them. Letters to the editors of women's magazines portray the financial struggles that many early twentieth-century women faced. Margaret, for example, wrote to *Good Housekeeping* magazine about how her husband John would get very angry when she needed more than her fifty-dollar monthly allowance to run the house, pay all bills, and buy clothes for herself and a baby. If Theresa Marabella, a forty-year-old homemaker, had had access to an institution like the Providence Ladies' HFLA, she might not have stolen ten dollars from her husband's trousers for a trip to New York. For her misdeed, according to a 1921 *New York Times* article, Marabella was sentenced to four months in a county jail.[15]

Given early twentieth-century gender roles, it is not surprising that far more men than women sought funds for their businesses. At the same time, however, it is very likely that more Jewish businesswomen benefitted from free loans than the data suggest. When women operated businesses jointly with their spouses—a relatively common occurrence—the husbands would have been the ones most likely to apply for loans. The records of a special émigré free loan fund administered by the Los Angeles Jewish Loan Fund during the early 1940s provide some helpful detail for exploring this issue. Between December 1940 and November 1942, sixty-seven loan applications were discussed in the minutes. The records make it absolutely clear that at least seven of the loans that were listed solely under male names were for businesses run jointly by husbands and wives. Adolph Mintz received money for a dry cleaning store he ran with his wife. Similarly, although a loan was listed under Peter Olinsky's name, the money was approved for a guest home administered by Mr. and Mrs. Olinsky. There was also one case of a husband, an immigrant from Hungary, who took out a ninety-dollar loan solely to be used by his wife who was a masseuse. She needed to buy a car to transport heavy equipment.[16] In general, statistics regarding entrepreneurship often disguise the actual role women play. The absence of women's names from official documents such as deeds, tax forms, and loan applications is not necessarily proof that women were not working as partners within family businesses or even as managers of their own businesses. Census data also underestimated women's enterprising roles. When census takers collected occupational data, husbands and wives often failed to report women's work in family-owned businesses, because they both viewed women as helpers, rather than owners, managers, or even workers. The historical role played by women in small businesses was, in the words of historical sociologists Lenore Davidoff and Catherine Hall, a "hidden investment."[17]

When storeowners and peddlers needed to borrow money for their businesses, how much could they expect to receive from a free loan society? The New York HFLS, which was the largest free loan organization in the country, granted approximately 670,000 loans totaling more than $32,000,000 between 1892, when it first opened its doors, and 1940 (see Table 3–1). It is perfectly logical that New

Ladies' Hebrew Free Loan Association

Organized June 15, 1931 — Prov. R.I.

REV. DR. B. DRACHMAN

CHAS. I. FLECK

JOSEPH SPECTOR

Hon. Vice President.

Hon. Secretary.

Chairman of Executive.

HARRY FISCHEL

DR. B. GORDON

Rev. Dr. L. Zinsler, President.

1st Vice President.

SIMON EPSTEIN

2d Vice President.

NICHOLAS ALEINIKOFF

Counsellor.

Treasurer.

Founders of the New York Hebrew Free Loan Society. Photograph from the collection of the New York Hebrew Free Loan Society.

◀ *Officers and Board of Directors of the Providence Ladies' Hebrew Free Loan Association. Photograph from the collections of the Rhode Island Jewish Historical Association, Providence.*

York City, which was home to over 40 percent of American Jews in 1925, would provide the most extensive free loan services. Even the Boston HFLS, another relatively large facility, expended considerably fewer loans than did the New York organization. Between 1913—the founding year of the Boston HFLS—and 1937, approximately 36,500 loans totaling $4,723,531 were granted (see Table 3–2). This figure represented about one-fifth as much money as was loaned in New York during the corresponding twenty-four-year period. What is less clear, however, is why New York's average loan was lower than the average loan in Boston (e.g., $92 versus $157 in 1925), as well as lower than the average disbursed by several other cities. Being situated in an area with a very large Jewish population may have required the New York HFLS to spread its resources more thinly than many other organizations.

The maximum borrowing amount varied from organization to organization. At the turn of the century, when the Industrial Commission on Immigration estimated that $50 was required to open a clothing shop, small merchants in New York were able to borrow a maximum of $100 from the New York HFLS, the nation's largest Hebrew free loan society. By 1918, the limit was augmented to $500. In 1911, its first year of operation, the Omaha Jewish Free Loan Society's loans ranged from $25 to $100. The Chicago Woman's Loan Association loaned up to $150 in 1918, while Boston's ceiling was $200. A decade later, the San Francisco HFLA lifted its ceiling to $500, followed by Los Angeles in 1942.[18] By the mid-1940s, many of the larger associations disbursed loans for up to $1,000. Only during the Depression did Hebrew free loan societies lower their limits. Otherwise, the maximum amount an individual could borrow increased as the capital needs of American Jews escalated.

At the Brooklyn HFLA, the second largest free loan society in New York City, the amount applicants could borrow depended on their occupational status. Borrowers were divided into three groups: working class, peddlers, and business people. In 1931, most working-class loans ranged between $25 and $50. Not a single loan for more than $75 was granted to members of this group. Meanwhile, every peddler loan fell between $60 and $125, while $100 was the minimum amount granted to a business person. Peddlers and business owners borrowed 65 percent of the total amount loaned by the Brooklyn HFLA in 1931.[19]

Upon making the final payment on a particular loan, borrowers

TABLE 3.1. *Loans Disbursed by the New York Hebrew Free Loan Society, 1892–1940*

Year	Number	Amount ($)	Average Loan ($)
1892	227	1,205	5
1893	505	4,779	9
1894	857	6,745	8
1895	774	7,016	9
1896	828	8,047	10
1897	2,662	38,113	14
1898	3,917	68,110	17
1899	5,353	101,800	19
1900	7,789	153,450	20
1901	10,883	230,646	21
1902	11,759	268,240	23
1903	13,143	320,740	24
1904	14,574	339,820	23
1905	15,226	364,480	24
1906	14,400	372,035	26
1907	15,797	445,355	28
1908	17,895	436,855	24
1909	18,625	471,625	25
1910	19,300	524,176	27
1911	19,949	560,025	28
1912	20,561	605,042	29
1913	21,302	632,410	30
1914	28,282	655,140	28
1915	23,934	670,505	28
1916	24,330	711,940	29
1917	23,403	765,500	33
1918	19,156	731,150	38
1919	17,395	913,855	53
1920	15,693	1,053,180	67
1921	14,489	967,575	67
1922	14,629	1,005,890	69
1923	13,715	1,026,515	75
1924	13,972	1,157,480	83
1925	12,837	1,185,160	92
1926	11,769	1,221,680	104
1927	11,082	1,222,720	110
1928	10,060	1,126,460	112
1929	9,551	1,129,850	118
1930	10,206	1,104,000	108
1931	10,669	1,036,560	97
1932	13,292	910,355	68
1933	15,465	871,220	56
1934	17,985	955,270	53
1935	20,279	1,055,515	52
1936	18,010	947,755	53
1937	17,288	1,000,555	58
1938	18,231	1,107,600	61
1939	17,520	1,129,785	64
1940	16,726	1,123,330	67
Total/average	671,294	32,747,259	49

were eligible to apply for more credit. Of a sample of twelve hundred New York HFLS loans between 1930 and 1932, at least half were renewals.[20] In Pittsburgh, Aaron Abrams, a peddler with four children, received two $100 loans from the local HFLA in 1934. The first loan was used to start his son in business, while the second was invested in his own stock. Between 1935 and 1940, he borrowed $150 for his business on ten different occasions. Philip Davidson took out seventeen loans for a total of $8,000 over a nineteen-year period. During the 1920s, an elderly Omaha woman borrowed $80 every few months to run her small business.[21] This renewal policy provided immigrants with a continuous source of funds.

TABLE 3.2. *Loans Disbursed by the Boston Hebrew Free Loan Society, 1913–37*

Year	Number	Amount ($)	Average Loan ($)
1913	193	15,105	78
1914	430	33,655	78
1915	690	51,812	75
1916	937	80,980	86
1917	1,189	117,545	99
1918	1,234	141,062	114
1919	1,389	180,489	130
1920	1,597	226,880	142
1921	1,521	190,020	125
1922	1,208	168,996	140
1923	1,206	184,715	153
1924	1,456	225,530	155
1925	1,467	229,820	157
1926	1,546	245,681	159
1927	1,530	237,347	155
1928	1,469	230,775	157
1929	1,655	253,540	153
1930	1,745	256,290	147
1931	1,820	259,650	143
1932	1,982	247,961	125
1933	1,920	219,204	114
1934	2,080	234,479	113
1935	2,121	241,500	113
1936	2,066	227,765	110
1937	2,041	222,730	109
Total/average	36,495	4,723,531	129

Depression and War

Even during as severe a crisis as the Depression of the 1930s, early twentieth-century Jewish entrepreneurs had access to their ethnic loan societies. When thousands of people were being thrown out of work and poverty statistics were escalating, the central mission of Hebrew free loan societies—helping people to remain in business—became even more urgent. At the height of the economic crisis, Julius Dukas, president of the New York HFLS said that the free loan was "usually successful in tiding them over a difficult place, in enabling them to get on their feet again, to pay pressing bills, to supply a shortage in money with which to carry on their business and, thus, it means continued employment for many who otherwise would be thrown out of their jobs."[22]

Business loans comprised one-third of the 1,772 loans granted by the Detroit HFLA in 1935. The 329 loans for living expenses made up the next largest category.[23] In his 1935 annual report on the San Francisco HFLA, the president said that "about fifty percent of the loans made are for business purposes, inasmuch as most of the borrowers are small business men—hucksters and proprietors of drug stores, grocery stores, clothing stores, delicatessen shops, etc." An even higher estimate was presented during the president's cumulative review of the organization's activities from 1930 through 1935. Seventy percent of the loans disbursed during these five years "were to persons we helped either to become or to remain self-employed." In 1931, a reporter for the *Cleveland News* described an elderly woman who came into the Cleveland HFLA office to make a payment. The borrower said: "If it wasn't for the money I borrow here I couldn't keep on in business. It's a hard business, selling stockings, dresses, whatever they will buy from me. But it keeps me alive. When you are as old as I am you are glad that they will buy anything from you."[24]

Pittsburgh applicants took out more than twice as many loans for their businesses as for all other reasons combined throughout the Depression era. Examples of individual borrowers illustrate the interconnection between free loans and business development during the Great Depression. In order to complete a 1932 bricklaying job, Ike Becker, a contractor and father of two children, relied on a $200 loan to buy materials. Between 1934 and 1936, Harry Ehrens,

Cover of the Pittsburgh Hebrew Free Loan Association Centennial Brochure.
Photograph from the collection of the Pittsburgh Hebrew Free Loan Association.
Illustration courtesy of the artist, © 1987 by Ilene Winn-Lederer.

a broom peddler, borrowed a total of $250 to purchase brooms. During the same two-year interval, Sam Bronstein, owner of a candy business, borrowed $500 to buy supplies. Between September 1935 and November 1936, Eva Bernstein, a widow with six children, took out three loans for a total of $550 to buy chickens for her poultry store. Irving Deutsch, who sold butter and eggs during the Depression, borrowed $100 for his business on three different occasions in 1933 and 1934. Rose Dorman, a widow and mother of four, peddled dresses to support her family and received five $50 loans between 1933 and 1936 for stock money. With two $100 loans in 1935, Moses Cronin expanded his business from nuts to potato chips and pretzels. Toward the end of the economic crisis, Esther Berger borrowed $200 to purchase machines for her gym and bathhouse.

Struggling to earn a livelihood in the face of economic depression was hard enough. Borrowers in some cities, however, faced additional burdens for which the Hebrew free loan societies provided special assistance. For example, residents of Long Beach, California battled a 1933 earthquake, while many Pittsburgh dwellers lost their homes and businesses to a devastating flood that swept through their city in 1936. In order to provide immediate relief, the Los Angeles Jewish Loan Fund and the Pittsburgh HFLA set aside special funds to help Jewish victims of these natural disasters. In a letter to the Pittsburgh HFLA, David Solomon, one of thirty-two flood victims aided by the organization, acknowledged the importance a free loan had for maintaining his business: "It is difficult for me to express in words my appreciation for your favor, especially since I was so badly in need of funds to enable me to continue in business after our terrible catastrophe of March 1936. All of us should take pride in knowing that there is in existence an organization such as yours to help, at least from a financial standpoint, in times when help is needed." Like Solomon, most of the other flood recipients were engaged in small enterprises.[25]

Throughout the Depression years, Hebrew free loan societies helped entrepreneurs hold onto the businesses they had started before the stock market crash. With the assistance of these ethnic credit associations, people were also able to embark upon new economic ventures during this time of crisis. A dentist who moved from Brooklyn to Cleveland because "the depression had ruined his chances of making a living where he had resided" borrowed funds from the Cleveland HFLA to start over again. In 1932, Bennie Chernin borrowed one hundred dollars from the Pittsburgh HFLA to start a tobacco factory. His attempt must have been successful, for the records indicate that he took out a loan for the factory in 1936. In 1934, Abraham Tulchinsky received a five-hundred-dollar interest-free loan from the San Francisco Rehabilitation Loan Fund in order to begin in either the cigar or candy business. Married and the father of two children, he had been the owner of a Sacramento clothing business before it failed in 1931.[26]

As more and more people like Abraham Tulchinsky lost their businesses and slid down the economic ladder, greater demands were placed on Hebrew free loan societies during the 1930s. Officers who had once bragged about how they had aided clients to become so financially secure that they were able to contribute to Jewish causes now acknowledged that many former philanthropists were appearing at their doorsteps for loans. Speaking at his organization's 1931 annual meeting, the president of the Pittsburgh HFLA noted,

> Never in the history of the Hebrew Free Loan was the demand so great as during 1930, not so much from our former clientele as from new borrowers and from people who in former years never would even think of coming for help to the Hebrew Free Loan. In previous years, we used to point with pride to former borrowers becoming contributors to the Federation. In 1930, we regretfully note that due to general business depression and unemployment former contributors have become borrowers.[27]

By creating a new fund for people "who prior to 1930 were generous supporters of philanthropic enterprises," the San Francisco HFLA made special efforts to accommodate this downwardly mobile group. These former philanthropists were able to receive loans of up to one thousand dollars, while the maximum for all other borrowers was set at five hundred dollars. In Indiana, the Lafayette Orthodox HFLA implemented a policy in 1934 to alleviate the shame felt by some of these new borrowers. To protect their anonymity, borrowers were identified by numbers, rather than by their names.[28]

Until the Depression, Hebrew free loan associations experienced a steady increase in the amount they loaned. Once the crisis struck, however, there was no longer one discernible pattern. At the same time that some associations suffered serious declines, others in-

creased their operations. Coming out of a period of relative in-
activity, both the Trenton and the Birmingham Hebrew free loan
associations were infused with new energy during the early thirties.
In a letter to the Los Angeles Jewish Loan Fund, the secretary of
the Trenton HFLA explained: "About 1931 the institution made a
new turn. A new Board of Directors was elected, an adequate book-
keeping system was installed, and, coincidentally, a Jewish federation organized. We began to grow." Similarly the Birmingham
HFLA was reorganized in 1930 and by 1932 had "produced marve-
lous results by lending immediate aid to large numbers of people
hard pressed for monetary relief." In contrast, the Lafayette Orthodox HFLA was in such dire financial straits during the Depression
that it began selling shares as a way to raise funds. The situation was
so precarious that by the end of the decade, the board of directors
seriously considered liquidation as a possibility.[29] Although many
free loan societies like the Lafayette organization struggled to stay
alive, there is no evidence of a single association closing its doors
during the economic crisis. There are records, however, of a few
new organizations emerging on the scene. On opposite coasts of the
country, for example, Providence and Los Angeles women founded
Hebrew free loan associations in 1931 and 1934, respectively.

The heterogeneous experiences of Hebrew free loan societies during the Depression are further depicted in Table 3–3, which exam-
ines ten Hebrew free loan societies analyzed at four junctures: 1925,
before the Depression began; 1932 and 1935, in the midst of the
crisis; and 1937, once the worst had passed. In 1932, four free loan
associations—Boston, Detroit, Los Angeles, and Seattle—disbursed
more money than they had before the Depression. While Boston and
Seattle loaned approximately 8 percent more in 1932 than they did
in 1925, Los Angeles loaned over 100 percent more, and Detroit over
200 percent more. The number of borrowers in all four institutions
increased, as well. After 1932, however, only Detroit and Los Angeles continued on an inclining path. The amount loaned by Boston
and Seattle decreased in 1935 and again in 1937.

The remaining six organizations loaned less in 1932 than they did
before the Depression. Baltimore and Providence loaned 10 percent
less, New York and San Francisco's decline was in the 20 percent
range, Newark disbursed almost a third less, and Cleveland's total
loan amounts declined by almost half. Only Newark, however, continued a progressive descent in terms of the amount it loaned in both
1935 and 1937. Two organizations—Baltimore and Cleveland—

TABLE 3.3. *Comparative Statistics for 1925, 1932, 1935, and 1937*

City	Number				Amount ($)			
	1925	1932	1935	1937	1925	1932	1935	1937
Baltimore	413	376	363	375	23,986	21,463	29,478	34,0
Boston	1,467	1,982	2,121	2,041	229,820	247,961	241,500	222,7
Cleveland	567	430	443	542	51,690	28,247	29,723	51,3
Detroit	640	1,585	1,772	1,808	42,316	131,580	148,450	186,7
Los Angeles	462	1,485	1,235	1,307	59,775	135,073	140,537	156,6
Newark	1,113	1,033	1,435	1,398	158,270	107,650	104,860	102,3
New York	12,837	13,292	20,279	17,288	1,185,160	910,355	1,055,515	1,000,3
Providence	462	420	426	406	60,495	54,410	70,049	69,9
San Francisco	436	428	293	292	97,487	72,204	56,640	64,6
Seattle (Ladies)	96	105	77	68	6,830	7,415	5,286	5,0

Source: Bureau of Social Research, Survey of Hebrew Free Loan Societies, ca. 1938, Out-of-Town F Jewish Free Loan Association, Los Angeles.

reversed directions after 1932, increasing the amounts they loaned in both 1935 and 1937. The other three associations—New York, Providence, and San Francisco—experienced "zigzagged" loan patterns. Neither a steady incline, such as existed before 1930, nor a steady decline, such as one might have expected, characterized Hebrew free loan societies during the Great Depression.

At the same time that Hebrew free loan societies were not immune to the ills of the Depression, they succeeded in serving as an economic cushion during the harsh financial times of the 1930s. The New York HFLS alone disbursed approximately one million dollars annually during the Depression years. Having had a network of ethnic loan societies in place before the Depression allowed Jews to survive the crisis better than many other Americans. Lloyd Gartner is one of several historians who has commented on how Jews, who were concentrated in white-collar and mercantile segments of the economy, were "less afflicted by unemployment than was unskilled and proletarian labor."[30] American Jews might not have been able to hold on to their businesses, however, if they had not had access to capital.

Helping refugees escape war-torn Europe became a central mission of Hebrew free loan societies during World War II. Between January and November 1941, 15 percent of the total amount granted by the Pittsburgh HFLA organization went to European émigrés. The short-lived Omaha Jewish Women's Loan Society started its operations in 1939 with the explicit goal of making funds available to people fleeing nazism and disbanded just four years later. By cooperating with the American Committee for Christian German Refugees, the New York HFLS pursued its nonsectarian loan policy.[31]

Refugees continued to borrow in the war's aftermath. During the fiscal year ending September 30, 1950, they borrowed more than half of the almost $105,000 disbursed by the San Francisco HFLA. According to the president of the San Francisco HFLA, "a very substantial part of these loans was used to establish [Jewish émigrés] in business such as cleaning and pressing, fruits and vegetables, household goods, variety merchandise, bakery, cattle, and poultry and egg producing."[32]

Along with the Emigré Service Committee and the Jewish Social Service Bureau, the Los Angeles Jewish Loan Fund (JLF) participated in the local Business Advisory Committee (BAC), a committee designed to aid refugees with advice and unsecured interest-free business loans. The BAC began meeting in late 1939 and by September 1940 was headquartered at the JLF office and administered by the JLF executive secretary. Of 111 cases discussed by the BAC between December 1940 and November 1942, at least sixty-seven dealt with loan applications.

Applicants to the BAC requested funds for a wide range of businesses including groceries, liquor stores, manufacturing firms, photography studios, rooming houses, and upholstery shops. For example, Alfred Kahn received a one-hundred-dollar loan for a lapel gadget business that he ran with his wife. In addition, the BAC gave him advice on licensing, arranged for him to use another client's business address, helped him to enter an art-and-gift exposition, and tried to influence him to learn American ways of doing business. Although the board members concluded that Kahn was unreceptive to BAC advice, they admitted that the Kahns were producing an excellent product. With the aid of a fifty-dollar BAC loan and the commitment from relatives to provide thirty dollars per month to cover rental costs, Charles Keller opened a delicatessen. Four months after he began his operations, a BAC report stated that Keller had purchased a refrigerator display case and was doing well. Three months after the report, however, he had to close shop because of high overhead expenses.[33]

In order to take advantage of landscaping opportunities offered by the Los Angeles building boom, seven BAC applicants requested loans for gardening businesses. With its relatively low capital requirements—enough to buy a car and equipment such as a lawn mower, hose, and tools—gardening offered newcomers a possibility for self-employment. For example, Ernest Kepler borrowed $105 to purchase gardening tools and a car; and Jacob Gerstein received $200 to buy equipment in order to engage in gardening maintenance work. In addition to granting Julius Lichter a loan, a BAC staff member accompanied him to the hardware store to help him purchase his gardening supplies.[34]

When BAC board members did not believe that an applicant's business plan was viable, they did not hesitate to dissuade that person from entering that particular line of work. For example, when Paul Brand wanted to start a rooming house, the BAC staff discouraged him because of inadequate capital. Similarly, they denied Max Dissenfeld's loan request for opening a grocery because of the store's poor location. Joan Ehrlich applied for a sixty-dollar loan for a dressmaking shop but was advised to find work as a seamstress. Based on his previous experience manufacturing shirts, pajamas, and dressing gowns in Europe, Franz Reimer sought BAC help for starting a similar business in California. Because of overcrowding in the field, BAC members discouraged Reimer from embarking on this entrepreneurial endeavor and helped him to find employment at a shirt company. Within one month, however, Reimer was fired and decided to join his family in New York.[35]

After the two Los Angeles loan organizations—the JLF and the HFLA—merged in 1948, the new Jewish Free Loan Association (JFLA) continued to help European émigrés establish enterprises. One fifty-year-old applicant who had owned a shoe business in Europe became ill shortly after his arrival in Los Angeles. After the Jewish Family Service subsidized him over a fourteen-month period, the JFLA helped this new American open a shoe store. The organization loaned him $2,000 from a special fund for émigré relief donated by the women's division of the American Jewish Congress, and helped him to secure a store location, merchandise, and a small line of credit. The JFLA continued to lend money to refugees throughout the 1950s. In 1953, the JFLA assisted 102 refugees with loans totaling approximately $51,000, of which $36,300 went toward fostering business development. Six years later, 123 of the 813

JFLA applicants were émigrés; and they borrowed nearly one-quarter of the $304,000 disbursed by the agency.[36]

Although many of the refugee loans went toward creating and maintaining businesses, the new immigrants also borrowed money to bring their relatives and friends from Europe. In a speech delivered in the midst of World War II, Herman Kretzer, executive secretary of the JLF, highlighted the urgency of providing loans to rescue people from Europe: "Human lives were saved because more than a score of loans enabled distressed relatives and friends, living here, to provide the means of getting a visa so that a dear one or a friend in some part of terrorized Germany or its occupied areas could escape the tortures and doom of German tyranny and a concentration camp."[37] Borrowing funds for transportation costs continued even after the war ended. In 1955, for example, nine of the forty-four émigrés who borrowed from the Los Angeles JFLA requested funds to pay for their families' transportation expenses.[38]

Assisting the European newcomers posed problems for some of the Jewish loan organizations. When the first émigré loan requests arrived, several Hebrew free loan association leaders feared that if they granted every loan, they would be without funds for other needs. Often, the newcomers were unable to provide endorsers, and their requests exceeded the maximum amounts set by the loan agencies. As a result, many agencies worked out arrangements with Jewish relief organizations to provide additional funds and to guarantee refugee loans. Just as the Los Angeles JLF collaborated with the Emigré Service Committee and the Jewish Social Service Bureau, the Seattle Hebrew Ladies' Free Loan Society worked with the Jewish Family and Child Service. Similarly, the Resettlement Committee of the Jewish Social Service Bureau guaranteed many of the émigré loans granted by the Detroit HFLA, while the United Jewish Fund and the Jewish Social Service Bureau contributed special funds earmarked for émigrés to the Pittsburgh HFLA.

Tension often erupted between émigré borrowers and officers of Hebrew free loan societies. Many émigrés arrived in the United States with considerable entrepreneurial expertise and resented the unsolicited advice offered by representatives from the credit facilities. In turn, those who worked within Jewish philanthropic loan associations became frustrated with what they perceived to be an intransigent and supercilious attitude on the part of some émigrés. Robert Stark, president of the San Francisco HFLA, complained how he and his staff encountered instances where our counselling efforts were re-sisted. Their sense of superiority over our American methods of doing business was indicated by a resentment to our efforts to demonstrate to them our concepts of doing business. Two cases of these "supermen" are known to us to be at present in difficulties. Our newcomers require in many cases a guardian-like supervision to assure their adjustment to our American way of living.[39]

Meeting the monetary needs of veterans was also on the agenda of Jewish loan activists. For two years the Los Angeles HFLA pro-vided ex-servicemen with twenty-five-dollar unsecured emergency loans. After the War was over, the San Francisco HFLA recruited forty businessmen to work with its ex-servicemen clients in order to "expedite the solution of problems that might appear to obstruct the adjustment of the veteran to civilian life."[40] In reality, however, Jewish philanthropic veteran loan programs never met with much success. Despite good intentions, the aid was not needed. With the support of the Veteran's Administration and the availability of G.I. loans, Jewish credit associations played a minimal role in the finan-cial lives of United States veterans.

By studying Hebrew free loan societies, we can see how ethnic institutions, even those with very explicit cultural roots, are shaped by the broader social context. Entrepreneurial opportunities led Jews, particularly Jewish men, into the field of business and precipi-tated a strong need for sources of capital such as philanthropic Hebrew free loan associations. Due to their societal roles, Jewish women borrowed far less frequently than men; and among those women who utilized the services of Hebrew free loan associations, most borrowed funds for personal and household needs.

Evidence for establishing a connection between Hebrew free loan societies and Jewish entrepreneurship includes the leaders' addresses and statements that consistently describe the organiza-tions as agencies for small business owners, as well as data collected on the reasons borrowers requested funds. Even during the Great Depression, small entrepreneurs applied for funds to create and maintain their businesses. By providing Jewish entrepreneurs with capital, these ethnic institutions expedited the process of Jewish economic mobility.

INSIDE HEBREW
FREE LOAN
SOCIETIES

HEBREW FREE LOAN POLICIES REFLECTED
the economic status of their clients. Unlike recipients of other philanthropies, free loan clients were not impoverished. Before requesting their loans, most applicants had achieved at least some modicum of financial stability, often through their own businesses. A reporter for the *Providence Sunday Journal* highlighted this difference between free loan associations and other charities. The fact that Jewish business owners can turn to a free loan association "does not mean that the member of the race who is pressed for money for other purposes, because of illness or other emergency, is left without possibility of aid from his own people. There are other associations which will help him. The loan associations, however, are designed primarily to assist Jews in business."[1]

Since the vast majority of free loan clients were employed, they had the ability to begin making weekly payments almost immediately after receiving their money. A short two-week grace period before making their first installment was typical. Furthermore, borrowers were in the financial position to take on the obligation to repay their loans within a relatively short period of time. Most societies required full payment within six months. This short-term loan policy allowed free loan associations to make maximum use of their funds. Turning over their capital two or even three times during a year was usual. Lending money, then, was far more efficient than other forms of relief. If a sum of money is loaned to an individual, the money is returned and can be borrowed by yet another person. In contrast, if that same sum is given to an individual, it is never seen again by the institution. During the era when thousands of immigrants were arriving monthly, expediency was of particular concern to Jewish communal leaders.

In addition to the payment schedule, the security requirements weeded out the truly disadvantaged from the ranks of free loan borrowers. There were two different forms of security that a borrower could offer: endorsers and pledges. While all societies accepted cosigners, some permitted applicants to borrow funds on collateral, as well. For example, of thirteen free loan organizations surveyed by the Bureau of Jewish Social Research in 1932, all accepted endorsers, and six also accepted jewelry.[2] Even among societies that accepted both types of security, cosigning was the more common. In Pittsburgh, only 12 percent of all loans were made on pledges. This society ran into difficulty when a burglar stole all the pledges from the safe in 1929 and the insurance company refused reimbursement because there had been no signs of forced entry.

The endorser system was clearly geared toward people who had risen above the bottom rungs of the economic ladder. To begin with, since endorsers were legally responsible for the loans, individuals would only agree to cosign if they were confident that a borrower had the means to make all the payments. And in the vast majority of cases, endorsers were correct in their assumptions. Only a very small proportion of loans were paid by endorsers. Second, being acquainted with people who could meet the guarantor standards suggests that borrowers belonged to social networks made up of individuals who had a foothold within the economy. Owning assets such as a business or property or being able to provide satisfactory bank references were key criteria for endorser approval.

Organizations took the task of investigating endorsers seriously and did not hesitate to reject an application on the basis of inadequate endorsers. In fact, unacceptable endorsers was the most common reason for refusing loans. During the first seven years of the New York HFLS's existence, officers denied over one-fifth of all applications on account of inadequate endorsers. By 1918, the New York facility utilized 150 volunteer investigators, who were responsible for some twenty-five thousand endorsements.[3]

While the vast majority paid their loans, every association had to contend with a small group of applicants who ceased making payments. Staff workers and officers would make every effort to collect from delinquent borrowers. Forthright letters, such as the following one written by the executive director of the San Francsico HFLA, were sent to pressure them to meet their responsibilities:

> It is most unfortunate that you should evidence so little appreciation of what has been done for you while you were living in San Francisco. You had a very hard start to make ends meet and if you did succeed in your effort to maintain your family, you did so only with such assistance as the Hebrew Free Loan Association of San Francisco was able to place at your disposal. . . . I spent considerable time in discussing your problems and advising with you. I called at your place of business on more than one occasion—not to gain any benefit or favors from you—but to ascertain whether I could be of further service to you. In spite of all the sincere effort spent in your behalf, you completely ignored your obligation to the Hebrew Free Loan Association. . . . The New Year has just turned. I do hope, for your sake, that your attitude has also turned and that you will favor us with the amount due, without further delay.[4]

Locating defaulters in order to remind them of their obligations was not always easy. The letter just quoted, for example, was mailed to an individual who had received a loan from the San Francisco HFLA and then moved south to Los Angeles. With the help of the Los Angeles Jewish Loan Association, the San Francisco organization was able to find its borrower. Societies often cooperated with each other in order to track down clients, as well as to warn each other that a person with a delinquent loan history had moved to a new area and might appear at the loan society office.

Once a society gave up on the possibility of collecting from a borrower, it would hold the endorser up to his or her financial commitment. If necessary, societies filed legal suits against cosigners. Of 191 summonses issued by the New York HFLS in 1913, 128 cases were settled out of court, and the remaining 63 went to trial. In August 1927, an endorser appeared before the board of the Los Angeles HFLA asking to be released of his obligation of $90 that was still owed on a loan. The association refused to relinquish him of his responsibilites; he was ordered to pay the full amount at $5 a month and told that if he failed to do so, immediate legal action would be taken. On one occasion, the Pittsburgh HFLA sent the sheriff to collect $179 from the endorsers of a borrower.[5]

The endorser method worked so well that most societies experienced extremely low annual rates of losses, usually under 1 percent. Based on a system of mutual trust between borrowers and endorsers, it provided clients with an intrinsic motive to return the capital back to the free loan treasuries. Since reneging on a loan would inflict hardship on friends, relatives, or business associates who had agreed to serve as cosigners, borrowers had a powerful incentive to fulfill their financial obligations. Furthermore, most borrowers would go to great lengths to avoid the stigma and humiliation that would ensue if their endorsers found out that they defaulted on their loans. Even in the relatively few cases when trust was eroded and borrowers defaulted, the associations' funds were still protected through their legal ability to collect from cosigners.

By ensuring that funds would be returned to institutional treasuries, the endorser system was central to the survival and viability of Hebrew free loan societies. Without such insurance, these ethnic loan facilities would have sustained serious losses. Indeed, when free loan associations experimented with special funds earmarked for applicants without security, they generally experienced high default rates. Poorer than typical borrowers, people who could not obtain endorsers were a minority of free loan clients. Even when philanthropic organizations, rather than individuals, cosigned loans, many borrowers failed to pay their loans. In Pittsburgh, for example, the Jewish Family Welfare Association had an arrangement with the local Hebrew Free Loan Association whereby the former organization guaranteed the loans granted to their indigent clients. Between 1926 and 1935, the Jewish Family Welfare Association endorsed loans totaling $9,740 and had to reimburse the Pittsburgh HFLA for over 50 percent of that amount. Similarly, when Jewish general relief agencies provided their own clients with unguaranteed loans, they, too, experienced considerable delinquency.[6] Between 1900 and 1913, the United Hebrew Charities of New York, through its self-support fund, gave out 1,480 loans for a total of $104,607. By 1914, 13 percent of the amount was repaid in full, 14 percent was repaid in part, 62 percent was considered to be lost, and 11 percent was still considered to be collectable. During the period 1890–1899, the Loan Department of Philadelphia's United Hebrew Charities collected only 22 percent of the $5,355 it loaned out. A representative of the Chicago United Charities reported that the "success we have met with is not the best, but we have received 20 percent of the money we have loaned out."[7] In the absence of the endorser incentive, many borrowers relinquished their financial responsibilities.

The administrators of philanthropic relief agencies, such as United Hebrew Charities, were well aware that by requiring endorsers they would witness a much higher repayment rate. Yet they chose not to implement a security plan because their mandate was to service a poor population who did not have access to reliable endorsers. Unlike officers of free loan societies, leaders of these philanthropies did not expect that the loans would be repaid. Rather than viewing unpaid loans as losses, they perceived any money that was returned to the treasury as a gain. A Chicago representative explained, "[On some loans,] we have received partial payments. In others, we have received nothing. But take it all in all, the society has not lost money, because we should have to give that money outright whether in the shape of a loan or in the shape of charity."[8] In contrast to clients of United Hebrew Charities, Hebrew free loan society borrowers were able to provide security and to pay back their loans due to their higher position on the economic ladder.

Before the 1930s, leaders of Hebrew free loan societies had acknowledged their effective endorser system and efficient methods at almost every public opportunity. During the Great Depression, however, their tone changed dramatically. Speeches at annual meetings reflected disquietude about their borrowers' financial predicaments. In 1934, the president of the San Francisco HFLA reported, "One of the major problems which has arisen during this depression period is the greater difficulty faced by would-be borrowers in securing endorsers. This is because fewer people are willing to endorse and the number of eligible endorsers has grown smaller. Thus, although the real demand for loans was greater, actually fewer loans were made during the year as compared with preceding years." Pittsburgh experienced an increased demand for loans; but because "endorsers are afraid to sign these days under present conditions, it has kept many people from getting loans." To address this serious problem, some Hebrew free loan societies relaxed their security requirements.[9]

In addition to being concerned about their borrowers' endorser problems, officers were very distressed about rising delinquency rates. In 1933, the board of directors of the Lafayette Orthodox HFLA made "a general plea to those borrowers who had fallen behind in their payments, asking them to make what effort they could to meet their obligation to the Free Loan Association." The president of the San Francisco HFLA complained, "Our financial situation is far from satisfactory. This is, in view of the present severe economic depression, to be expected. The earnings and the consequent paying ability of our borrowers having been seriously impaired." According to an annual report of the Los Angeles Jewish Loan Fund, 1930 was a particularly hard year: "Not only has the need been much greater, and the demands far in excess of our means, but poor business conditions, sickness and unemployment forced even the most regular of our clients into delinquency."[10]

Twelve of seventeen Hebrew free loan societies surveyed by the Bureau of Jewish Social Research in both the United States and Canada reported that the number of borrowers who were behind in their payments increased during the Depression. Four organizations provided no data on this issue; and only one—the Hamilton (Ontario) HFLS—indicated that it experienced little change. The delinquency rate of the Boston HFLS increased by about 50 percent between 1931 and 1932. One-quarter of the Minneapolis Gemilus Chesed Society's loans were delinquent in 1932, compared to 10 percent in previous years. Montreal borrowers were slower in making their payments and were having difficulty obtaining endorsers. Since late 1929, delinquencies had been increasing rapidly among San Francisco HFLA applicants; and by 1932, a full 60 percent of the accounts were delinquent. Over a third of the Seattle Hebrew Ladies' Free Loan Society's accounts were delinquent in 1932.[11] To accommodate their clients' needs during this crisis, many Hebrew free loan associations extended their payment periods.[12]

That borrowers were paying off their loans more slowly than they had in the past does not necessarily mean, however, that they were defaulting any more often than they had in the pre-Depression era. In fact, most eventually repaid their loans in full. Throughout the 1930s, officers continued reporting that their losses remained under 1 percent per year. The nominal losses sustained by the San Francisco HFLA—less than one-fourth of 1 percent between 1930 and 1936—illustrated to the president the extent to which his organization "weathered the ravaging storm of the economic Depression." The Boston HFLS's losses for 1932 were only three-eighths of 1 percent and "disclosed a remarkable financial situation in spite of the depression."[13] Having the resources to continue making loan payments during an era when welfare rolls were swelling strongly suggests that Hebrew free loan clients occupied a higher economic status than the typical beneficiary of philanthropy.

Sources of Funds

Hebrew free loan societies were unusual philanthropies in terms of the population they served. They catered to the economic needs of a nondisadvantaged clientele. At the same time, however, independent Hebrew free loan associations were perfectly conventional philanthropies in terms of how they raised their capital. Until the second and third decades of the twentieth century, Hebrew free loan societies relied heavily on annual membership dues in order to finance their activities. While membership accorded voting privileges and eligibility for election to the board of directors, it was not related to borrowing rights. Borrowers and members were generally distinct from one another, with the former being of a lower socioeconomic class. The dues charged varied according to the organization's size. For example, the largest institution, the New York HFLS, had four categories of membership in 1905: members, patrons, life members, and members in perpetuity. The first group, members, was divided into three classes which paid annual fees of three, five, and ten dollars, respectively. Patrons contributed $25 annually; life members, $100; and members in perpetuity, $250. Members and patrons were by far the largest categories. In 1907, there were 4,230 members and patrons, 91 life members, and 12 members in perpetuity. On average, dues comprised 54 percent of the New York HFLS's total income from 1892—its first year—until 1914. During the same period, the smaller Cleveland HFLA charged all members three dollars. The fee structure of the Providence HFLA ranged from $3 to $100 with a life membership costing $250 during the 1920s.[14] Some societies employed collectors who worked on a commission to collect the dues.

Annual stipends from Jewish Federations and community chests (umbrella organizations that coordinated fund-raising efforts and distributed funds to local organizations) began to replace membership dues as the primary sources of capital during the first decade of the twentieth century. In some cities, electing to join the federation brought automatic membership in the nonsectarian community chest. The Cleveland HFLS joined the local Federation in 1905; the New York HFLS in 1916; and the Los Angeles HFLS in 1927. Although a stipulation for joining the Federation was the cessation of organized fund-raising events, including membership drives, without special permission, affiliates were permitted to continue accepting donations. Available statistics for the years 1917–1938 indicate that the Federation allotment for the New York HFLS comprised over three-quarters of the loan association's annual income.

Federations often extended extra help to their constituent free loan societies during difficult economic times when funds were especially low. During the 1930s, the Los Angeles HFLA relied on the Federation of Jewish Welfare Organizations for temporary loans. When the Cleveland HFLA borrowed five thousand dollars from its Federation during the early years of the Depression, it took more than three years to repay the loan.[15]

While Hebrew free loan societies and Federations often cooperated with one another, tension between the two groups was also frequent, particularly over the amounts of annual stipends. Leaders of Hebrew free loan societies easily took offense when their organizations were allocated less than they had expected. From their perspective, low budgets were insulting and reflected a lack of recognition for the importance of their work. Within months after the Los Angeles HFLA voted to join the Federation, it threatened to withdraw from the community chest because of a funding dispute. The president of the free loan association wrote the general manager of the community chest, "you are hereby officially notified that we are withdrawing from the Community Chest on December 31, 1927, and you are hereby strictly forbidden to use the name of this Association during the 1928 Chest appeal, as we will absolutely not permit, that with the use of our name, thousands of dollars shall be gathered for others." The letter ended, "We remain Free and Independent as ever. Hebrew Free Loan Association." Six weeks later, when it became absolutely clear that the community chest would not augment the stipend, the loan society backed down from its threat and voted to remain within the community chest. Tension surfaced again during the 1930s when the Community Chest repeatedly denied the loan society's requests for fund-raising drives.[16]

Relations between the Federation for the Support of Jewish Philanthropic Societies and the New York HFLS began on a much more cordial note. Julius Dukas, who was president of the New York HFLS between 1906 and 1940 and a trustee of the Federation, was at first very enthusiastic that the free loan organization joined the Federation. At a February 1917 New York HFLS meeting he remarked that the year opened

*Julius Dukas.
Photograph from the
collection of the New
York Hebrew Free
Loan Society.*

with our Society placed in the enviable position of having joined the Federation for the Support of Jewish Philanthropic Societies, which came into being on the first of the year and which means that our struggle for funds and members is at an end, for, as a constituent part of this great Federation, we expect to have placed at our disposal such sums as may be necessary to meet the growing demand of our borrowers.[17]

The enthusiasm for the Federation that was voiced during the early years of the alliance became muted in the 1920s. Officers frequently complained that their annual allotment of $38,128 remained constant between 1918 and 1940. The year 1919 marks the first public hint of discontent. While Dukas still voiced his "heartiest support" of the Federation, he also expressed hope for an increase in funds. Throughout the 1920s and 1930s, the complaints escalated. At the annual meeting in 1924, Dukas claimed that the New York HFLS was the only institution that had not had its stipend increased. The board of directors believed that the Federation was not favoring the New York HFLS.[18]

Dissatisfaction with the amount allotted by the Federation continued to mount during the late 1930s and early 1940s. In October 1939 Dukas reiterated that the New York HFLS was one of the few organizations for which the Federation has not increased its allowance "in spite of the fact, that by the very nature of our work we are able to decrease the demands for help made upon other institutions in the Federation." The president went on to ask, "Have we not, then, the right to ask additional funds from the Federation in order to meet the constantly increasing expense of continuing our work?"[19] In 1940, Dukas again charged the Federation with singling out his organization for unfair treatment.

> I think we are the only organization in Federation that has not had an increased allowance in its annual budget. . . . There is, I feel, too little realization on the part of Federation and of the general public that . . . we have in our history undoubtedly saved the charitable institutions of New York millions of dollars by rendering effective aid to individuals in time to prevent the need for outright charity. Does not this fact and this fact alone, demand recognition and are we not entitled to ask and to obtain larger funds in order to permit us to extend this usefulness, which reaches into every philanthropic undertaking in New York, for, as is well known, our loans are not restricted to those of any race or creed.[20]

Free loan societies further supplemented their treasuries with donations, often in the form of bequests. To attract contributions, many organizations instituted loan funds named after individuals. Only the New York HFLS, however, had a sizable number of upper-class contributors, often of German origin, who regularly supported its work. The president of the San Francisco HFLA acknowledged that this source of revenue provided the New York HFLS with an advantage over other societies. "A great deal of their funds came from Americanized Jews. Fully 95% of our loan capital came from foreign-born Orthodox Jews. . . . The meagerness of our funds—that is, before 1922—is illustrated by the fact that, prior to that year, we received only one contribution of $1,000.00 and one of $500.00. The others were for much smaller amounts."[21]

A cursory glance at the list of New York contributors yields the names of many distinguished New York families: Buttenweiser, Guggenheim, Lauterbach, Lehman, Lewisohn, Marshall, Schiff, Straus, and Warburg. They were impressed with the organization's emphasis on self-reliance, its low rate of delinquency, and its simulation of a business atmosphere with tellers standing behind cashier windows. These wealthy philanthropists admired the Hebrew free loan society's reputation as "the poor man's bank," where applicants were made to feel like bank clients rather than recipients of charity. In their opinion, the New York HFLS's preventive approach to poverty merited strong communal financial backing. Between 1892 and 1938, donations comprised, on average, one-third of all the New York HFLS's income.

Jacob Schiff—philanthropist, banker, and Jewish leader—was one of the New York HFLS's greatest benefactors. Born in Frankfurt am Main in 1850, he emigrated to the United States at age eighteen. As a leading partner in the banking firm of Kuhn, Loeb, and Company, he became one of the wealthiest and most influential Jews in the country. Between 1893, when he made his first contribution, and his death in 1920, Schiff donated over fifty thousand dollars to the New York HFLS. Between annual donations and a large twenty-thousand-dollar bequest, his son Mortimer contributed nearly the same amount. In early 1897, the elder Schiff proposed a plan whereby he would "consent to bear part, say one-quarter or one-half of each loan made by the Society." There is no evidence, however, that this plan was ever implemented. When discussions began, in 1913, about opening a branch in the Brownsville section of Brooklyn, Schiff offered his enouragement by pledging one thousand dollars. In December 1915, several months before the Brownsville branch office opened, Schiff wrote to the free loan society's president that he received a two-thousand-dollar pledge from the New York Foundation for this venture, provided that an additional three thousand dollars be raised from other sources. In the same letter, he agreed to provide half of that needed sum. Schiff also supported the purchase of a building at 108 Second Avenue to house the free loan office. In 1917, he sent Julius Dukas, president of the New York HFLS, a check for eight thousand dollars to "wipe out the cost of the reconstruction on your building which will then be free of debt." This wealthy philanthropist influenced others, including the Baroness Clara De Hirsch, to donate money to this favored charity. Schiff addressed many annual meetings, and his presence lent much prestige to the organization. It is no surprise that free loan leaders referred to Schiff as a "guardian angel" and "our best friend."[22]

In addition to his involvement with free loans, Schiff was also vice president of the New York Charity Organization Society for many years and a founding contributor to both the Provident Loan Society—a New York remedial loan association—and a loan fund

Interior of the New York Hebrew Free Loan Society. Photograph from the collection of the New York Hebrew Free Loan Society.

*Building of the New York Hebrew Free Loan Society at 108
Second Avenue. Photograph from the collection of the New
York Hebrew Free Loan Society.*

connected to the United Hebrew Charities. While he was proud that he helped to establish the Provident Loan Society, in Schiff's view the Hebrew free loan society did better work.[23] The *American Hebrew*, a national newspaper, summarized Schiff's remarks about the New York HFLS:

> Mr. Schiff referred to Mr. Carnegie's recent utterances on wealth and its uses and of the degenerates that were found in wealthy families. Work, said he, work was the only palliative for evils in this world, and they (the free loan society) were encouraging honest work. . . . No society in this city was conducted with such care, efficiency, and such economy as theirs.[24]

For Schiff, the New York HFLS maintained "the dignity and self-respect of those whom it benefit[ed], by enabling them to become or remain self-supporting instead of becoming subjects for charitable relief."[25] By encouraging people to rely on their own initiative rather than on "handouts," the New York HFLS gained Schiff's esteem and financial support.

Louis Marshall, another prominent Jewish leader and supporter of the HFLS, was also impressed with the methods employed by the New York organization. He wrote to Dukas that "without exaggeration, I consider your institution as one of the most beneficent in this community. . . . You are performing the exalted duty of brotherhood, not by giving alms or stimulating pauperism, but by acts of justice which leave no sting of shame or of humiliation, but arouse a sense of manhood both on the part of him who is aided and of him who lends a helping hand."[26]

The New York HFLS was even able to depend on its wealthy contributors during the Great Depression. Between 1930 and 1935, the organization received on average more than ten thousand dollars in donations and bequests each year. Meanwhile, other free loan associations were suffering from a severe shortage of funds.[27] The *Newark Sunday News* ran the following story about the financial troubles faced by its city's free loan society:

> During the depression pleas for help ran into hundreds of thousands of dollars annually. Sometimes the association's treasury went broke and the officers and members dug down into their own pockets to keep going. Once the association drew all its money out of the regular bank where it keeps its funds, and

Jacob Schiff.
Photograph from the
collections of the
Institute for Jewish
Research of the
Yiddish Scientific
Institute (YIVO).

Slavitt [president of the Newark HFLA] mentioned to the bank president that they didn't even have enough to pay all the loans already promised. The bank president made out his own personal check for $25, apologizing because—in those days—he couldn't afford to give a larger donation.[28]

While membership dues, Federation stipends, and donations were the main sources of funds, free loan societies sought other avenues for revenue, as well. Fund-raising events, such as annual dinners, bazaars, and fairs, were popular.[29] The five auxiliaries of the Los Angeles HFLA—two consisted of women, one of young adults, one of "little lenders," and the fifth had been formed in honor of a past president—organized banquets, theater events, Hannukah balls, picnics, and an auto raffle. During the Depression years, for example, the ladies auxiliary raised nine thousand dollars. Rose Schwartz remembers that her mother "used to get dressed and go to everybody and sell the [theater] tickets at 25 cents apiece" in order to raise money for Daughters of Peace, a women's free loan society in New York City. The mayor of Paterson, New Jersey spoke at a 1909 local free loan fair, where refreshments, jewelry, silk, cigars, and flowers were sold and musicians performed in an evening recital. Leading New Yorkers such as Robert DeForest, president of the

Charity Organization Society of New York City, and Julia Richman, assistant superintendent of schools, attended annual meetings of the New York HFLS, spurring newspaper coverage of the organization's endeavors.[30]

During periods when demands were high and capital was short, organizations resorted to borrowing from institutions and individuals.[31] When the effects of the Depression first struck, the Los Angeles HFLA took out a series of loans from a commercial bank, synagogue, and friends of the organization. Officers often complained of the hardship entailed by borrowing money with interest from banks and then lending it to applicants interest-free. Mergers with smaller societies augmented the treasuries of the larger groups. In December 1936, the board of directors of the New York HFLS voted in favor of merging with Daughters of Peace, a women's free loan association. Two conditions were agreed upon by both organizations: first, that the Daughters of Peace would relinquish the majority of their twenty-five-thousand-dollar fund, and second, that a member of Daughters of Peace would be elected to the larger organization's board. As a result, the New York HFLS acquired its first woman board member.[32]

Women as Lenders

As indicated by the existence of the Providence Ladies' HFLA, the Seattle Hebrew Ladies' Free Loan Society, and the Chicago Woman's Loan Association, women administered their own institutions.[33] A tradition of autonomous Jewish women's associations in America dates back to the early nineteenth century, when women organized their own benevolent societies at least partly as a response to men's exclusionary practices. The first known women's society, the Female Hebrew Benevolent Society, was founded in 1820 by a group of New York women affiliated with Shearith Israel in order to aid indigent females and their families: "In 1847 the society took a bold step in giving a dinner and ball conducted by a group of male patrons. The account of this function stated that 'it was indeed a novel thing for ladies to appear at a public dinner and hence the plan met with some opposition'." At least eight Jewish women's associations existed in New York City by the late 1850s.[34]

Following this trend, American Jewish women began creating free loan societies at the close of the nineteenth century. Often called ladies' free loan associations, they existed in many communities, such as Baltimore, Boston, Chicago, Cleveland, Columbus, Hartford, Jersey City (New Jersey), Lawrence (Massachusetts), Los Angeles, New York, Omaha, Philadelphia, Providence, Rochester, Salem (Massachusetts), Scranton, Seattle, South Bend, and Springfield (Massachusetts). While all these organizations were administered exclusively by women, most loaned money to members of both sexes.

In 1897, the Chicago Woman's Loan Association, one of the earliest Jewish women's credit organizations, granted its first loan from the drugstore of Mrs. I. J. Robin, the head of the loan committee. Beginning with eighty-seven dollars in its treasury, by 1918 the society was disbursing as much as thirty-three thousand dollars per year, with minimal losses of 1 to 1½ percent of the total amount borrowed. Membership was limited to fifty, composed "entirely of Russian women."[35] Ten women constituted the loan committee, which met weekly to review the applications. Expenses were kept at a minimum, since, with the exception of the investigator, there were no paid workers.

Originally members of a local relief organization, the founders of the Woman's Loan Association felt strongly about the advantages of loans over conventional almsgiving. Loans preserved recipients' dignity, while monetary gifts were humiliating. Minnie Low represented her organization's view:

> Loan a small amount to a man struggling for existence, let him invest it in a legitimate occupation, let him by thrift manage to keep body and soul together; let him at the same time repay the loan in small installments, without flinching, and without shirking his responsibility, and what greater proof do we require that undaunted courage, ambition, honor, and manliness are virtues of the poor? Not to annihilate but rather to preserve these sterling qualities is the mission of the loan organizations.[36]

The Woman's Loan Association was one of the few free loan societies that insisted on the merits of investigating borrowers in order to maximize the benefits of any given loan. Only loans considered to be for a worthy purpose were approved. In contrast, most free loan associations deliberately did not investigate their clients because they did not want to probe into their lives by asking personal and potentionally embarrassing questions. The officers of the Woman's Loan Association, however, feared that a lack of information about the borrowers would lead to fraud, as well as to inappropriate loans for luxury items.

An ardent supporter of women's rights, Low was proud that women administered this Chicago loan facility. At a 1914 national meeting on Jewish philanthropy, not long after the state of Illinois voted in favor of women's suffrage, she boldly asserted,

> no man has ever had an active voice in the affairs of this Association. As contributing members, men have been granted the courtesy of affixing their names to the subscription list, otherwise all privileges have been denied them. What bearing woman's emancipation in our state will have in extending the privilege of the vote to the sterner sex, the future alone will tell. At the present time the sentiment is still against the open door policy.[37]

Low was thirty years old when she helped found the Woman's Loan Association. Despite a history of poor health, (she dropped out of high school in her first year because of illness), she was very active within Chicago's social service agencies such as the Maxwell Street Settlement, the Juvenile Protective League and the Central Bureau of Jewish Charities. Low achieved national recognition for her abilities when her colleagues elected her president of the National Conference of Jewish Charities in 1914.

Within her leadership capacity, Low actively fought for women's equality within the broader field of Jewish social work. She protested when she found out that all thirty-one presenters scheduled to speak at a Conference of Jewish Social Workers were male. David Bressler, president of the National Association of Jewish Social Workers, defended the speaker selection process by saying that the executive committee "did not think in specific terms of men and women" when they made up the program but, rather, "selected the names in accordance with our best judgement."[38] Low responded with the following letter:

> Women not only like to vote, but they like to talk once in a while, and particularly in the presence of a crowd of brilliant

co-workers of the other sex. In fact, if you want to retain the interest of the rank and file, you must give women a chance to be heard. It is not a question of favoring my sex, but it is merely a question of justice, because surely you could have found one fair dame in the width and breadth of this land, who could bring something valuable to the Conference.[39]

Further west, Seattle women also organized a loan facility. According to a brief history compiled by an organization member, the Seattle Hebrew Ladies' Free Loan Society began when in 1909, a group of women from a local synagogue, Congregation Bikur Cholim, organized a whist and sewing club with dues of twenty-five cents a month. By 1913 they had accumulated sixty-four dollars in their treasury and began making small loans to Jewish residents of Seattle. However, the women had first approached their rabbi and offered to buy something for the synagogue with their dues money. It was only after he refused their offer (he considered the funds gambling money) that they appropriated the money for free loans.[40]

The Seattle Hebrew Ladies' Free Loan Society and the Chicago Woman's Loan Association were typical of most women's free loan organizations; they were run by women but had male and female clients. In contrast, the women who founded the Providence Ladies' Hebrew Free Loan Association in 1931 had the goal of providing funds for women only. A group of Providence women formed this organization because they were denied loans at the local Hebrew free loan society unless they acquired their husbands' signatures.[41]

Discrimination against women was evident in other cities, as well. In Canada, the Montreal HFLA rejected "applicants not of age, women married or endorsers unsatisfactory."[42] The Seattle HFLS (administered by men and different from the Seattle Hebrew Ladies' Free Loan Society) only began accepting women members in 1955. A differential dues structure based on gender was in place as recently as 1982.[43] Although the constitution of the Lafayette Orthodox HFLA in Indiana had stipulated that any Jewish resident of the greater Lafayette area was eligible for membership, women were denied membership as late as the early 1970s. When Lillian Kaplan, a crusader for women's equality within the Lafayette Orthodox HFLA, was nominated for a board position in 1973, one male director tried to bar her election with the claim that only men could be on the board since the organization's constitution referred to a director with the pronoun *he*. His argument, however, was refuted

*Minnie Low.
Photograph from the
collections of the
Chicago Jewish
Archives.*

*Pauline Perlmutter
Steinem. Photograph
from the collections of the
Toledo–Lucas County
Public Library.*

by the legal counsel present at the meeting. Kaplan won the election, making her the first woman board director of the Lafayette Orthodox HFLA.[44]

Not all of the male-dominated free loan societies, however, practiced such overt forms of sex discrimination. Although women borrowed less often than men, women's names appear regularly on loan listings with endorsers who are not their husbands. Women sometimes even served as cosigners, as illustrated by a 1901 loan given by the New York HFLS to a man on his wife's endorsement and by a 1938 loan granted by the Cleveland HFLA to a man on the endorsement of his two employed daughters. Clara Appelbaum, a Pittsburgh woman who owned property and borrowed for tax purposes in the early 1940s, endorsed her father's two-hundred-dollar loan for a truck license and stock money. In 1935, Rebecca Bernstein endorsed loans for both her mother and brother through the Pittsburgh HFLA. During the 1930s, the Los Angeles HFLA implemented a policy requiring wives' signatures before approving loans to their husbands.[45]

A few of the male organizations allowed some degree of women's participation on an administrative level. Leah Goldstein, Jennie Gordon, and Celia Grosberg, members of the North End Loan Association, were among twenty-eight people present at the very first meeting of the Boston HFLS in 1912. The group appointed all three women to a seven-person committee responsible for drafting bylaws for the new organization and voted that the women be listed on the organization's charter "provided however that said North End Loan Association will hand over their funds to our society." Also, by way of a financial merger, Rose Schwartz became the first woman director of the New York HFLS after the Daughters of Peace, a free loan society in which both she and her mother had been very active, relinquished its twenty-five-thousand-dollar treasury. In at least one case, a woman was elected as an officer of a nonwoman's organization. Pauline Perlmutter Steinem, born in Poland, educated in Germany, and the grandmother of noted feminist Gloria Steinem, was president of the Jewish Free Loan Association in Toledo, Ohio, in 1908. A suffragist who spoke before the United States Senate, she was a prominent citizen who became the first woman to be elected to public office in Toledo.[46] Steinem was an anomaly, however, within free loan history. For the most part, women could ascend to high leadership roles only within the context of women's institutions.

The ability to control their own organizations motivated women to establish their own Hebrew free loan societies. In contrast, helping women to obtain access to funds was not high on their agenda. By establishing separate institutions with their own ladders of achievement, leaders of women's free loan associations secured some degree of power and status. As founders and officers of economic institutions, Jewish women moved outside of the private sphere and into the public world of communal service.

Irrespective of Race, Creed, or Nationality?

Whether or not to lend funds to Jewish women never emerged as a serious debate within Hebrew free loan circles. In contrast, the "Non-Jewish Question"—whether Gentiles should be allowed to borrow funds—occupied the minds of free loan activists. Meetings, correspondence between activists in different cities, and surveys were devoted to this issue. The ideological split that developed around the question of servicing non-Jews mirrored discussions within the broader Jewish community about how best to relate to Gentiles, a discussion that was particularly American and could not have emerged in the more segregated European context. On one side of the debate, free loan activists who advocated a closed-door policy followed an avoidance strategy for minimizing the possibilities of intergroup conflict. On the other side, supporters of an open-door approach believed it would be a mistake for Jews to separate themselves from the larger community. Rather, the proponents argued, in order to prevent the eruption of anti-Semitism, Jews must contribute to society's general welfare and create arenas in which positive interactions between Jews and non-Jews could take place.

Those who argued against lending to Gentiles feared that if a non-Jewish applicant were either refused a loan or brought to court for nonpayment of a loan, anti-Semitism might result. In his response to a 1942 survey conducted by the executive director of the San Francisco HFLA, N. S. Fineburg of the Montreal organization voiced his strong opposition to an open-door policy:

I may further state that we have long ago abandoned the practice of publishing in the Gentile Newspapers and Press any information as regards our loan statistics, objects, functions and purposes, because the aftermath was numerous applications from Gentiles and the situation became very delicate and terribly embarassing to us as administrators who are always anxious and zealous to protect the Jewish Community and its reputation, and so avoid ill-feeling which can easily be fanned into anti-semitism.

It is my considered, definite and emphatic opinion, after at least twenty-five years of continuous, active guidance of this Institution that no Gemiluth Chasodim Institution [*hevra gemilut hasadim*] anywhere should adopt as a general policy, with the usual publicity, that it lends "irrespective of race, creed or nationality."[47]

Fineburg feared renewing the age-old image of Jew as moneylender. In addition, he believed that the entire concept of a free loan society was alien to the non-Jew.

I find that after painstaking efforts in explaining the function and scope of our work, the traditional idealism and Hebraic philosophy forming its background, the spirit which is wrapped up in this idealism of the Gemiluth Chesed, all of these even when thoroughly expounded to our Gentile friends, even when they thoroughly comprehended everything, they cannot thoroughly grasp what the whole thing is about, because to me it is a matter of blood and it is only the Jew, with a Jewish or Hebraic background, who can understand the spirit and idealism of a Gemiluth Chesed.[48]

Although excluding non-Jews contributed to a tense relationship with its principal benefactor, the local community chest, San Francisco's HFLA refused to change its application policy:

As far back as 1928, we had comments from Chest workers that people had refused contributions to the Chest because it supported a sectarian loan organization. . . . Almost annually our representative had to appear before the Budget Committee to justify our Budget and at each of these meetings there were always one or two members of that Committee who expressed surprise that the Chest should be supporting a loan organization.[49]

While a disagreement over interest charges catalyzed their final break in 1942 (see chapter 5), more than a decade of conflict over the religious question fueled their mutual distrust.

Abraham Gribetz, manager of the New York HFLS, strongly disagreed with a closed-door approach. Gribetz, who worked at the loan society from 1923 until his death in 1971, was convinced that advancing loans to non-Jews alleviated anti-Semitism because of the good will generated by an open-door policy. He claimed, "[The New York HFLS] has received the praise of the Press and of many leading Gentiles and leading Catholic and Protestant organizations. It has done a great deal to lessen Anti-Semitism in this community." At a 1902 annual meeting, the president of the New York HFLS recited,

> Our motto shall be:
> Come, may it be Gentile or Jew,
> if support be your demand,
> we're ever ready to help you,
> ready to give a brotherly hand.

In 1914, approximately 15 percent of all New York HFLS loans were allocated to non-Jews. By 1942, 22 percent of the borrowers were not Jewish.[50]

Fifteen percent of Los Angeles Jewish Free Loan Association borrowers were non-Jews in 1949: "However, money-wise, or in terms of amount of loan capital extended, the percentage was much less." Several years later, this organization granted nineteen loans to Native American families who had left their reservations and moved to Los Angeles, worked with the Catholic Welfare Bureau, and was honored by a local labor organization for its unprejudiced policies. According to the Pittsburgh HFLA constitution, loans were extended "irrespective of creed, color or nationality." In practice, however, there were only one or two non-Jews who borrowed from the Pittsburgh organization during a forty-three-year period.[51]

During the 1930s, board members of the Cleveland HFLA discussed strategies for broadening their constituency. One speaker at the 1935 annual meeting stressed "that the *gospel* of the Free Loan should be brought to non-Jews (emphasis mine)." When the issue of keeping the office closed on Saturday came up, the president addressed his board: "Is it wise from our viewpoint to keep closed if we are anxious to acquire members of all denominations? A great

Abraham Gribetz. Photograph from the collection of the New York Hebrew Free Loan Society.

number of our board members discussed the question of procuring non-Jewish loans. If we do this then our office should keep its doors open Saturday until noon." The board supported its president and the office operated on Saturdays. Twenty years later, the Cleveland HFLA was extending one-fifth of its loans to non-Jews.[52]

The debate about lending to non-Jews continued throughout the 1950s. The San Francisco HFLA conducted another survey in 1950 and found that most societies' experiences with lending to non-Jews were "unfavorable." The Detroit HFLA, for example, stated that the majority of loans to non-Jews had to be written off. Gribetz continued to defend the New York HFLS's non-sectarian policy. In 1957, when he received yet another inquiry about his organization's success with loans to Gentiles, he responded, "Our experience as to repayment of loans has been the same with non-Jews as with our people."[53]

From the 1880s through the early decades of the twentieth century, American Jews created a large network of philanthropic loan societies throughout the United States. The organizations discussed in these last two chapters shared a common vision of facilitating Jewish entrepreneurial roles. By targeting small entrepreneurs, leaders of Hebrew free loan societies catered to clients who were atypical recipients of relief. They had the means to repay their loans within a relatively short period of time and were able to convince endorsers to vouch for their financial credibility. That organizations experienced very few losses, even during the 1930s, also attests to the economic status of free loan clients.

At the same time that Hebrew free loan societies were united in their commitment to serve Jewish business needs, they differed in terms of size, policies, and gender composition. For example, some leaders chose to extend their services to non-Jews, while others limited borrowing privileges to Jews. The question of whether or not to lend to non-Jews was an American dilemma that would not have arisen in the European setting, where the lives of Jews and non-Jews were far more separate and expectations of interethnic help far weaker, if not nonexistent.

Variation between Jewish philanthropic loan associations also existed on one other important dimension: the levying of interest fees. While the majority of organizations provided borrowers with interest-free loans in accordance with Jewish law, some philanthropic leaders consciously moved beyond cultural constraints by creating loan societies that charged applicants a modest interest rate.

PHILANTHROPY AND SIX PERCENT

Why loans from $50 to $200 should be made without interest charged I do not understand. . . . Why place the self-respecting man in a position where he receives something for nothing. He would much rather pay a small interest charge, and not feel under obligations to anyone.

SO ARGUED JULIUS GOLDMAN OF NEW ORLEANS AT THE 1914 National Conference of Jewish Charities.[1] He and several other delegates felt that free loans, an important source of capital for early twentieth-century Jews, did not go far enough to protect the integrity of borrowers. As we saw in the last chapter, free loan activists argued that loans were preferable to alms because by returning the funds, borrowers kept their self-esteem intact. According to Goldman, however, free loans still made borrowers feel like recipients of charity, since they were receiving funds for "free." By charging interest, the New Orleans representative argued, organizations would be able to simulate business transactions more closely and thereby obviate feelings of degradation.

Goldman was not alone in his views on interest. Actually, his was the dominant perspective expressed by leading philanthropists and social workers of the day. Influenced by the prevalent philanthropic trends, Goldman and a small group of Jewish leaders—often acculturated and well-established German Jews—advocated aiding the East European newcomers with philanthropic loan societies that charged interest. These institutions, known within the general society as remedial loan associations, exemplified the principle of "philanthropy and 6 percent."

Scientific Philanthropy and the Remedial Loan Movement

Remedial loan associations were innovated by nineteenth-century communal leaders who subscribed to an ideology known as "scientific philanthropy." This philanthropic approach emphasized the importance of encouraging the poor to be self-sufficient. In addition, maximizing efficiency—eliminating interagency service duplication, investigating applicants, and professionalizing welfare services—became central concerns of philanthropists and social workers.

"Scientific philanthropy" developed in England and the United States during the last half of the nineteenth century as a response to the soaring costs of charity work. In Brooklyn, approximately one-tenth of the population received some form of public relief by 1870. In London, the number of people annually assisted by official charity increased from 85,000 to 120,000 during the 1860s; expenditures increased proportionately from four million to seven million pounds. In order to reduce expenses and deliver services at the "smallest cost to the benevolent," communal workers attempted a preventive approach.[2]

A corresponding ideology emerged to suit the cost-cutting agenda of charitable organizations. Adherents of "scientific philanthropy" professed that "handouts" were psychologically degrading and perpetuated poverty by encouraging dependency. Instead, they advocated encouraging individual initiative and responsibility as the most effective antidotes to poverty. Scientific philanthropists believed that "each must learn in the last analysis to bear his own burdens, to live one's own life and to do his own work. . . . that the ability to 'paddle one's own canoe' is always worth conserving, that self-direction is a real social value."[3]

Scientific philanthropists proposed new methods to prevent pauperism and thus obviate the need for alms. They created work rooms, where women received employment training as nursemaids, laundresses, and seamstresses, penny savings funds to encourage thrift among the poor, and employment agencies to enable people to support their families. According to this modern approach, philanthropy encompasses more than material relief. Friendly visitor programs provided poor people with "personal kindness, even the alms of understanding, prudence, discretion, counsel, friendship."[4] Visitors were specifically instructed not to give doles; they went to the "abodes of misery with empty purses, and pledged to withhold every penny from their personal resources."[5]

Aiding the poor with loans, rather than with alms, was another key strategy of scientific philanthropists. Loans were preferred because they are an efficient and relatively inexpensive form of charity. If a sum of money is given to an individual, it is never seen again by the institution. If that same sum is loaned to an individual, the money is returned and can be borrowed by yet another person. Furthermore, loans promoted self-respect and responsibility among borrowers by requiring them to repay all funds. In order to encourage the disbursal of loans, remedial loan societies were established in many cities throughout the United States. They were semiphilanthropic institutions: funds were donated and then loaned at rates "high enough to cover legitimate costs of operation and to yield a fair return on the capital invested, but no higher."[6]

Scientific philanthropists had yet another agenda when they promoted remedial loan associations: to offer small borrowers alternatives to unlicensed lenders who plagued urban areas with their excessive loan-sharking practices. As discussed in chapter 2, it was not unusual for borrowers to pay interest rates of several hundred percent per year.

The two oldest remedial loan societies—the Collateral Loan Company and the Workingmen's Loan Association, both in Boston—began business in 1859 and 1888, respectively. In New York, Saint Bartholomew's Loan Association and the Provident Loan Society were both organized in 1894. Similar societies were organized in Worcester, Massachusetts, in 1896 and in Providence, Rhode Island, in 1898. Between 1909, the founding year of the National Federation of Remedial Loan Associations, and 1915, the number of loan societies grew steadily from fifteen to forty.[7]

The Provident Loan Society of New York was by far the largest of all the remedial loan institutions. A 1930 study reported that the Provident Loan Society advanced forty-one million dollars per year, compared with a total of fifty-nine million dollars loaned by all twenty-seven remedial loan associations combined. Furthermore, it pointed out, one out of every thirteen people in New York City borrowed from this one facility every year. By the end of 1900, the Provident Loan Society had $250,000 in its treasury and had made loans for a total of $810,000. Thirty years later, the organization maintained fourteen offices throughout New York City.[8]

Leading German–Jewish businessmen and philanthropists such as James Speyer, Jacob Schiff, and Seth Low were integrally involved in the New York Provident's creation. At the same time, according to an institutional history published in 1944, Jews predominated among the Provident's New York borrowers. Through branch offices in Williamsburg, Brownsville, and the Lower East Side, East European immigrant Jews took advantage of this remedial loan association. In 1911, when two existing Lower East Side offices could no longer accommodate the Jewish community's demand for credit, the Provident Loan Society purchased its third building in this ethnic neighborhood.[9]

There is almost no evidence available about the ethnicity of Provident borrowers outside of New York City. According to H. Joseph Hyman, president of Indianapolis' Jewish Welfare Federation, the local remedial loan association "does not meet the need of the small Jewish business man. This type of organization is quite foreign to him. . . . His attitude towards this type of organization is akin to buying herring in a chain store."[10]

Unfortunately, we also lack general statistics on Jewish remedial loan associations. Maurice Karpf's 1938 study, *Jewish Community Organization in the United States*, is the only published work even to mention Jewish remedial loans. Even Karpf, however, does not discuss independent associations but only briefly outlines statistics on Jewish social agencies that provided clients with remedial loans. For 1935, he recorded that twelve agencies loaned close to ninety thousand dollars.[11] The paucity of historical references to Jewish remedial loan societies suggests that these institutions were far less common than Hebrew free loan societies.

The Interest Debate

As the concept of remedial loans became popular within the general society, the question of whether to charge interest was passionately debated within Jewish philanthropic loan circles. At the 1914 National Conference of Jewish

Charities, Julius Dukas of the New York HFLS defended the policies of Hebrew free loan societies against Julius Goldman's criticisms. Dukas did not base his defense, however, on the biblical and talmudic injunction against charging needy Jews interest. Rather, he offered a rational argument focused on the bottom line: fund-raising.

> If we were to charge interest, the public would not support us as liberally as it now does; we should be told that since we charge interest and require endorsers on loans, the same as a bank, we do not need subscribers; since we do not charge interest, we have a membership of 6,000, with an income of more than $30,000, where 6 per cent interest would only yield us $6,000 and the public would probably not care to support such an organization. Our society is thus strengthened day by day by its policy, and the longer we are in operation the more people can we help.[12]

In fact, two decades earlier, the issue of charging interest had been seriously explored by the founding leaders of the New York HFLS. Advocates of implementing an interest fee had temporarily prevailed and the organization, which began in 1892, was reincorporated in 1895 as the Hebrew Loan Association of New York City. Not bound by Jewish cultural prescriptions, this new institution charged interest; and loans were made on pledges of personal property and mortgages, rather than on endorsers' signatures. Twelve directors were listed on the new papers, many of whom had been officers of the predecessor free loan society; and they subscribed for a total of six hundred shares worth three thousand dollars to be used as loan capital. But this new plan did not last for long. Within the year, the organization resumed its former status as a free loan society. In 1897, Leopold Zinsler, first president of the New York HFLS, explained why the Hebrew Loan Association failed:

> Great objections arose, in regard to this system of loaning based on the following reasons. First: Our aim is a pure charitable one, and in the sense of the Jewish ethics, we are not allowed to take interest. Second: our aim is to help deserving people only, and this cannot be observed by loaning on pledges, for then and there we might assist a gambler or thief. Third: (main objection). If we shall loan, even on a small interest, in the course of time, our problem and purpose may dissolve and the society would become a regular office.[13]

Zinsler claimed that by charging interest, philanthropic loan societies had the potential of becoming standard banking establishments, since they "look for the pecuniary interest of the stockholder," rather than after the interests of the poor.[14]

At its very inception in 1912, the founders of the Saint Louis Jewish Loan Association, later renamed the Jewish Aid Association, similarly debated about whether or not their organization should charge borrowers interest. Oscar Leonard recounted the beginning of this credit institution:

> One of the first questions discussed was that of interest charges. Some of the organizers wished to make a Free Loan Society. Others thought a small interest charge would be desirable. The speaker, acting as manager for the Association, argued in favor of charging interest. While the amount charged is small, it gives the transaction a business aspect. I argued at the time that the Association must be a philanthropic organization from the point of view of the members. It must be a business proposition to the borrower. . . . We hope our borrowers will some day do real banking and we wish them to learn that the use of money must be paid for.[15]

Opponents argued that according to Jewish law an interest charge would be "illegal and unjewish."[16] Furthermore, it was not clear to them what constituted a fair interest for a benevolent association. They reasoned that if some of the applicants were uncomfortable with receiving a free loan because they viewed the loan as charity then let only those individuals pay interest. Interest fees, they insisted, should be optional and not mandatory. The traditional camp lost, however, and after much discussion, the board of directors voted to charge 6 percent interest. The funds accumulated from interest fees were slotted to defray organizational expenses and not to pay members dividends.[17]

In 1902, Minnie Low of the Chicago Woman's Loan Association voiced pride in her organization's policy of not charging clients interest. Over time, however, she switched to the other side of the interest debate. At the 1914 National Conference on Jewish Charities, she announced, "In my heart, I believe a small interest should be charged, and I think the time will come when we shall do it in Chicago."[18]

Sometimes Hebrew free loan associations were pressured by outside forces, such as Jewish Federations and local community chests, to charge their clients interest in order to help cover administrative costs. These attempts, however, were always unsuccessful. When the community chest insisted that the San Francisco HFLA implement an interest policy, the consequence, according to the loan association's president, was "to be expected by those familiar with our idiology [*sic*], we withdrew from further participation in the chest."[19] Without community chest funding, the San Francisco HFLA office was forced to cut back its personnel and limit some of its services.[20] Similarly, the New York HFLS ignored the local Federation's policy recommendation to implement a service charge in order to cover operating expenses. At the 1940 annual meeting, the HFLS president explained that "the suggestion has been made that after all these years we should alter our policy and make a slight charge for our servcies or exact a nominal interest. This we resolutely refuse to do."[21] The New York Hebrew Free Loan Society's refusal to heed Federation's advice contributed to the interorganizational tensions described in chapter 4.

That American Jews organized remedial loan associations far less frequently than they created free loan societies suggests that the Jewish public was less persuaded by the need for interest fees than by the arguments in favor of free loans. Yet at the same time, the existence of Jewish credit institutions that charged interest is significant for understanding how culture evolves within new settings. To assume that the character of ethnic associations is static—that they are transplanted by all members of a group from one setting to another—and that cultural heritage is an ascribed monolith is simplistic.[22] The fact that some American Jews organized credit institutions to resemble the modern philanthropic loan associations of the general society points to the dynamic nature of ethnicity. I shall highlight portraits of three Jewish remedial loan associations: the Mastbaum Loan System in Philadelphia, the Jewish Loan Fund in Los Angeles and the Haas Loan Fund in San Francisco.

The Mastbaum Loan System

Concerned with the acute credit problems faced by Philadelphia's Jews, Jules Mastbaum, owner of a chain of movie theaters that stretched from New York to West

Virginia, founded the Federated Loan Association (FLA) in 1920, later renamed the Mastbaum Loan System (MLS). Since Philadelphia, one of the largest immigrant communities outside of New York, never developed an active free loan society, the FLA filled a large vacuum.[23] Mastbaum was aided in this philanthropic venture by other upper-class Jewish Philadelphians: Samuel Fels, Louis Gerstley, Ellis Gimbel, Albert Greenfield, David Lit, Lessing Rosenwald, Horace Stern, and Morris Wolf. Except for Greenfield, all the founders of the FLA were of German extraction. Greenfield, owner of the city's largest real estate business, was one of the first East European Jews to penetrate the German establishment, as evidenced by his acceptance as a member of the German-dominated Mercantile Club, one of the two elite clubs where the loan association's board meetings were often held.

All of these prominent men were actively involved in philanthropic work, particularly within the Jewish Federation. But Jules Mastbaum, president of the FLA, stood out for his level of communal commitment. Described by a noted historian of Philadelphia Jewish life as "the most prominent, most influential, and most generous Jew in Philadelphia," Mastbaum was on the executive board of many local Jewish institutions, headed the Federation building fund drive, served on the executive committee of the sesquicentennial exhibition in Philadelphia, and established a museum of Rodin sculpture.[24]

The FLA generated its loan capital by selling stock to wealthy individuals. Most subscribers purchased at least ten shares at the price of $100 per share. Although it was chartered as a business corporation, stockholders did not receive dividends on their investments. Within the organization's first three years, shareholders subscribed for a total of $134,500 worth of stock, a considerable sum of money for the time. This sound capital base allowed the organization to purchase a building and hire a full-time manager, William Hirsch, as well as a clerical staff. In 1921, the credit institution issued 857 loans for a total of $138,225. Four years later, borrowers received over a quarter of a million dollars.

Applicants who supplied two adequate endorsers and whose loan purposes were deemed worthy by the board of directors were able to borrow sums ranging from twenty-five dollars to five hundred dollars at a flat discount rate of 6 percent. After a two-week grace period before the first payment was due, borrowers then had to repay the loans in fifty-three weekly installments. While these were

Jules Mastbaum. Photograph from the collections of the Philadelphia Jewish Archives Center at the Balch Institute.

the general loan guidelines, the organization was flexible enough to allow for exceptions to be made in terms of amounts loaned, security required, and the repayment schedule. For example, the President's Endowment Fund, a five-thousand-dollar fund that originated from a gift made on the founder's birthday, was established for borrowers who could secure only one endorser.[25]

Hirsch disapproved of the name Federated Loan Association from the outset. In early 1922, he attempted to persuade the board of directors to replace *Federated* in the title on the grounds that the word gave the public the false impression that the credit organization was under the auspices of the Jewish Federation. Hirsch was convinced that many people desisted from borrowing from an organization that they believed carried the stigma of a charitable institution. Furthermore, Hirsch reported, borrowers who were under the assumption that the FLA was affiliated with the Federation were less likely to repay their loans. The board, however, did not approve a name change at that time. Five years later, Hirsch again raised the issue. This time, he complained that borrowers who willingly told their acquaintances about credit institutions that had higher interest fees than the FLA's were not recommending the FLA because they were ashamed to admit that they borrowed from an institution that people thought was connected with the Federation. Two months later—

December 1927—the issue was offically resolved when the stock-holders voted to change the name to the Mastbaum Loan System. Jules Mastbaum had died a year before and in his will bequeathed the sum of one hundred thousand dollars to the loan society.[26]

Hirsch was adamant that loan societies function independently of federations. In a letter to the executive director of the Jewish Federation of Saint Louis, Hirsch insisted that the city's Jewish Aid Association should not be housed in the Federation building because it was "degrading for a person not seeking aid in the form of philanthropic relief to be made to appear frequently in a so-called relief building."[27] On principle, the MLS manager was opposed to loan societies' affiliating with Federations.

A significant ingredient of the MLS's self-definition was as a social service agency, as well as a lending facility. Actually, according to Hirsch, "lending at the Mastbaum loan office has always been a secondary function. The problem of the family and the definite need for the loan is of first importance."[28] Investigating the needs—material, medical, and psychological—of each family member was central to the MLS's loan evaluation process. This emphasis on the family was consistent with prevailing trends in social work. The most popular theories within the field of social service highlighted the relationship between an individual's rehabilitation and his or her family's stability.[29]

The Mastbaum staff routinely advised clients on financial and family matters and did not hesitate to refuse a loan if the purpose was deemed unworthy. At one of his last board meetings, Jules Mastbaum reported that approximately 40 percent of applicants did not have their loans approved because "in the first place, the loan is not a necessary one, neither consumption nor industrial; and, secondly, because the client requires services which he received and which are more beneficial than the loan which becomes unnecessary."[30] Arranging business partnerships, figuring out innovative ways to clear debts, particularly debts owed to personal finance companies, aiding sick family members, and securing applicants with employment opportunities were all tasks that the MLS staff viewed as part of their mandate.

Examples of individual borrowers illustrate the service component of the MLS's work. A woman who was diagnosed with cancer requested a one-thousand-dollar loan in 1928 to cover the costs of radium treatments and an operation. Before approving the loan, the Mastbaum staff made inquiries about her doctor's reputation and discovered that "the man's methods were faulty, he was not an expert in the use of radium, and that the operation which he proposed to perform would not be performed by him but by someone engaged by him and who was not qualified to do the work."[31] After arranging several appointments for her with "leading" surgeons, she was finally persuaded to switch doctors. The applicant would not, however, accept the new surgeon's offer to operate without charge and insisted on paying him five hundred dollars for his services. After discussing this case, Hirsch pointed out that if this woman had approached a bank for the loan, the commercial institution would have simply lent her the money without investigating her doctor's abilities. He concluded, "We could have made a $1,000 loan in this case with fairly good collateral security, but instead we obtained for her the right service and granted a loan of only $500 and obtained results."[32]

In 1927, a male applicant who had a wife and five children approached the Philadelphia association for a three-hundred-dollar loan to pay general bills such as mortgage payments, taxes, groceries, and medical expenses. The applicant claimed that he was in financial trouble because of illness. As a result of the investigation, Hirsch deduced that the real source of the applicant's pecuniary problems was the small size of his apartment, which led to unsanitary conditions. The borrower was advised to get another room to properly house the family. By obtaining more space, "the amount of illness is decreased, the working time of the bread-winner increased, and with it the elimination of all the discouraging elements of an overcrowded establishment. Illness was only a by-product, but improper housing was the problem."[33]

Arthur Bloch, the person who succeeded Jules Mastbaum as president of the MLS, referred the following case to the organization. A woman who worked part-time in sales and was a mother of a twelve-year-old girl, found herself in difficult financial, as well as emotional, straits after her husband, an insurance adjuster, had a serious stroke and was confined to a wheelchair: "He would accept no hospital treatment, was abusive, foul mouthed, and a danger in the home. The child was suffering untold hardship, was not permitted out of his sight and the wife was constantly in danger of physical harm, as a result of the man's proclivity to hurl any object at her that he could lay his hands on." To make matters worse, the husband "had been squandering his monthly checks, sending money by mail for objects he did not need, and for years had been borrowing money from a personal finance company at commercial rates." A plan was put in place by the MLS to have the husband permanently hospitalized. When the husband entered Philadelphia General Hospital in order to be treated for a broken shoulder that he suffered "when he fell out of his wheel-chair in a rage, trying to go after his wife," arrangements had been made in advance to have him evaluated psychologically. He was diagnosed as insane and, as a result, was committed to a state hospital. At the same time, the MLS negotiated an amicable settlement with the Household Finance Corporation and interceded with the husband's insurance company, which had been reluctant to turn the monthly checks over to the wife. An application that began with a standard request for funds "evolved into an 8 month's job for complete straightening out of the entire family situation."[34]

Mastbaum Loan System workers made a particular effort to provide services for men released from prison. Alfred Fleisher, a stockholder, praised the organization's work in the field of prisoner rehabilitation. In 1924, Fleisher reported that of eighteen clients who had been prisoners, "seventeen have proven to be completely successful."[35] For one former convict who was finally pardoned after serving a three-year jail term, they secured a partnership in an automobile agency. In addition, they provided him with a one-thousand-dollar loan through the President's Endowment Fund.[36]

According to Mastbaum leaders, service was the critical ingredient that distinguished their organization from other loan facilities such as the Provident Loan Society, credit unions, banks, and even Hebrew free loan societies. They accused these agencies of having no commitment to their clients beyond ensuring prompt repayment of funds. The Provident Loan Society was criticized because it "makes no special inquiry as to the need for loans."[37] In response to an article praising Jewish credit unions, Hirsch pointed out that the "credit union does not serve the purpose in its entirety. . . . Credit without service is not credit. Helping the marginal man who wants credit must have a much more useful purpose than merely the granting of loans."[38]

Their attitude toward banks was more ambivalent. On the one hand, Mastbaum associates took credit for the development of small loan departments within a number of commercial lending facilities. They were particularly proud of the MLS's influence on the National City Bank of New York, and Philadelphia's Corn Exchange National Bank and Trust Company, and the Pennsylvania Company. On the other hand, they disapproved of banks because they will never "do the work we are doing. They will be lending agencies but not social service agencies."[39] At a 1942 annual meeting, Hirsch made the following indictment of commercial lending institutions:

> The banks grant no indulgences over extended periods, indulgences required to give the client breathing space. The bank is not interested in the health and well-being of the family, or in the need for convalesent care of a member of the family. The bank depends on the reliability of the co-maker on the note for repayment as soon as a note looks shaky. The bank is not interested to help the man to anything better for the welfare of his family. Their purpose is to lend money, get the money back and earn the interest.[40]

The harshest attacks, however, were reserved for the Hebrew free loan societies. Not only did free loan associations focus all their energies on ensuring that their money was returned, but they were a drain on the Jewish community because they were subsidized by Federations. While Hirsch and other Mastbaum workers viewed free loan societies as liabilites, they portrayed their own organization as a communal asset because it prevented people from burdening the welfare rolls. At a 1936 annual meeting, Hirsch commented:

> May it be said to our credit that while we have taken clients off the hands of Philadelphia social service agencies which include the clients of the J.W.S. [Jewish Welfare Society], the Family Society of the Welfare Federation, Penn[sylvania] Prison Society and even the Lansdowne Family Society, succeeding with them to a greater degree than would the organizations themselves had they advanced the money, probably one-tenth of one per cent of our clients have fallen back to relief agencies.[41]

Furthermore, Hirsch was convinced that borrowers preferred the MLS to free loan societies. Once Mastbaum began operating, he claimed that Hebrew free loan clients migrated to the new agency because "they would not accept charity if they could obtain a loan at an interest rate within their means."[42]

While the records clearly reflect a sentiment of superiority over free loan societies, they also indicate a sense of feeling threatened by the success of their perceived competitors. For example, questions arose at one meeting about why some Hebrew free loan societies, such as the Boston HFLS, were handling a larger volume of loans than the MLS. One conjecture put forth was that the leadership and clientele of free loan associations both consisted of Eastern European Jews while within the MLS, elite German–Jewish officers served a predominately lower-class Eastern European group of borrowers.[43] At the following board meeting, the members decided to contact some young men of Eastern European origin for "whatever help they can offer in the form of suggestions."[44] The records contain no further evidence of discussion about this issue.

Class and cultural differences most likely did create a gulf between Mastbaum lenders and borrowers. In addition, borrowers may have also resented having to subject their lives to the scrutiny of the Mastbaum management in order to obtain a loan. As we saw in the earlier example of the man who was ill and asked for a loan to pay debts, he was instructed to get a larger apartment. While the Philadelphia organization was insistent on the careful investigation of each borrower, the Hebrew free loan societies tended not to ask questions in order not to embarrass their applicants. Only endorsers were investigated under the free loan system and applicants' reasons for needing funds were generally not questioned.

Borrowing Experiences

While the MLS's primary agenda was to aid Philadelphia's Jewish community, the organization served clients of any religion and race. Sometimes the minutes and loan records would explicitly refer to a black, Catholic, or Irish applicant; and occasionally, a priest's name would surface. During the early 1930s, approximately 16 percent of Mastbaum clients were non-Jews. By 1940, Hirsch reported that there were only seventy-five non-Jewish borrowers, a lower figure than in previous years. If all seventy-five had borrowed the funds within the previous year, which is a safe assumption, then non-Jews represented 10 percent of all loan applicants in 1939.[45]

In terms of marital status, the vast majority of borrowers were married and had children. In early 1929, for example, only 15 percent were not married at the time of their loan application.[46]

While the records provide cases of individual women and men borrowers, there is no statistical breakdown on gender.

A significant percentage of Mastbaum borrowers owned their own businesses. Of a 289-person sample from 1927, 38 percent were small entrepreneurs.[47] Three years later, the Mastbaum staff completed a study of borrowers' occupations over a one-year period, November 1929–November 1930. Twenty-two percent owned their own stores and an additional 4.5 percent were stand keepers and peddlers. Another 22 percent worked for others while the remaining borrowers were in sales and insurance (12 percent), clerical positions (5 percent), professions (4 percent), and a variety of other occupations (24 percent). Five percent were unemployed.[48] By 1935, the percentage of business owners increased, while the proportion of workers declined. Thirty-nine percent were peddlers and shop owners, and 7 percent were manufacturers. Only 15 percent were categorized as workers. The percentage of professionals (10 percent) more than doubled in this period, as well.[49]

Approximately one-third of borrowers requested funds for their businesses in both 1930 and 1935.[50] In early 1928, after her partner backed out of their mutual arrangement, Rose Perlman approached the loan association for a four-hundred-dollar loan to fix up a tea room that she had opened in Philadelphia. Hirsch described the restaurant as a place that is "quaintly furnished and is attracting a good clientele" and Mrs. Perlman as an "exceptional fine manager [*sic*]."[51] She borrowed an additional three hundred dollars later that year and another four hundred dollars in 1930. At the time she requested her first loan, Rose was separated from her second husband after divorcing her first. She had two children, ages fourteen and sixteen, from her first marriage, four stepchildren, and a four-month-old baby from her second marriage. According to the Mastbaum investigation, Perlman separated from her second husband because of "inability to get along with the children and husband's poor earning capacity unable to provide for seven children [*sic*]."[52] A diamond and jewelry dealer in Germantown sought out the MLS's help after his shop was burglarized. He lost forty thousand dollars worth of merchandise for which he was uninsured. Since his business had been prosperous, the jewelry dealer had enough capital to cover his debts but was left without any funds to start anew. For seven consecutive years he borrowed three hundred dollars from the MLS; and by 1936, he was sufficiently established in his new store that he no longer needed financial help.[53]

One-third of the borrowers cited illness, bills, and debts on their loan applications. Jacob Rudinsky, a widower aged fifty-five, received $450 to cover the payment of his health policy premium, as well as his rent expenses. He was about to be operated upon for glaucoma when he requested the loan in 1939.[54] Within the same year, Herman Backman received $500. He had just had a major operation from which he was not fully recovered; and his wife, who was seriously ill, was about to undergo surgery.[55]

Finally, one-third of MLS borrowers needed loans for assistance to relatives, college tuition, taxes, mortgage interest, and other miscellaneous expenses. Student loans were disbursed on a different basis from regular loans. Unlike Hebrew free loan societies, which required students, just like other borrowers, to begin payments shortly after they received their loans, the MLS did not expect to be reimbursed until after the borrower graduated and entered a profession. Furthermore, student loans generally exceeded the five-hundred-dollar limit. However, there was a price to pay for this flexibility; the security for each student loan was "in the form of cash advanced by persons interested in the student or by strangers to the student who became interested through the intervention of [the MLS] office."[56] At a 1943 meeting, Hirsch described some students who were helped by his organization:

> In Berkeley, California, there is a young man enjoying a teaching fellowship at the University. We advanced to him more than $900.00, beginning at a time when he had a partial scholarship studying with Albert Einstein. At Brown University we have a young man, an associate, teaching mathematics and physics. He had previously been a student at the University of Pennsylvania, had received five offers of appointments and accepted a teaching fellowship at Leland Standford [*sic*] University in California. He recently was called to Brown. Both boys come from the poorest surroundings in the City and neither of them could possibly have completed his work had we not found the money for them.[57]

Student loans were not the only loans that exceeded the five-hundred-dollar maximum. Under special circumstances, the board of directors also approved other loans for large amounts. In some cases, exceptions were made for people who were active in communal affairs. In 1932, a couple—a physician and his wife—applied for a twenty-five-hundred-dollar loan to pay for their mortgage and taxes. As a result of an illness, Dr. Jacobs had to cut back on his practice, and the couple had to take in boarders, as well as rent out first-floor rooms as offices to other physicians. At a board meeting in which this loan was discussed, Hirsch noted that Dr. Jacobs was a prominent physician and that Mrs. Jacobs was a Federation campaign worker and a board member of the Jewish Welfare Society (JWS).[58] When Leon Grossman, a Hebrew teacher for over twenty years developed a growth in his throat that prevented him from continuing in his profession, the MLS provided his wife, Jennie, with one thousand dollars to open a business "either in a grocery, delicatessen or meat line."[59] The MLS collaborated with the Talmud Torahs Association and the JWS to locate the proper business location. Another applicant's fifteen-hundred-dollar business loan was approved because of the "man's previous history and his community consciousness when he was able to participate in community affairs."[60] While MLS board members were prohibited from borrowing institutional funds, an exception was made when one member, who was forced into bankruptcy by the Depression, needed two thousand dollars to embark upon a new manufacturing business. Before the economic downturn, he had earned a good living and had even made provisions in his will for a twenty-five-thousand-dollar MLS loan fund.[61]

Having a good credit history with the MLS also helped one to qualify for a large loan. Mr. Korvitz, who had finished paying off a three-hundred-dollar loan that he received from the organization in 1922, needed additional funds six years later for his expanded candy business. He was in financial difficulty because his competitors had been spreading false rumors about his business's solvency.[62]

Under extraordinary circumstances, the MLS issued loans without any security. In 1932, a barber who had received a twelve-hundred-dollar loan two years previously and on which there still remained a balance, applied for another two-hundred-dollar loan. Since applying for the first loan, his wife had died, and both properties he owned were lost through a sheriff's sale. The barber desperately needed a new loan because he had to move his shop immediately to another location. Since Hirsch considered him to be a good risk, the loan was approved.[63]

In the cases of borrowers who could not provide security, most received loans through a special arrangement with the JWS whereby the JWS guaranteed the loans. Between 1921 and 1930, more than eighty JWS loans for a total of $14,500 were granted through the loan association. Of that amount, JWS had to only cover $2,000 because of defaults.[64] Rarely did JWS borrowers fail to pay any part of the loan.[65] One JWS client, a diabetic and father of ten children, sought out JWS assistance when his original business failed. He listened to the advice of the JWS and found employment compatible with his health. "But," says an MLS annual report, "we soon found that the change from a business man to a working man played havoc with the man's mentality and, upon medical advice, it was necessary for him to give up his job."[66] As a result, the MLS loaned the client $1,000 to start a business with the condition that he was to find a business partner: "An ad was accordingly placed in the Jewish World, and, lo and behold! a capitalist with $1,000 appeared in answer to the ad."[67] In another instance, a complicated plan was devised between the Eagleville Sanitorium, the JWS, and the MLS to help Reuben Rabinowitz open a garage. Reuben had been a tuberculosis patient for six months at the sanitorium and, due to his illness, could not return to his trade as a plasterer. The sanitorium agreed to guarantee $400, the JWS $450, and the MLS an additional $450.[68] On a JWS endorsement, a refugee couple obtained $584 to make improvements on their chicken farm in rural Pennsylvania.[69]

For every JWS client who repaid his or her loan, the JWS was relieved of the need to provide that individual with alms. Being able to save the JWS money was a source of pride for those involved with the MLS. Therefore, when the JWS requested that the MLS cancel the amounts the JWS owed due to its clients' defaults, MLS officers refused. In their opinion, they were already saving the JWS considerable sums of money. On the whole, however, the JWS seemed satisfied with the lending arrangement. Based upon the results of a study it conducted on the relationship with the MLS over a two-year period, the JWS decided to endorse more loans than it previously had.[70]

The Depression inflicted hard times on the MLS. Loans declined from $272,400 in 1930 to $127,800 four years later, and delinquency rates increased from between 10 and 15 percent during the 1920s to between 20 and 25 percent during the next decade: "Clients who had always been able to meet the requirements began to fall behind so that though paying their accounts there are intermittent lapses of from one to two weeks. In some cases payments stopped for two to three months before they were resumed."[71] While many borrowers were late making their payments, very few actually defaulted on the loans.

When first approached in 1934 with requests to aid German refu-

gees fleeing Nazi Europe, the board of directors of the Mastbaum
Loan System decided that "it was definitely not the province of the
organization."[72] By 1941, however, the Philadelphia remedial loan
organization was approving émigré loans on a regular basis. Along
with the Allied Jewish Appeal, the MLS had established a $20,000
revolving loan fund for refugees "who desire to have purchased
steamship tickets and who can furnish at least One-third (1/3) of the
cost of such steamship ticket, provided the Allied Jewish Appeal
endorse or guarantee each borrower's notes to the extent of Fifty
Percent (50%) of the amount thereof."[73] Thirty MLS refugee loans
amounting to nearly $9,000 were granted that year. For example,
one couple who had been in the United States for less than a year—
he was a metalurgist and she had a coffee route—received a $250
loan to purchase a steamship ticket to bring a relative from Berlin via
Lisbon. While the ticket cost $500, they were able to contribute $250
from their own savings.[74]

Although the MLS did not aim its efforts toward borrowers with
any special interests, some Jewish loan associations had more specific loan agendas. For example, the Abraham Haas Memorial
Fund (AHMF), based out of San Francisco, was established with the
purpose of aiding farmers in Northern California, and Los Angeles'
Jewish Loan and Housing Association (JLHA) targeted homeowners in Southern California. These two California organizations
were founded within one year of each other: the AHMF in 1922
and the JLHA in 1923.

Real Estate and Chicken Farms

Caesar Samuels, an immigrant
from Germany, was the JLHA's first president and benefactor.
When he presented the JLHA with his first installment of a fifty-
thousand-dollar pledge made in memory of his wife, he instructed
that the funds were "to be administered by your association for the
purpose of assisting worthy Jewish families in obtaining moderately
priced homes."[75] The articles of incorporation signed the next
week, reflected Samuels' directions. The document explicitly stated
that a central purpose of the JLHA was to "assist families in acquiring homes on easy payment plans."[76]

While many other ethnic groups created scores of loan societies to help finance the purchase of homes, an organization like the JLHA was relatively uncommon for American Jews. Early twentieth-century Jewish immigrants, who had relatively low rates of home ownership and high rates of entrepreneurship, tended to focus their communal energies on developing institutions that would help them in their business ventures. In 1930, of ten Chicago ethnic groups for which comparable data are available, Jews were the least likely to own their own homes. Czechs, who were the most likely to be homeowners, were also the most actively involved in the city's building-and-loan associations.[77]

From its inception, the JLHA helped borrowers with funds to buy and repair homes. During its first seventeen months of operation, fifty families were helped with real estate loans.[78] Jake Stern, for example, was aided with a four-hundred-dollar loan in 1925 to build a "store and rooms." Fourteen months later, he received an addional three-hundred-dollar loan for installing a bathroom and to pay his taxes.[79] In 1926, the board of directors approved a five-hundred-dollar loan to Esther Meyers "for the purpose of reconstructing her partly destroyed residence."[80] That same year, Joe Pred received one thousand dollars, the maximum amount documented in the records, to build a house.[81] In addition, the institution purchased lots, which it then sold to its clients.[82]

In actuality, the JLHA was a combination of a remedial and free loan association. At its very first meeting in January 1923, the board of directors decided to charge a 6 percent interest fee on loans greater than one hundred dollars, while smaller loans were to be interest-free. Throughout the 1920s, a higher number of free loans were disbursed than interest-bearing ones; but the amount of the average free loan was considerably smaller than the average interest loan. In 1926, for example, borrowers received more than five hundred free loans for a total of approximately fifty thousand dollars, and close to eighty interest loans for slightly less than thirty-four thousand dollars. The average interest loan, then, was four-and-a-half times greater than the average free loan. This trend became even more pronounced during the early 1930s. By 1932, less than 10 percent (134 out of 1,485) of the loans were made with interest. By the middle of the decade, however, the proportions shifted, and interest loans were issued with greater frequency than free loans.[83]

The Los Angeles organization went through a number of changes during the Depression era. It changed its name to the Jewish Loan

Fund, experienced increased delinquency rates, and ceased making real estate loans. With the onset of the crisis, real estate loans became very risky, and the officers became more concerned with helping their clients to earn a livelihood rather than to purchase homes.[84] The revised goals are articulated in a 1932 annual report:

> An effort is made to assist small merchants so that their business may be made more secure and profitable by the aid of additional capital; and in such cases wherever feasible, a small interest charge is made. Also to assist tradesmen and skilled workers to establish themselves in business, as a measure of solving their unemployment. . . . Small fruits and junk peddlers need constant attention for the purchase or upkeep of their equipment, trucks, and stock in trade, all are making a desperate effort to maintain themselves and but for the aid of this organization, would be handicapped beyond hope without financial assistance of a small loan timely made.[85]

With seven acres, a shack, a small poultry house, and five hundred pullets, Sam Melnick, an immigrant from Lithuania, became Petaluma's first Jewish chicken farmer in 1904. Within four years of his pioneering effort, four Jewish families joined Melnick in this Sonoma County community situated forty miles north of San Francisco, to be followed by other immigrants who wanted to pursue a pastoral life. By 1930, the Jewish community of Petaluma grew to ninety families out of a total population of 8,245 individuals.[86]

In this center for poultry production known as the Egg Basket of the World,[87] chicken farming became the mainstay for three-quarters of Petaluma's Jewish families. By 1930, they owned sufficient acreage—an average of six acres each—to accommodate 380,000 chicks and over a quarter of a million growing and grown chickens. Among the remaining Jewish household heads, there were six poultry buyers, one poultry wholesale dealer, one hatchery owner, one hides dealer, one feeds dealer, two women's clothes dealers, one hardware merchant, one grocer, one automobile shop owner, one gasoline station owner, one tinsmith, one barber, and one bags and sacks dealer. By the end of World War II, the 175 Jewish families residing in Petaluma made it one of the largest Jewish farming communities west of the Delaware River.[88]

Similar to their ethnic counterparts who earned their livelihoods from urban businesses, these farmers needed funds for their rural enterprises. Since 1918, the Hebrew Free Loan Association in San

Francisco aided Jewish agriculturalists from a five-thousand-dollar special Farm Loan Fund allotted by the Federation. It soon became apparent, however, that this credit source was not sufficient to meet the farmers' pecuniary needs. In 1919, I. Irving Lipsitch, the Federation's superintendent of social service, wrote to the Jewish Agricultural and Industrial Aid Society (JAIAS) in New York City to explore whether JAIAS would provide loans to Petaluma's chicken farmers. It took eleven months (partially due to a long bureaucratic delay in finding an appropriate person to investigate the situation) for Lipsitch to receive a response. Based on an investigator's negative assessment, the JAIAS denied his request.[89] The investigator, a professor at the University of California, concluded that the majority of Petaluma's Jewish poultry farmers were conducting their businesses along irrational lines: "They do not realize the details or essentials to the building up of a high class poultry industry and are interested in quick returns and large profits. . . . If the loans are to be considered from the standpoint of a business proposition, they cannot, in my opinion, be termed either sane, safe, or sound."[90] Except for a few isolated loans, Petaluma's Jewish chicken farmers did not benefit from JAIAS services until 1945, when it opened a western branch in Los Angeles.

Lipsitch continued to pursue alternative credit sources for the poultry farmers, particularly in the face of an emerging farm crisis that precipitated a sharp decline in the price of eggs. In June 1922, he wrote to the president of the Federation of Jewish Charities, summarizing the status of the Hebrew Free Loan Association's Farm Loan Fund. Since 1918, Lipsitch reported, sixty-nine loans aggregating $32,400 were made to forty individuals with no anticipated losses. The superintendent then pointed out that the utility of the Farm Loan Fund was seriously hindered by two conditions: first, farmers needed to borrow more than the $500 maximum allowed; and second, the loan had to be repaid in relatively large installments, the first of which was due shortly after the loan was issued. Lipsitch concluded that "a larger fund could remove all these objections, and could enable the farmers through larger loans to really help themselves."[91] Two months later Fannie Haas, one of San Francisco's wealthiest German Jews, pledged $50,000 to establish a loan fund in memory of her husband, Abraham. In her letter on behalf of herself and her children, she wrote, "We desire loans to be made at a low rate of interest to individuals who are engaged, or expect to engage, in agriculture in California."[92] The organization,

known as the Abraham Haas Memorial Fund, was chaired by Daniel Koshland, Haas's son-in-law as well as nephew; and Lipsitch
served as secretary.

Aiding East European immigrant farmers was a popular cause
among German–Jewish philanthropists. In order to prevent the
formation of poor urban ghettos, well-established German Jews
devised many schemes to encourage as many East European immigrants as possible to move out of the congested cities into rural
areas. Furthermore, there was a sense that the prevalence of Jewish
farmers would enhance the image of all Jews. If, said an editorial in
the weekly *American Hebrew*, Jewish immigrants penetrated the agricultural sphere, then "the arguments would be removed from the
traducers of our race, that the Jews are a nation of money-lenders
and traders. A return to the pastoral pursuits which were followed
by our forefathers will enlighten the ignorant that the Jews were
once tillers of the soil."[93] Many prominent New York German Jews
such as Jacob Schiff, Jesse Seligman, Julius Goldman, Emanuel
Lehman, Leonard Lewisohn, and Oscar Straus worked with the
Baron de Hirsch Fund to settle immigrants in farming colonies in
sparsely populated areas of Louisiana, Oregon, Arkansas, Colorado, Michigan, the Dakotas, and New Jersey.

On the other side of the United States, California businessman
and philanthropist Abraham Haas also supported Jewish farming
efforts. According to Lipsitch, Haas "was always extremely interested in promoting agriculture among Jews. . . . He endeavored to
persuade the trustees of the Pacific Hebrew Orphan Asylum to
locate its new institution in the country instead of the city, in order
that the children might secure a training in agriculture."[94] The
AHMF, then, was a fitting tribute to this leading citizen who began
his career in a family grocery business and went on to be president
of the largest wholesale grocery in the Southwest; builder of Los
Angeles' twelve-story Haas Building; pioneer entrepreneur in the
field of hydroelectricity; and director of the San Francisco Savings
and Loan, the California Insurance League, and the Union Sugar
Company. Within Jewish communal life, Haas was a benefactor of
many institutions such as the Eureka Benevolent Society, the Federation of Jewish Charities, and the Pacific Hebrew Orphans' Asylum and Home Society.[95]

In accordance with Fannie Haas's wishes, AHMF loans were
made at 4 percent interest. From its inception through 1926, the
AHMF granted 110 loans to seventy farmers, the majority of whom

were chicken farmers in Petaluma, for a total of $160,930.[96] Borrowers from other parts of California engaged in "stock raising, fruit growing, alfalfa and truck gardening."[97] Second mortgages, chattel mortgages, and endorsed notes secured the loans; and applicants made their payments in eight quarterly installments over a two-year period. Only one loan, a $120 loan that was made to an agricultural school student, was written off as a loss.

Tension erupted between the AHMF and the San Francisco HFLA when the former organization attempted to augment its treasury by acquiring the latter's five-thousand-dollar Farm Loan Fund. Shortly after the creation of the AHMF, Lipsitch wrote to William Weiss, the executive director of the HFLA:

> It occurs to me that little by little the Hebrew Free Loan Association ought to retire from the business of granting loans for agricultural purposes, so that the work can be undertaken entirely by the "Abraham Haas Memorial Fund Committee." . . . May I respectfully suggest that without undue pressure and in the course of events, the $5,000 fund which the Federation set aside for this purpose should be eventually added to the "Abraham Haas Memorial Fund Committee" which will then be in a position together with such additional sums as it will get, to handle the entire matter."[98]

Lipsitch ended the letter with a list of borrowers' names and balances "which ought to be cleaned up and which have possibly escaped your notice."[99]

Weiss clearly disliked both the tone and content of Lipsitch's request. In his response, Weiss made the following defense: "As to the accounts enumerated by you, which you indicate have escaped my notice, some of them are being paid very slowly. Unfortunately, our failure to receive money from them is not due to inattention to these accounts, but rather entirely due to the inablility of the borrower to pay."[100] As to the emergence of the AHMF on the loan scene, Weiss informed Lipsitch, "I am of the opinion that the 'Abram [sic] Haas Memorial Fund Committee' is conducting a duplication of our work."[101] Not long after this interchange, however, the five-thousand-dollar fund was turned over to the AHMF.[102]

Our most detailed portrait of Petaluma borrowers comes from a 1929 report entitled "A Survey of the Petaluma Jewish Community with Special Reference to Borrowers of the Abraham Haas Memorial Fund," completed by Myer J. Heppner for the AHMF. Based on six days of interviews and observations, Heppner described the borrowers' farms, assessed the impact of the AHMF on the farmers' lives, and compared Petaluma's Jewish and non-Jewish inhabitants. At the time of the report, the poultry industry was entering a period of stabilization after experiencing several rough years. Poor market conditions combined with widespread diseases such as bronchitis, chicken pox, and ruptured yolks, wiped out entire flocks and forced many farmers off the land.

According to Heppner, without the AHMF, many Jewish farmers would have incurred heavy losses during the difficult years. The investigator supported his conclusion with quotations, made with "much emotional feeling," from twenty-eight borrowers. According to one farmer, the AHMF "helped immensely in that it saved ranch for me. Put me on my feet and placed ranch on a solid basis. The fund is like a saving hand to a drowning man going down for the third time." Another said, "Business conditions of industry were in such a crisis that if it had not been for the fund I would have been wiped out."[103]

Further evidence for the importance of the AHMF is the higher rate of farm losses among non-Jews than Jews. Moreover, of the non-Jewish farmers who survived the depressed economic conditions, many took on work outside of the farm. "As far as I could determine there is not a single Jewish rancher who is doing outside work. His energies are being devoted entirely to his ranch."[104] J. H. Gwinn, vice president of the American Trust Company in Petaluma, told Heppner that there is a need for a similar fund for non-Jewish ranchers.

This scenario—Jewish farmers' weathering with the help of an ethnic credit association a farm crisis with greater ease than their non-Jewish neighbors—is ripe for the eruption of conflict. Heppner, however, did not dwell on intergroup tensions. Rather, he highlighted the positive feelings and relationships that existed between Jews and non-Jews. He wrote that the Jewish farmers "are highly respected in the community and looked upon as among the best chicken men in the locality."[105] For example, L. T. Langworthy, manager of the Poultry Producers of Central California, observed that "a higher percentage of the Jewish than non-Jewish members bring in better grade eggs." Langworthy attributed the Jewish farmers' success to their "having an inherent characteristic to make money if there is any to be made, they do their utmost to bring in first-class eggs whereas, the majority of the non-Jews will not take the necessary precautions to strive for eggs of this type. Seeing that first-class eggs bring in a premium of four cents a dozen over dirty eggs they do their utmost to get all their eggs in the higher grade."[106] Heppner did not seem to detect any ill will on Langworthy's part. He noted that "Mr. Langworthy considers the Jews among his best friends and on numerous occasions goes to their homes for dinner. He, in return, frequently has them at his home."[107]

Jewish geographic dispersion throughout the Petaluma region, according to Heppner, was directly correlated to the good relations between Jews and non-Jews: "This is a good thing in that it allows [Jewish farmers] to become more intimate with a much larger number of fellow ranchers than would be the case if they were in one group. . . . As it is, Jew and Gentile, one's ranch next to the other, exchange ideas each giving the other the benefit of his experiences, both good and bad. Such a feeling is bound to build up a stronger community that knows or cares nothing about class distinction."[108]

A second and final report by Heppner provided details about borrowers outside of Petaluma. This group was at a distinct disadvantage compared to Petaluma's Jewish farmers. Most rented the land they occupied, and many devoted a considerable amount of time working outside their farms. For example, David Bilder, who tended an orchard in Oakley, was forced to take a job at a steel mill when his entire crop was lost due to frost. Harry Raskin of Pacoima worked in town as a painter while someone else cared for his two thousand chickens. In Arcadia, Harry Kanter was employed as a trunkmaker, and his wife tended the chickens.[109]

In his second report, Heppner provided several profiles of borrowers. Jake Epstein of Pomona bought and sold cows and calves. In addition, he kept a few calves on his rented two-and-a-half-acre plot for fattening purposes. Heppner was skeptical of Epstein's future plans to devote all his attention to the fattening of calves, because the small amount of land could only support a few head of stock at any one time. Philip Feinberg had a four-and-a-half-acre ranch in Lakeview, almost entirely planted with apricot trees. Heppner reported that "the orchard, consisting of bearing trees, is in splendid shape for which Mr. [Feinberg] should be given credit seeing that his entire crop was frosted early in the spring. When he first came on the place he started with nothing but the land and trees."[110] He also had several well-stocked chicken houses. Max Keller and Victor Caplan, partners in a dairy business, requested an extension on their loan after they were forced to relocate from Arcadia because of a city ordinance that prohibited cows within the city limits. Subsequently, they rented a dairy ranch in El Monte, where they ran a herd of forty-eight cows. Heppner was particularly impressed with the ranch's cleanliness:

> This care exercised along sanitary lines is well rewarded in that their raw milk, in which they specialize, brings them a premium of from two to four cents per quart over similar milk supplied by all other Los Angeles dairies. They are naturally well proud of this seeing that the equipment for chilling, bottling, sterilizing, etc. is not of the latest design.[111]

Egg prices plunged again during the Great Depression, causing severe hardship for California's poultry farmers. Basha Singerman, a chicken farmer who arrived in Petaluma in 1915, remembered how she and her husband "almost lost everything we had" and survived the crisis by selling nine acres of their twelve-and-a-half-acre farm.[112] The Singermans' experience of struggle and sacrifice was common for the era, and only a minority of Petaluma's Jewish farmers became so destitute that they were forced to foreclose on their property. Although officers of the AHMF became much more cautious in their lending policies during the Depression and, as a result, loaned less money during each successive year of the early 1930s—$31,540 in 1930; $18,870 in 1931; $6,720 in 1932; and only $2,600 in 1933—they probably played some role in the relatively high survival rate of Jewish farmers.[113] According to one observer, "it was this fund, more than any other individual factor, that has stabilized the struggling Jewish settlement in Petaluma, both during the pioneering years as well as the more recent, and so much more critical, depression days."[114]

The Jewish farmers who lived outside of Petaluma often lived in isolated conditions: "Being widely separated none of them has the opportunities afforded the Petaluma group in the way of social and other similar gatherings."[115] Petaluma's Jews enjoyed a rich cultural life. With the help of a twenty-five-hundred-dollar loan from the AHMF, they constructed a Jewish Community Center. At the cornerstone ceremony in March 1925, Fannie Haas had the honor of laying the stone of the building that eventually "brought the community together and displayed the diversity and richness of the local Jewish culture."[116]

The Jewish Community Center was built with the goal of accommodating the needs of both secular and religious Jews. It housed a synagogue and library and was the meeting place for many political, literary and fraternal organizations. Basha Singerman reminisced: "When we built the Center in 1925 we built a *shul* in it. You know what a *shul* means? Synagogue! We built a big hall, a smaller hall, the kitchen and the synagogue. I was never in the *shul*, to tell you the truth. I don't know how it looks. I wasn't interested. It didn't occur to me to go in there."[117]

In subsequent years the Jewish Community Center was the scene of fierce political battles. During the 1930s, the members of the communist Jewish Cultural Club were barred from using the facilities. The political climate in Petaluma was so charged that a member of the Jewish Cultural Club was tarred and feathered by a vigilante group because of his support for a migrant workers' strike. The Jewish Community Center was again the locus of a political struggle during the McCarthy era when left-wing Jews were prohibited from the building.[118]

Basha Singerman and her husband at their Petaluma chicken ranch. Photograph from the collection c Kenneth Kann.

With three hundred families, Petaluma's Jewish farming community reached its peak during the early 1950s, comprising approximately one-tenth of all poultry farmers in Sonoma County. From then on, however, Jewish life in Petaluma declined, as did the entire region's chicken industry. Family ranches were displaced when they could not compete against large southern enterprises that produced low-priced packaged frozen poultry. In 1972, the AHMF formally dissolved. This time the farm loan funds—some seventy-three thousand dollars—were transfered to the HFLA.[119]

It is not a historical coincidence that many of the advocates of "philanthropy and 6 percent" who appear in this chapter (e.g., Caesar Samuels, Jules Mastbaum, and Fannie Haas) were German Jews. Since German Jews tended to be more acculturated than the newer East European arrivals, they were more aware of, as well as responsive to, current American trends, such as "scientific philanthropy." When scientific philanthropists organized remedial loan societies in the society at large, some prominent German Jews replicated these institutions within the Jewish community. Developments within American philanthropy shaped the emergence of Jewish remedial loan associations, pointing to a positive relationship between context and ethnic institutional patterns.

A Jew of German descent also played a prominent role in shaping the emergence of another "non-Jewish" loan facility, the credit union. Recognized as the "father of the credit union movement," Edward A. Filene became one of its principal leaders and financial supporters.

BONDS OF
COOPERATION

IN EARLY FEBRUARY 1907, EDWARD A. FILENE,
the German–Jewish department store owner from Boston, stopped
in India during his trip around the world. A self-educated man who
wanted to learn about life in rural India, Filene hired a car and
chauffeur to tour the remote and impoverished villages of Bengal.
He observed a great deal about Bengali survival strategies and was
particularly impressed with their system of cooperative credit. This
introduction to cooperative credit associations inspired Filene's life-
long commitment to the credit union movement in the United
States.[1]

Indian credit cooperatives, initiated by European colonialists,
have their roots in the small towns of mid-nineteenth-century Germany.[2] Herman Schulze-Delitizch, a former member of Parliament,
pioneered the movement when he founded the first cooperative
credit association in 1850. Although a group of wealthy contributors provided the initial funds, his credit facility differed from existing philanthropic loan societies. By paying a small monthly fee,
members helped to defray operational costs.

Within a few years the Schulze-Delitizch cooperative credit association moved even further away from a philanthropic model. The
role of donors was eliminated, and members assumed full responsibility for generating their institution's loan capital. They had to pay
an entrance fee, buy at least one share, and deposit their savings in
the treasury. If the credit association needed further funds, then it

borrowed money with the understanding that all members shared liability for the debts.

Known as a people's bank, the credit facility was run on democratic principles. Each member, regardless of the number of shares owned, had one vote. Members elected individuals to serve on administrative committees that deliberated on loan applications and supervised the institution's day-to-day activities. The credit cooperative's success inspired Schulze-Delitizch to establish other societies in Germany. By the end of the 1850s, 183 people's banks existed, with a total of eighteen thousand members.[3]

While Schulze-Delitizch focused his energies on urban communities, his contemporary, Friedrich Wilhelm Raiffeisen, innovated agricultural cooperative credit associations. Impressed by Schulze-Delitizch's work, Raiffeisen reorganized the Heddesdorf Welfare Organization, a general relief society, as a democratic farmers' credit union in 1864. For Raiffeisen, Christian principles provided the basis for his cooperative ventures while Schulze-Delitizch relied on a secular philosophy of self-help.

Initially, the Raiffeisen credit unions spread more slowly than the Schulze-Delitizch urban cooperatives. By 1869, Raiffeisen had only succeeded in organizing thirty-three credit unions throughout Germany. Over time, however, the Raiffeisen credit societies became even more popular than the Schulze-Delitizch institutions. Between 1913 and 1915 there were approximately seventeen thousand rural credit cooperatives in Germany, compared with about fifteen hundred urban people's banks.[4]

From Germany, cooperative credit associations spread to other parts of Europe and the world. Luigi Luzzatti, an Italian Jew and professor of political economy who went on to become Italy's premier and home secretary, pioneered credit cooperatives in his native country. In 1900, after corresponding with leaders of the European cooperative banks and studying the literature on cooperative credit, Alphonse Desjardins established the first credit union in North America, La Caisse Populaire in Levis, Canada. Although Desjardins and Pierre Jay, Massachusetts' first commissioner of banks, corresponded about the possibility of introducing cooperative credit to the United States, the American credit union movement did not begin until Filene's return home from his travels abroad.

It is not surprising that this Bostonian would be attracted to the concept of cooperative credit. A progressive reformer and philanthropist, Filene believed in the merits of a free enterprise system but sought changes to make it more equitable and democratic. In his mind, the inability of most early twentieth-century Americans to borrow capital was a serious social ill that needed rectifying. Filene believed that credit unions, self-sufficient organizations that were independent of philanthropic funds, could make an important contribution to filling the existing credit vacuum and facilitating achievement of the American Dream.

In addition to promoting credit cooperatives, Filene, the social activist, also fought for workmen's compensation and minimum wage laws. Along with attorney Louis D. Brandeis, Filene founded the Public Franchise League in 1900 to protect the public from the increasingly powerful transit and utilities companies. Three years later, Filene created the Industrial League, later renamed the Twentieth Century Fund, to promote research on public questions such as medical care, the tax structure, the role of big business and employee–employer relations. To fight religious discrimination within elite social clubs, Filene created a men's club—the City Club—where Jews and Catholics were welcome. To make businesses more responsive to societal concerns, he organized the chamber of commerce on local, national, and even international levels. Unfortunately for Filene, neither the City Club nor the chamber of commerce developed into forces of reform. The City Club "soon became as conservative as the city's other institutions and a force for protecting the status quo," and the chamber of commerce "became a powerful force for reaction and repression."[5]

His department store, William Filene's Sons Company, became his own special laboratory for industrial democracy. A maverick in his day, Filene instituted many employee benefits such as free medical care, an insurance fund, an arbitration system, and an employee's cafeteria. At the turn of the century, Filene created the Filene Cooperative Association, which gave the department store workers control in governing each of the above benefits, as well as the power to decide store hours, wages, and personnel issues such as hiring and firing. Filene's ultimate vision was a department store owned by the workers themselves. His brother Lincoln and senior executive Louis Kirstein, however, had no intention of handing the store over to the employees and effectively blocked Edward Filene's plans.

Soon after his return from his 1907 travels, Filene became involved in the American credit union movement. When Alphonse

Desjardins, founder of Canada's La Caisse Populaire, visited Boston in November 1908, Filene was one of a small group who met with him to explore how similar institutions could be introduced in Massachusetts. A few months later Filene testified in a hearing before the Massachusetts Banking Committee about the merits of credit union legislation. With his support, the Massachusetts legislature passed the country's first credit union law, enabling credit cooperatives to be incorporated as credit unions and to be supervised by the state banking commissioner.

Based on the Schulze-Delitizch model, American credit unions operated on a very different premise from philanthropic loan societies. In the latter associations there were two classes of people, who were generally distinct from one another: contributors who provided the loan capital and borrowers who made use of the funds. Credit unions, in contrast, were cooperative and generated their loan capital from the borrowers themselves. The institutions received members' savings in the form of purchased shares and deposits, and, in turn, provided members with interest-bearing loans. When members joined they usually paid a small membership fee and bought at least one share of stock. A certain percentage of credit unions' profits were disbursed annually to the members in proportion to their shares in the organization. Credit union members—each and every one had voting privileges—elected a board of directors, which, in turn, chose the officers.

The credit union movement progressed slowly during the early years. Disillusioned with the work of the Massachusetts Credit Union (MCU), an umbrella organization Filene had helped to establish in 1914 in order to promote cooperative credit within his home state, Filene replaced it with a new organization, the Massachusetts Credit Union Association (MCUA) in 1917. Several years later, Filene financed the Credit Union National Extension Bureau to foster credit union development on a national scale.

The enormous credit growth that took place after 1915 suggests that Filene's strategies were successful. During a fifteen-year interval (1915–30), the number of organizations multiplied over twenty times, from 48 to 1,017 (see Table 6.1). In contrast, the number of remedial loan associations declined during this same period. By 1930–31, the number of credit unions exceeded the number of remedial loan associations by a factor of forty.

During the movement's formative years, a disproportionate number of credit unions were centered in Massachusetts and New York,

TABLE 6.1. *Growth of Credit Unions in the United States, 1915–30*

Year	Number	Membership	Outstanding loans ($)	Assets ($)
1915	48	7,600	420,000	471,000
1920	142	39,800	3,100,000	3,568,000
1925	257	130,700	19,000,000	21,165,000
1930	1,017	292,800	36,000,000	40,910,000

Source: Louis N. Robinson and Rolf Nugent, *Regulation of the Small Loan Business* (New York: Russell Sage Foundation, 1935), 153.

the first two states to pass credit union legislation. Massachusetts passed its credit union law in 1909, followed by New York four years later. According to a 1916 Russell Sage Foundation study (published in Yiddish) that detailed the history and philosophy of credit unions, over three-quarters of the nation's 107 credit unions were concentrated in these two northeastern states alone. The others were located in Connecticut, New Jersey, North Carolina, Delaware, Oregon, Tennessee, Texas, Utah, Wisconsin, and Rhode Island. By 1920, Massachusetts' 64 credit unions and New York's 70 credit unions comprised 94 percent of the total number of agencies nationwide. As credit unions spread throughout the rest of the country, Massachusetts and New York continued to play a prominent role, although their proportion of cooperatives declined. By the beginning of the Depression, Massachusetts and New York credit unions dropped to 42 percent.[6]

Ethnic Leadership

Corresponding with sociologist Milton Gordon's observation that people tend to confine their social participation to members of their own "eth-class"—a social class within an ethnic group—Filene mainly approached other wealthy Boston Jews to take leadership positions within the credit union movement.[7] His colleagues included Felix Vorenberg, president of Gilchrist Company, a men's clothing store; Max Mitchell, vice president of the Cosmopolitan Trust Company; and Abraham Cohen, a municipal judge. All three gentlemen became officers of the MCUA. An MCUA-sponsored history of Massachusetts credit unions acknowledged that the movement was "started, financed and directed almost entirely by Jewish men who believed this among the most fundamental methods of helping their fellow men and who were thus effectively answering the historic accusation of Jewish usury."[8] At one MCUA Finance Committee meeting, for example, Mitchell and Filene each pledged $12,500, while each of the remaining members of the committee—Vorenberg, Charles Weil, Edwin Dreyfus, and Joseph Morse—offered to contribute $1,000. But even before the MCUA was created, a conscious decision was made to solicit funds for the credit union movement only among Jews.[9]

Filene preferred working with members of his own ethnic group, particularly when it came to fund-raising, despite his high degree of acculturation and prominence. He shied away from institutional religious life and distanced himself from secular Jewish organizations. Although Filene contributed funds to Boston's Federated Jewish Charities, he refused to become a member, because, according to his long-standing assistant Lillian Schoedler, it "was against his established custom of many years to become a member of any organized religion or sectarian charitable or educational movement."[10] In the philanthropist's own words, "It must be as clear to every thinking man as it is to me that I cannot have belief in any organized religion or organized theology thrust or forced upon me."[11] Nevertheless, even such a public-spirited individual as Filene, who was in contact with world leaders such as Georges Clemenceau, Mohandas Gandhi, Vladimir Lenin, Franklin D. Roosevelt, and Woodrow Wilson, felt most comfortable asking other Jewish men to help him in his credit union venture.

Part of Filene's inclination to work on this particular financial endeavor with fellow ethnics stemmed from his desire to emphasize that not only did American Jews oppose usury but that they would take active steps to combat the nefarious practices of loan sharks. In his 1930 article, "The Spread of Credit Unions," he explained:

> Now some of the loan sharks were Jews, and some of the agitation against them was anti-Jewish propaganda. It should be recorded, then, that the first promoters of credit unions in America were also Jews. They were not thinking of themselves as Jews in doing the work they did. They were simply citizens sincerely interested in rescuing other citizens from the jaws of

the loan sharks; but the fact that they were Jews, I think—and I thought at the time—was strategically important. So when I broached a plan for the organization of a society in Massachusetts to promote the credit-union idea, I saw to it that the Jewish citizens became its first organizers and directors.[12]

While the men who financed and initiated credit union development were Boston Jews, they hired non-Jews to manage the MCUA. Following the recommendation of Felix Frankfurter, Filene hired John Clark Bills, a Harvard Law School graduate and head of Puerto Rico's Bureau of Labor, but only after being reassured that Bills was not anti-Semitic. Filene was informed about Bills's candidacy, "While he is not of the same race as the members of the Directorate, he appears to have no prejudices."[13] In 1917, Bills became the first managing director of the MCUA. Because Bills did not make much progress organizing new credit unions, his tenure with the MCUA did not last long. After three years, Filene replaced him with Roy Bergengren, another non-Jewish Harvard Law School graduate, who was to play a pivotal role in developing credit unions throughout the nation. Bergengren went on to become executive secretary of the Credit Union National Extension Bureau and then managing director of the Credit Union National Association.

Jewish domination of the credit union movement brought forth criticisms. William Stanton, general manager of the MCU, relayed to his superiors that the president of the Shawmut National Bank and officials of the Boston Chamber of Commerce complained that credit union activity "should be contributed to by a more interracial set of financiers and business men" and that the leadership should be expanded to include "a number of people of other than the Jewish faith."[14] When the Massachusetts state treasurer began to limit state charters to prospective credit unions, Filene attributed his actions to "racial antipathy."[15] In a 1918 letter to Arthur Ham of the Russell Sage Foundation, Alphonse Desjardins, founder of the first credit union in North America, wrote that Jewish merchants should not be allowed to organize credit unions, because "nothing will hurt more your movement than such so-called credit unions organized for the sole benefit of a class of people looking only for their personal advantage and *nothing* else" [emphasis original]. He ended his letter by emphasizing that credit unions should be protected from Jewish influence, "for I fear the Jews and much more the merchant Jews above all."[16]

While some people were critical of Jewish domination, the leaders were proud of their participation as Jews. They wanted to portray an image of Jews' helping to solve society's problems. A talk by Nathan Sallinger, a credit union activist, was summarized in a *Boston Post* article: "Each and every person of the Jewish faith, he said, should do his utmost and make every sacrifice to make this movement stand out as a monument to the State and their people showing the world at large an accomplishment for all mankind."[17] They believed they had a special responsibility to show society that the "Shylock of history and drama is not representative of the Massachusetts Jew of the twentieth century."[18] In a 1916 speech, the rabbi of Boston's Temple Israel encouraged Jewish support of credit unions on the ground that it "helps make people realize that not all Jews are alike, that not all are bad, that not all are money lenders or usurers, that there are Jews who are ready to serve, to help, to give, to lend, not for what they can get out of it but for the good they can thus do."[19] Twelve years later, the editors of the *Jewish Advocate*, a Boston newspaper, praised the Jewish leaders of the credit union movement for having "initiated the most successful movement of its kind to combat usury in the United States. Especially significant is it because Jews are sometimes accused of being money lenders and usurers!"[20] In response to this editorial, the secretary of the New York State Credit Union League wrote to the newspaper that Jews were leaders not only in Massachusetts but also in New York, where seven of the ten officers and directors of the league were Jews.[21]

Filene's desire to "fight an age old prejudice that all Jews were usurers" contributed to his active involvement within the credit union movement.[22] His critical financial support and guidance, especially during the movement's vulnerable and uncertain early years, earned him recognition for being one of the foremost leaders of credit unionism: "His picture hung on the office walls of many credit unions. He was the subject of constant tributes, and audiences listened raptly to his discussions of ways and means to achieve economic democracy in America. . . . More than any other man, he brought the movement to the place where it could be self-sufficient."[23] As a tribute to his credit union accomplishments, a plaque was erected in Filene's honor in the Boston Common.

Filene's dedication to the credit union movement stemmed from his belief that cooperative credit was part of a universal endeavor to improve the lives of average American citizens. While his goal was

*Edward A. Filene.
Photograph from the
collections of the
Credit Union National
Association, Madison,
Wisconsin.*

to help society in general, his efforts were of particular benefit to members of the Jewish community.

The Creation of Jewish Credit Unions

Just as American Jews moved beyond their culture to establish remedial loan associations, they also organized credit cooperatives—modern institutions that charged interest and had no roots within Jewish law. While credit cooperatives existed in nineteenth-century Russia, it is unlikely that East European immigrants had had much, if any, familiarity with cooperative credit before they arrived in the United States. The first credit cooperative among Russian Jews, the Loan and Savings Kassa of the Artisans and Small Merchants of Vilna, was not established until 1898. The growth of these organizations proved to be slow among Jews because of restrictive government legislation. It was not until 1906, when new regulations were put into effect, that Jewish credit cooperatives were organized in significant numbers.

Two hundred and fifty existed in Russia by the end of September 1907. At the outbreak of World War I, there were 680 Jewish credit cooperatives with over 450,000 members and a capital of forty million rubles.[24] Credit cooperatives were organized, then, at about the same time in the Jewish communities of Russia and America; they were not transported from one country to another.

That credit unions had no cultural basis, however, does not necessarily suggest that they were in transgression of Jewish law. In his published volume of religious rulings, Rabbi Moses Shohet, an immigrant from Lithuania who lived in New England before settling in Jerusalem in 1933, addressed the following question: Since Jews were prohibited from charging other Jews interest, were credit unions, organizations that charged interest on loans, in violation of religious law? Shohet concluded that participating in a credit union was permitted, since the interest collected by a credit union augmented the institution's general funds and thus benefitted the entire group. Since no one individual profited by the interest charges, credit unions were not in violation of Jewish law.[25]

While Jews founded only a handful of remedial loan societies, they created scores of credit cooperatives. Until the post-Depression era, a disproportionate number of credit union members were Jews of East European descent. In 1916, Jews operated half of all urban credit unions in New York State; and by the early years of the Depression, 85 (73 percent) of the state's 117 credit unions had a predominately Jewish membership.[26] Jewish participation was particularly high in New York City. In 1918, ten of this large metropolitan area's 23 credit unions were composed almost entirely of Jews.[27] Twelve years later, the 79 Jewish cooperatives comprised 68 percent of New York City's total number of credit unions, owned 77 percent (close to $8,500,000) of all organizational assets, and granted 82 percent (over $11,000,000) of the total volume of loans. The average Jewish credit union loan was $396, compared with $242, the average loan granted by New York City's non-Jewish institutions. The Jewish facilities, then, were relatively large in terms of both membership and resources.[28]

In Connecticut, Jews also actively organized credit cooperatives. By the early 1950s, Hartford Jews organized 46 of that city's 65 credit unions, such as the Kief Protective Mutual Benefit Society and the Victory Loan Mutual Benefit Association, named after the allied victory in World War II.[29] In neighboring Massachusetts, 172 (55 percent) of the state's 311 credit unions that existed in 1930 had mostly Jewish members.[30] Over three-quarters of Boston's 139 credit unions listed by the banking commissioner in his 1927 annual report, had either explicitly Jewish names or a board of directors and a group of officers that were at least two-thirds Jewish.[31] Collectively, their assets were worth over two million dollars. According to a different 1927 study, one that focused on eight credit unions, of which seven were in Boston, "the great majority [of the borrowers] were American born, largely of Irish, English, and Russian–Jewish stock."[32]

Massachusetts credit union leaders recognized the potential for recruiting members from the Jewish community. In 1914, Max Mitchell, then an officer of the MCU, hired a credit union organizer who had been affiliated with the Roxbury Credit Union and was able to speak Yiddish. At his own expense, Mitchell hired another man

Organizers of the Worcester Credit Union, April 17, 1910. Seated left to right: Berkowitz, Abelson, Lederman, Joseph, Cohen, Joseph, Parker, Mazur. Standing left to right: Saltzman, Weisman, Abelson, Lubarsky. Photograph from the collection of the Worcester Historical Museum, Worcester, Massachusetts

"to bring the credit union system before the various Jewish lodges, synagogues, etc." Stanton, general manager of the MCU, reported to the board of directors that he was in close contact with Jews in various parts of Massachusetts and that according to his assessment, credit unions "among the jewish [*sic*] residents of Springfield and Holyoke may be organized in the near future." The board also sent Jacob de Haas as a delegate to the 1914 National Conference on Jewish Charities in Memphis. There he made contacts with such prominent Jewish figures as Cyrus Sulzberger and, through a representative, Julius Rosenwald.[33]

Extant MCU minutes reflect that considerable effort was extended toward organizing credit unions within the Jewish community. In contrast, only once did Stanton mention the contacts he made within other ethnic groups. He had interviewed prominent Armenian, Syrian, Greek, Polish, and Italian men but, according to his own report, "did not waste any time on these projects, but simply took odd times when it was convenient for me to call."[34] Stanton, unfortunately, did not expound upon why he invested so little energy on the non-Jewish groups. It is possible, as historians J. Carroll Moody and Gilbert C. Fite suggest, that Stanton shaped his priorities in response to the low level of interest exhibited by most ethnic leaders. By 1920, only isolated facilities (e.g., the Skandia Credit Union in Worcester, the predominately Finnish Workers' Credit Union in Fitchburg, and the Polish National Credit Union in Chicopee), emerged among non-Jewish communities. As late as 1927, only one Boston credit union, the Independent Order Sons of Italy Credit Union, was identifiably Italian; and ten years later, Italians administered only 4 of the state's 419 credit unions. Although the Saint Jean Baptiste Parish Credit Union (Lynn, Massachusetts) and the Saint Mary's Parish Credit Union (Manchester, New Hampshire) were two of the earliest cooperatives in the country, parish credit union development made little headway until 1930.[35]

Roy Bergengren was highly critical of credit unions that "were organized within groups with no other than racial group significance."[36] He accused them of having high interest rates, lacking honest administrators, and being vulnerable to liquidation. Every New York credit union that failed during the Depression, Bergengren claimed in early 1933, was a racial credit union "with an open charter."[37] Since, by his own accounts, these racial credit unions existed only in New York and, to a lesser extent, in Massachusetts, it is clear that Bergengren's criticisms were primarily directed at institutions with heavy Jewish constituencies.[38] It was not at all unusual for early twentieth-century Jews and non-Jews alike to categorize Jews as a racial group.

There are several possible explanations for why Bergengren was antagonistic toward Jewish credit unions. He may not have been opposed to Jewish credit unions per se, but, rather, to their high percentage of "open" facilities which any Jew could join. Open credit unions lacked sufficient common bonds that united members, an ingredient that according to Bergengren, was central to a successful operation. He favored "closed" credit unions that were sponsored by employee groups such as telephone and postal workers and parish credit unions that benefitted from the guidance of priests, as well as from "the parish community spirit."[39]

The vast majority of Bergengren's critical comments were reserved for racial credit unions in New York. At times, he even praised open Jewish credit unions in Massachusetts such as the Beacon Hill Credit Union, Blue Hill Neighborhood Credit Union, Lord Beaconsfield Credit Union, Salem Credit Union, and Traders' Credit Union.[40] This contradiction suggests that Bergengren's antipathy had less to do with Jewish credit unions and more to do with his attitudes toward credit union development in New York. New York was the one region in the entire country where Bergengren was not allowed to do his organizing work. The Russell Sage Foundation had jurisdiction there, while the MCUA—and, later, the Credit Union National Extension Bureau—supervised credit union development throughout all other states.

Being excluded from New York was a source of frustration for Bergengren. He was convinced that the Russell Sage Foundation was not providing "the right sort of supervision or leadership" and that many opportunities for establishing employee credit unions were being ignored.[41] In 1928, when Bergengren approached Leon Henderson of the Russell Sage Foundation about visiting New York in order to form credit unions "of the right sort," he was told in no uncertain terms to keep away from the area.[42] His dissatisfaction continued to mount; and in 1930 he wrote the following letter to Filene, his employer:

> In New York for eight years I tried in every way I knew how to get the Russell Sage Foundation to carry on the credit union work adequately in that one state. In all of the other states our work is coming along in uniform and excellent fashion. In

New York State the credit union work has been botched, mismanaged, and improperly conducted from the very start. All of the serious operating problems we have in credit union work are in New York State. . . . For years and years we tried every diplomatic trick we knew to have the Foundation carry on a typical credit union development in New York.[43]

Shortly thereafter, the Russell Sage Foundation relinquished its control over New York and Bergengren was allowed to enter this one remaining field. Under his jurisdiction, state-chartered open membership credit unions declined significantly from eighty-one in 1928 to forty-nine in 1937, despite the New York Credit Union League's unqualified support of open facilities.[44] In 1931, the league resolved to promote the "advancement of that type of credit union, . . . render every assistance possible to such open credit unions as now exist, and propose such legislation to further the interests of this type."[45] Not surprisingly, considerable tension existed between the leadership of the New York State league and Bergengren.

Bergengren's opposition to Jewish credit unions may have also stemmed from his discomfort with being affiliated with a movement that had such a strong Jewish presence. Years later, when he was managing director of the Vermont Credit Union League, he continued to voice uneasiness with New York's Jewish character. In a 1952 letter to Agnes Gartland, who had been his assistant executive secretary for many years, Bergengren attributed New York's credit union problems to the need for "an office outside New York City and a good field man of Gentile persuasion."[46] Some of his criticisms may have even been tainted with prejudice. Certainly accusations that racial or Jewish credit unions charged high rates of interest and were run dishonestly are reminiscent of anti-Semitic canards. In 1951, Gartland wrote to her former employer that two individuals, including "our Jewish lawyer," were to blame for poor legislation in California, suggesting that negative ethnic references were tolerated by Bergengren.

Jews also formed credit unions outside of the Northeast. Just weeks after the devastating stock market crash that shook at the core of America's economy in 1929, the Indianapolis Jewish Federation initiated the Jewish Community Credit Union in order to provide small entrepreneurs with a steady and reliable source of capital. The Indianapolis Jewish Community Credit Union was unique; no other credit union experienced such a close relationship with a Federation.

The Indianapolis Jewish Federation entered the credit union business because, according to its executive director, H. Joseph Hyman, neither the local Hebrew free loan society nor the city's nonsectarian remedial loan association adequately solved the Jewish community's credit problems. Furthermore, they did nothing to encourage savings and thrift among their clients. Due to limited resources, Hebrew free loan societies loaned amounts too small to be really useful; and its policy of not charging interest made it a charitable facility. In contrast, Hyman argued, the credit union

> adds another step in the direction of dignity and security. It is a mutual organization; the borrower must be a member; he must save simultaneously with the repayment of his loan; he benefits by the earnings in the form of a dividend on his stock; he has a voice in the management of the Credit Union, since every member, irrespective of the amount invested, has equal voting power.[47]

The executive director went on to equate the Hebrew free loan society with "the relief society several decades ago," and the society's borrower with "an honest Schlemiel."[48]

While representatives from the Jewish Federation, the Jewish Welfare Fund, and the Jewish Family Service Society sat on the Jewish Community Credit Union's board of directors, the credit union office was deliberately located away from the Federation building so as to avoid any stigma attached with being affiliated with a philanthropic institution. Sometimes, the Jewish Family Service Society would refer its clients to the Jewish Community Credit Union and endorse their notes. The delinquency rate of this group, however, was high. In 1931, only three of the seventeen Jewish Family Service Society borrowers were making regular payments.[49]

Leo Kaminsky, who became president of the Jewish Community Credit Union, was very active within his state's credit union movement. Known as the "father of the Indiana credit union act," Kaminsky organized the state campaign that led to the passage of crucial legislation in 1923. That same year, he organized the first credit union in the Midwest for employees of Wasson and Company, an Indianapolis department store.[50]

That Jews such as Leo Kaminsky and Edward A. Filene comprised the leadership of the credit union movement may have contributed to the popularity of credit cooperatives among Jewish immigrants.

While these institutions probably would have been attractive to East European Jews regardless of the leaders' nationalities or religions, the pronounced Jewish character of the leadership may have encouraged Jewish rank-and-file participation in credit unions.

Aktsiyes

Technically, an organization did not become a credit union until it was legally incorporated under a state's credit union law or, after 1934, under federal law. Many Jewish credit unions, however, had their origins as informal credit cooperatives known in Yiddish as *aktsiyes*.[51] *Aktsi* has its etymological roots in *Aktiengesellschaft*, the German word for a society of shareholders or joint stock company. The primary distinction between a credit union and an *aktsi* is that the former was government-regulated, while the latter had no legal status.

During the first decades of the twentieth century, experts on credit observed the widespread use of *aktsiyes* by Jews. Estimates of the annual amount loaned by *aktsiyes* during the 1920s and very early 1930s range from fifty million to sixty million dollars, far greater than the amount loaned by Hebrew free loan societies.[52] Over 70 percent of this large volume of capital was centered in New York where, according to a 1930 study, "literally hundreds of these axias [*aktsiyes*] are now operating, making loans in all amounts, and some of these have grown to large proportions. . . . In one building in New York City twenty such organizations have offices."[53] Similarly, in Hartford, "every night in the labor lyceums, in synagogues, in homes, in basements, they had *aktsiyes*."[54] Writing about the early 1920s, Rolf Nugent, a Russell Sage Foundation staff worker in charge of credit union promotion in New York State, noted the existence of large numbers of *aktsiyes* among Jews in Boston, Chicago, Newark, New York, Philadelphia, and Saint Louis.[55]

Beginning in the 1920s, credit union activists sought to bring all cooperative loan societies, including *aktsiyes*, under state supervision. As a result, many states passed laws requiring all credit cooperatives within their jurisdication to apply for state charters. Different states, however, enacted legislation in different years. For example, Massachusetts passed its law in 1926, inducing 156 associations, most of which were *aktsiyes*, to become licensed credit unions by the end of that year. Connecticut, meanwhile, did not mandate regulation until 1945.[56]

This trend toward regulation was prompted by a concern that unlicensed cooperatives were mismanaged and had high rates of embezzlement. In some *aktsiyes,*

> excessive fees and charges are not infrequently used by "insiders" as a means of obtaining a lucrative income. Even more common is the dangerous tendency to use the "axia" [*aktsi*] as a convenient source of credit for themselves and their friends without adequate security. Within recent years there have also come to light numerous instances, where the "insiders" embezzled the funds of the organization, the prosecution revealing a glaring disregard of ordinary business principles.[57]

The secretary–treasurer of the Mansfield Community Mutual Benefit Association in Connecticut, described how his organization functioned before state regulation: "At first we didn't charge interest rates. We worked off the kitchen table, nobody got salaries, there were no offices and no bonding and it wasn't all that unusual for the treasurer to skip town with the assets in his pocket."[58] Nugent corroborated that many *aktsiyes* were liquidated because of "accounting errors, defalcations, and favoritism."[59] The New York State Credit Union League opposed *aktsiyes* because members did not have adequate legal protection and in some cases were subject to usurious interest rates, as well as to officers of "questionable integrity." Between July 1931 and May 1932, the New York State attorney general forced 102 *aktsiyes* to cease their operations.[60]

Many people involved with *aktsiyes* opposed what they perceived as government interference in their affairs. They feared that *aktsiyes* would lose their Jewish character because once under government jurisdiction, they would not be allowed to deny non-Jews access to their institutions. If non-Jews joined their organizations, the economic role of *aktsiyes* might not be threatened but their social function would probably be transformed. For example, one former *aktsi* member reminisces how "we would get together in somebody's home, get our business done, and then we'd all have a little schnapps."[61] A Connecticut credit union publication describes the changes that occurred in Connecticut after regulation took place in the mid-1940s:

Oxies [*aktsiyes*] lost their specialized flavor of being exclusively Jewish and opened their doors to the larger community. They tightened up their operations, began to pay salaries, rented offices, and in modernizing gained a measure of security while forfeiting some of the old ethnic flavors that had made them as much a social organization as an economic cause.[62]

Yet despite these fears, many cooperatives were able to maintain their predominately Jewish composition during the transition from *aktsi* to a formal institution. The largest credit union in Cambridge, Massachusetts, had operated as an *aktsi* for ten years prior to receiving a state charter in 1926. By the late 1930s the majority of its membership—two-thirds—was still Jewish. Similarly, the Lynn Credit Union, the largest credit union in that Bay State city, functioned as an *aktsi* for eight years prior to government regulation. On the eve of World War II, it retained a membership that was almost 90 percent Jewish. Hartford's extant Kief Protective Mutual Benefit Society was an *aktsi* for many years before Connecticut passed its regulatory law. As recently as the 1980s, Jews still comprised 50 percent of the membership of this three-million-dollar facility.[63]

Not all *aktsiyes* survived the era of regulation with equal success. Massachusetts, for example, experienced a 5.7 percent decline in its number of credit unions between 1929 and 1933, not so much because of a depressed economy but, rather, because many of the *aktsiyes* that became credit unions were not able to satisfy the new mandatory requirements that took effect in 1926. At the time, dozens of *aktsiyes*

> came before the state board of bank incorporation as applicants for credit union charters. To refuse them would have meant that their activities, which in general were quite proper, must terminate. A lenient policy in granting charters was therefore pursued, even though it was maintained by many, including leaders in the credit union movement, that a large number of the associations would probably not continue to qualify under the regulation of the banking department. Many of the associations were informal loan clubs or family groups whose managers were not qualified by experience and inclination to do the bookkeeping and other systematic administrative duties necessary for credit union operation under the law.[64]

141

With regulation, *aktsiyes* quickly became a forgotten chapter of the American Jewish experience and of credit union history. Only a small group of contemporary credit union members who had been former *aktsi* members themselves or who remember their parents making their weekly visits to their local *aktsi*, continue to refer to Jewish cooperatives by their original Yiddish term.

Agricultural, Business, and Consumption Credit

Many of the earliest Jewish credit unions were organized not in cities but in rural areas. Actually, Jewish farmers were in the vanguard of the agricultural credit cooperative movement in the United States. In 1911, when Jewish farmers founded their first three credit unions, including the first credit union in New York State, agricultural credit was virtually nonexistent in the United States. Noting Jewish cooperatives as the one exception, E. W. Kemmerer, professor of economics at Princeton University, voiced chagrin at the lack of credit facilities for American farmers:

> To the American the surprising thing about it all is that such cooperative banks are practically unknown in the United States, although there has been a remarkable development here in recent years of other forms of cooperation among farmers. This surprise is the greater when one bears in mind that [quoting George K. Holmes, statistician of the U. S. Department of Agriculture] "whole counties have been populated in the Northwest by European agriculturalists who came from neighborhoods where they were familiar with agricultural cooperative credit, and yet not a society of cooperative credit for these immigrants has been established from the beginning to the present time."
> A real beginning in the direction of cooperative agricultural credit was made last year through the influence of the Jewish Agricultural and Industrial Aid Society.[65]

In response to two congressional bills advocating a commission to go abroad in order to investigate agricultural credit cooperatives, an *Indianapolis News* editorial argued, "We do not need commissions to hunt knowledge. We need simply to follow the lead of these Jews and set to work to provide credit. And we need to do it just as they did—which is, simply to do it."[66] Similarly, the editors of the Minneapolis journal *Cooperation* praised Jewish agriculturalists for initiating credit unions without first seeking government help and criticized American farmer organizations that were demanding that Congress pass laws in favor of low-interest governmental loans to farmers. Two decades later, Jewish farmers took the lead again when they pioneered the first federally chartered agricultural credit union in Perrineville, New Jersey.[67]

The JAIAS promoted credit unions among Jewish farmers. Founded in 1900 with funds from Baron Maurice de Hirsch's large philanthropic legacy, the organization's primary agenda was to encourage East European immigrant Jews to move away from densely populated cities to settle in more remote areas. Granting loans to farmers in order to help them purchase land, as well as equipment, seed, and livestock, was an important organizational strategy.

Through its general manager, Louis Robinson, the JAIAS was very visible within the general credit union movement. He had close ties to the Russell Sage Foundation, the organization that coordinated credit union activity within New York State, and he assisted in drafting New York's credit union law and published extensively on small loan agencies. In 1914, Robinson coauthored the handbook *A Credit Union Primer* with Arthur Ham, the first director of the Russell Sage Foundation's Department of Remedial Loans.[68]

Relying on the German Raiffeisen system as a model for rural credit, the JAIAS organized its first three credit unions in 1911: one in New York and two in Connecticut. By the end of their first year, they had a combined membership of 84 and had loaned approximately forty-five hundred dollars. In 1912, the JAIAS initiated five new credit unions, and the following year an additional nine. By the end of 1913, the seventeen existing rural credit unions had 517 members and made loans aggregating more than seventy-three thousand dollars.[69] The number of Jewish agricultural cooperatives peaked in 1915, when a total of nineteen existed; one in Massachusetts, five in Connecticut, five in New Jersey, and eight in New York.[70]

After each facility raised at least five hundred dollars through the sale of shares, it became eligible for a one-thousand-dollar low-interest JAIAS loan. Specializing in short-term loans—a critical need for farmers who are particularly strapped for funds during certain times of the year—JAIAS credit unions granted loans for a maximum of one hundred dollars, to be paid back within six months at a rate of 6 percent. Robinson explained: "With the approach of the Spring [the farmer] is usually at his wits' ends to find the wherewithal for seed, fertilizer, and general Spring work. If he is hampered in his Spring work, he not only loses that season, but is frequently handicapped for some time."[71]

Through the JAIAS, Jewish farmers had a communal infrastructure to help them succeed in farming.[72] A member from one of the Connecticut credit unions described how,

> previous to the formation of the Credit Union when a farmer had an accident—a horse died, or a cow died—there was no help for him, and when he applied for help to the other farmers he could not get it, but now when we have a Credit Union, when a farmer applies for help it does not take more than an hour for him to get the money.[73]

But despite this economic help, most Jewish attempts at agriculture failed. In the eastern states the soil was often poor; production costs were high; and, in general, it was difficult to compete with farmers who owned large tracts of land. As their farming ventures declined, Jewish agriculturalists quickly exhausted their credit union funds. New York State credit unions encountered particular financial difficulties. After the state legislature enacted its credit union law in 1913, "physical conditions in farming communities were such as to make compliance with these regulations difficult, and there was therefore a laxity in living up to them."[74] As a result, in 1918, the New York State department forced the dissolution of three JAIAS cooperatives. Not long after, the remaining sixteen organizations ceased their operations, as well. The JAIAS "liquidated its entire stake in these credit unions which almost all had died a natural death."[75] In contrast to these short-lived rural cooperatives, credit unions organized for Jewish business development were far more viable and remained on the scene for a considerably longer period of time.

Securing funds for Jewish entrepreneurs was a central mission of both *aktsiyes* and credit unions. A representative of the Russell Sage Foundation informed the 1934 National Conference of Jewish Social Service that *aktsiyes* "were essentially agencies for financing the small Jewish entrepreneur" and that credit unions "were organized primarily by small Jewish business men in order to secure credit for their businesses."[76] And since credit cooperatives had greater resources than did Hebrew free loan societies, their impact on Jewish business development was far stronger. In Omaha, for example, for every dollar disbursed by the free loan society, nine were loaned by the Jewish credit cooperatives.[77]

In Massachusetts, the majority of loans made by three Lowell Jewish credit unions—the Lowell, Highland, and Ideal—were for business, rather than personal needs. Members often joined two, if not three, of these institutions, thereby maximizing their borrowing capacities. Similarly, the Lynn Credit Union—its membership was 90 percent Jewish during the 1930s—also catered to the financial needs of entrepreneurs. Very few loans were issued to help clients purchase real estate. In contrast, most of the loans made by these two cities' French Canadian credit unions—two in Lowell and one in Lynn—were for real estate purposes and very few were to aid businesses. Among these two non-Jewish Lowell facilities, business loans accounted for less than 10 percent of all loans.[78]

The need for credit among Jewish entrepreneurs was especially pressing once the Depression hit. Hyman, founder of the Indianapolis Jewish Community Credit Union explained:

> Economic depression whether caused by war, or by the swing of the business cycle, always means a special problem for our people.
> Unemployment, the major ill for the community, generally is secondary with us. Except in a few cities, our people are not the workers in the mills, the mines and the factories. They are in the main, small tradesmen. Their particular distress in normal times, and aggravated during depressions, is the lack of capital for business purposes.[79]

During the beginning years of the economic decline, most of the Jewish Community Credit Union's borrowers applied for loans for entrepreneurial purposes. In 1931, 68 percent borrowed for their businesses; and within the first four months of 1932, this increased to 71 percent (see Table 6.2). One borrower had been an executive of a large business and a member of a country club until he lost his job and savings. With a Jewish Community Credit Union loan, he "was able to embark into a little business and is today struggling

145

along, at least tiding over the bad times until the possibility will again present itself for him to go back into his former work."[80] Other Depression clients were a plumber who had mortgaged his tools, truck, and furniture to loan sharks and an elderly couple who needed money to establish a fruit stand and market.[81] In general,

> the grocer, the restauranteur, the small dry-goods merchants, who had their funds tied up in defunct banks, were aided to keep their business going through [the Jewish Community] Credit Union. The young physician who required funds to establish himself, similarly, the young lawyer who required the same sort of service, also, the young man who was elevated to the position of manager of a store, but who had to put up a cash bond, and the young man who had secured a position with an insurance company which required a cash bond,—all of these were served through the Jewish Community Credit Union, and all of these are paying their loans regularly.[82]

Down south, Jewish entrepreneurs in Fitzgerald, Georgia, organized the Hebrew Commercial Alliance during the early years of the

TABLE 6.2. *Number of Loans Disbursed by the Indianapolis Jewish Community Credit Union, 1930–32*

Purpose	Year ending 12/31/30	Year ending 12/31/31	First 4 mos. 1932
For business purposes	70	85	32
To pay debts	23	12	6
To pay taxes	8	12	3
To pay insurance premiums	2	1	—
Medical and hospital bills	4	3	—
Cash bonds to secure employment	4	—	—
Aid to relatives in Europe	4	2	2
To tide over because of funds in defunct banks	4	—	—
Professional establishment	3	7	2
Moving expenses	1	3	—
Total	123	125	45

Source: "Discussion of Adolph Held's 'Community Provision for Reconstruction Through Credit'." *Jewish Social Service Quarterly* 1 (December 1932): 129.

crisis to keep their businesses solvent. Morris Abram, a former resident of Fitzgerald, describes the importance of the Alliance: "All of the Jewish merchants or most of them within a fifty-mile radius joined the Alliance and one or another in most cases borrowed from it during some period of the economic decline. . . . [The] Jewish community was really built on the Alliance."[83] With branches in South Carolina and Florida, the Hebrew Commercial Alliance specialized in providing loans to southern Jewish shopkeepers.[84]

Jews who worked within similar occupations often banded together to form a credit union. In 1912, Boston Jewish peddlers and small shopkeepers started the West End Credit Union, the first credit cooperative in Massachusetts to own its own building. The Traders' Credit Union, founded in 1914, also targeted Boston Jewish merchants. In 1923, Jewish hotel owners in the Catskills created a credit union. By the late 1930s, Atlanta Jewish grocers had established a credit union to help their members buy merchandise. This credit union was affiliated with the Atlanta Savings Stores, a cooperative formed to help grocers not only with loans but with other economic necessities, such as advertising.[85]

As with Hebrew free loan associations and remedial loan societies, only people with at least some small degree of economic security were able to join credit unions. Very poor people were generally excluded. Marie Chesler remembers that her family lived "in an atmosphere of poverty and 'credit' of one kind or another" while she was growing up in New York City. "We did not join any 'Jewish Credit Unions' for many reasons: (1) we had no credit because we were poor, poor; (2) you had to be *introduced* to a credit union by some one who already partook of it; (3) we were too proud to ask for help in any way."[86]

In order to fund their businesses, Jews established credit unions under the auspices of already existing organizations. In some cities there were credit unions affiliated with synagogues and *landsmanschaften*. In Buffalo, "virtually every synagogue except the very old ones established such facilities [credit unions]."[87] The decline of Synagogue B'rith Sholem, for example, was halted by the emergence of the B'rith Sholem Credit Union.[88] Similarly, "[those Buffalo *landsmanschaften* that] adjusted to the changing needs of the people survived longer. One way of adjusting to the needs of a newer day was to convert a social organization that had outlived its usefulness into a credit union."[89] For example, members of the First Warsawer Beneficial Club founded the First Warsawer Lodge Credit Union in 1913. It was subsequently chartered as a federal credit union and still exists in Buffalo.

The Workmen's Circle (Arbeiter Ring, in Yiddish), a national Jewish socialist organization, sponsored credit unions in many states. In 1927, Massachusetts Workmen's Circle chapters operated seven credit unions in Boston, Brockton, Lynn, and Worcester. During that same year, a New York Workmen's Circle Credit Union had 205 members and loaned close to thirty thousand dollars.[90] In the Midwest, three Omaha credit cooperatives—the Omaha Workmen's Loan Association, the Independent Workmen's Loan Association and the Mutual Loan Association—were aligned with the socialist fraternal organization.

On the one hand, it is understandable that socialists would be attracted to the cooperative and grassroots nature of credit unions. On the other hand, it is ironic that people who prided themselves on being anticapitalist promoted institutions designed to stabilize the American economic system and deter the masses from the lure of socialism. By having access to capital, Filene and other leaders believed that average citizens would be able to enter the mainstream economy; and if content, Americans would be less likely to embrace a socialist ideology. Jacob de Haas of the MCU articulated this view when he addressed the National Conference of Jewish Charities: "I am fully persuaded that we have in the credit union the most practical antidote for all that natural discontent which finds its expression through Socialism."[91] Despite the reality that credit unions ultimately supported the status quo, Jewish socialists became active members and utilized these ethnic institutions. Practical needs, such as building up businesses and achieving a stable middle-class existence, steered even socialists toward this source of capital.

Credit unions clearly reflect the dual nature of the socialist Workmen's Circle. The socialist organization "embodied both the desire to be part of American society and the determination to correct its evils."[92] Oliver Pollack, a historian who researched Omaha Jewish credit associations, concluded that while the financial organizations "were a byproduct of the Yiddish socialist fraternal brotherhood," the goal was the "integration of its members into capitalist America. The loan associations had socialist origins, became depoliticized, and ultimately became *social* groups."[93]

I have mentioned that three Jewish credit cooperatives in Omaha were connected to the socialist Workmen's Circle.[94] The Omaha

Workmen's Loan Association (OWLA), the oldest and largest of the organizations, was incorporated in 1917 but began its operations about six years earlier. In 1924, OWLA members who lived in South Omaha and Council Bluffs split from the parent organization and formed the Independent Workmen's Loan Association (IWLA).

In order to join the OWLA, applicants had to pay a $1 entry fee ($3 after 1929) and be voted in by the membership. Shares cost $25, and members paid twenty-five cents per week for each share owned. By 1940, members could borrow a maximum of $750. In order to be approved for a loan, an applicant had to have one member serve as cosigner for each $100 requested. After receiving the funds, borrowers repaid the loan at 6 percent interest, and if they were late in making payments, a penalty charge was levied. Similar to a free loan society, the OWLA turned to the guarantor when a borrower defaulted and to the courts if the guarantor also refused to pay.

For many years, the OWLA held its meetings in the Labor Lyceum, an institution built by two local Workmen's Circle chapters. Indicating a shift from its socialist roots, the OWLA leadership voted in 1926 to move its meeting place to the newly erected Jewish Community Center. The vote, however, was a tie, which the president broke by casting the deciding ballot in favor of leaving the Labor Lyceum. From this point onward, the OWLA had little overlapping membership with the Workmen's Circle.

The leadership of the OWLA was proud that its membership included people with a multiplicity of political viewpoints, as well as members from different social classes. According to a 1939 annual report the "membership today represents a genuine cross section of Omaha Jewry, with German, Russian, Polish, Rumanian and American elements, rich and poor, Zionist and non-Zionist, Rabbi and layman, professional man, worker, and business man, conservative and radical believer and free thinker."[95]

The defection of the OWLA from the Labor Lyceum led Workmen's Circle Number 173 to establish the Mutual Loan Association (MLA). Incorporated in 1926, the MLA met at the Labor Lyceum until the building was sold in 1940. As a result, it, too, moved to the Jewish Community Center but had a short life in its new home. The MLA dissolved later that year for failure to pay taxes.

At their height, the OWLA, IWLA, and MLA had 300, 250, and 150 members, respectively. These figures "in an Omaha Jewish population never greater than 10,000 (approximately 2,400 families) means the role of the commercial loan society was significant."[96] Within its first ten years of existence, the IWLA disbursed $250,000 to its members without experiencing a single loss. Over an eleven-year period, the MLA loaned $360,000. Until its demise in the 1970s, the OWLA loaned over one million dollars.

Although women did not serve as either officers or directors of the Omaha loan associations, they did borrow from these ethnic facilities: "Rose Blumkin, founder of Nebraska Furniture Mart, a major midwest retailer, was a leading borrower from the Independent Workmen's Loan Association, which she joined on September 15, 1943. She, her husband, Isadore, and her mother Chasia Gorelick, borrowed about $20,000 from 1943 to 1951."[97] Similarly, Jewish women had access to other male-dominated credit unions. In the Dorchester district of Boston, women comprised one-third of the membership of the Blue Hill Neighborhood Credit Union during the mid-1920s. Unlike the high percentage of single women who borrowed from the Pittsburgh HFLA, over 80 percent of Blue Hill Neighborhood female clients were married.[98]

Just as women administered their own free loan societies, they also founded their own credit cooperatives. In a discussion of Jewish credit unions in Massachusetts, Michael Freund, of the Bureau of Jewish Social Research, commented on the "establishment of credit unions in connection with various women's organizations."[99] Of the 104 Jewish credit unions in Boston in 1927, eleven (10.5 percent) were administered exclusively by women. These included the Jewish Women's, Mother's, the Roxbury Ladies' and the Sisters' Social credit unions. In contrast, there were no non-Jewish cooperatives in which women comprised all of the officers and directors and only one—the Industrial Credit Union, a relatively large facility created by the Women's Educational and Industrial Union in 1910—that had a majority of female board members. According to a longtime activist very familiar with Boston's credit unions, Jewish women formed separate organizations because of their difficulty securing loans elsewhere without their husbands' signatures. He concluded that women's credit unions were "the forerunner of Women's Liberation."[100]

The Boston Jewish women's credit cooperatives, however, were small compared with those run by their male counterparts.[101] While the largest of the women's institutions, the Hill Credit Union in Roxbury, had one hundred members and assets totaling close to

$15,000, the largest Jewish men's organization, the Blue Hill Neighborhood Credit Union had over twenty-five hundred members and assets of $430,000. The assets of the average men's organization was five times larger than the average women's credit facility.

Since there are no extant records of the borrowers of women's credit unions, we cannot make any conclusions about the reasons they applied for money. At least some women's credit unions, however, were organized for consumption purposes by homemakers who lived near one another. In his talk before the National Conference of Jewish Charities, de Haas briefly mentioned women's credit cooperatives:

> I am enthusiastic on the formation of neighborhood housewive's credit unions. Let a decent woman buy a $5.00 share by small installments and you put her in the position of borrowing at 6 per cent for her winter's coal, the family insurance or that doctor's bill, which is inevitable in the multiplication of the family. This credit thrift will save her 100 per cent on these particular domestic bills.[102]

Credit organizations that catered to the needs of housewives were not unique to the Jewish community. Based on models that had existed in their country of origin, turn-of-the-century Japanese–American women organized rotating credit associations, known as *ko* or *tanamoshi-ko*, through their churches, classes, and clubs. In groups of about twenty, Japanese women generated their own loan funds by pooling together money earned through sewing and domestic work. Each woman made a monthly contribution of between five and twenty dollars; and every month, a different woman borrowed the combined funds. After each woman had a borrowing turn, the *ko* disbanded. According to sociologist Evelyn Nakano Glenn, the *ko* "was a serious savings device that enabled women to accumulate a large lump sum of money for special expenses, such as a winter coat, a trip to Japan, or school clothes for children."[103] Japanese women, like Jewish women, borrowed primarily for consumption purposes.

Jewish men also organized credit unions within their own neighborhoods. Residents of Blue Hill Avenue in Dorchester established the Blue Hill Neighborhood Credit Union (later known as the Blue Hill Credit Union) in 1919. Each of the eighteen people who was present at the initial meeting deposited five dollars and pledged to save at least fifty cents weekly. The organization grew steadily; and in 1925, the credit union loaned out thirteen times as much money as it did four years previously (see Table 6.3). When Jews migrated from Dorchester to Brookline, they eventually transported their neighborhood credit union with them. Until it was acquired by the Grove Bank in 1991, it functioned on Harvard Street in the center of Brookline.[104] Similarly, the Washington Credit Union, organized by Dorchester Jews, moved to West Roxbury in 1969. After the relocation, its amended constitution still reflected extant ties to the old neighborhood: "Membership in this Corporation is limited to those who are presently or formerly residents of the Dorchester District of Boston, MA or are presently or formerly members of the Washington Credit Union or members of their families."[105]

TABLE 6.3. *Blue Hill Neighborhood Credit Union Statistics, 1921–25*

Year	Members	Borrowers	Loans ($)
1921	347	118	11,321.50
1922	553	225	26,644.50
1923	679	276	49,435.35
1924	931	394	80,645.26
1925	1,249	555	149,949.35

Source: "Blue Hill Neighborhood Credit Union," ca. 1926. Blue Hill Federal Credit Union, Brookline, Massachusetts.

The credit unions discussed so far were either exclusively Jewish or overwhelmingly Jewish in their membership. There were other credit unions, however, that served a heterogeneous clientele but had a significant minority of Jewish participants. For example, many members of credit unions organized by garment workers' trade unions in New York City were Jewish. Herman Frank, author of a 1929 Yiddish article on Jewish credit unions in the United States, estimated that one-third of the members of the credit union formed by the Amalgamated Clothing Workers were Jews. By 1928, five years after it was established, the credit cooperative had seventeen hundred members and loaned out over $380,000. In 1926, the Amalgamated founded a second credit union in Rochester.[106]

Through their neighborhoods, jobs, and organizations, Jewish men and women created credit cooperatives to meet their monetary needs. In particular, their role in the economy helps us to understand the emergence of large numbers of *aktsiyes* and Jewish credit unions during the first half of the twentieth century. These financial organizations, which were self-sufficient and independent of outside pecuniary support, provided entrepreneurs with a viable means for generating capital. While most Jewish credit unions were established in urban areas specifically for small entrepreneurs, Jews also pioneered in the field of agricultural credit.

Not only were Jews active as rank-and-file members of the credit union movement, but they also comprised much of the leadership. Edward A. Filene, the wealthy and progressive Boston merchant, was a principal financial supporter and had an important role in shaping the national movement's direction and goals. When this prominent citizen launched the cooperative endeavor, he solicited help solely from members of his "eth-class."

Unlike Japanese and Chinese immigrants, who relied solely on a model that they imported from their native countries, early twentieth-century Jews had several credit options: modern credit

Blue Hill Credit Union, 1970. 1151 Blue Hill Avenue, Dorchester, Massachusetts. Photograph from the collection of Paul Levenson.

unions and remedial loan societies, as well as traditional Hebrew free loan associations. All three types of loan facilities provided East European Jewish immigrants with a needed source of capital, particularly for their expanding business enterprises.

7

DECLINE AND
TRANSFORMATIONS

WHEN HERMAN KRETZER OF THE LOS ANGELES
Jewish Loan Fund complained to William Weiss, executive director
of the San Francisco HFLA, that only one-half of his organization's
funds was being used in 1942, Weiss responded, "It should be com-
forting for you to know that fully two-thirds of our capital is idle."[1]
Similarly, the Philadelphia MLS granted 28 percent less in 1942
than it had in 1939, while the AHMF loaned just $2,250 between
1941 and 1944. During the early 1940s, many Jewish credit unions
also experienced a period of decline. Between 1927 and 1941, for
example, the number of Massachusetts Jewish credit cooperatives
fell from 188 to 115 and from 67 percent of the state's total number
of facilities to under 25 percent.[2]

This downward trend was repeated virtually everywhere during
the post-Depression era. In 1940, 25 percent of the Boston HFLS's
funds were in disuse. Between 1941 and 1943, the total amount
granted by the Boston agency fell by two thirds from nearly
$150,000 to approximately $50,000. Forty percent of the Detroit
HFLA's capital was inactive as of September 1942. Between 1941
and 1942, Detroit loans dropped by 31 percent; and during the first
nine months of 1943, loans fell to 52 percent below the corresponding period in 1942 and to 64 percent below the corresponding
period in 1941. New York HFLS loans declined from over one
million dollars to slightly more than $345,000 from 1939 to 1945;
in Pittsburgh they dropped from approximately $70,000 to less

than $9,000; and in Providence from about $73,000 to $24,000. As fewer people utilized the services of the Cleveland HFLA, the directors explored the possiblity that their organization had "outlived its usefulness in the community."[3]

Investing idle funds in war bonds became common practice among Hebrew free loan societies. By the end of the war, the Los Angeles HFLA had $15,000 invested in war bonds. The San Francisco HFLA and Boston HFLS had bought $32,000- and $33,000-worth of bonds, respectively. Meanwhile, Providence HFLA board members contributed to wartime needs by volunteering as a group for civilian defense work. A plaque listing the names of members and sons of members fighting with the Allies was displayed in the office.[4] But patriotism was not the only reason why Jewish free loan activists chose to invest organizational funds in government bonds. That a large proportion of their capital was inactive during the 1940s provided a crucial impetus.

Discussions about curtailing or even terminating loan operations were frequent throughout the 1940s and early 1950s. And over the decades, liquidations became a reality. In 1946, stockholders of Omaha's IWLA decided "that the Association should continue for at least one year more and at the next annual stockholders' meeting a decision should be made about the continued operations of the Loan Association."[5] The IWLA survived for another two decades, dissolving in 1969. The OWLA followed the IWLA, closing its doors one year later. In 1953, members of the Seattle Hebrew Ladies' Free Loan Society considered donating their organizational funds to various charities out of concern that their facility had "outlived its usefulness and that the days of small free loans had passed."[6] After consulting with an attorney who advised them against appropriating loan funds for outright gifts because "[e]xisting funds of the Society and income therefrom must continue to be used for the object and purpose as now provided by the Constitution and By-Laws," the officers did not close their organization's doors at that time.[7] In 1973, however, the Seattle Hebrew Ladies' Free Loan Society merged with the Jewish Family and Child Service.[8] During the 1940s, the Chicago Woman's Loan Association lost its autonomy when it turned over its funds to the Jewish Social Service Bureau. After donating five thousand dollars to the Building Fund for the Aged of Rhode Island in 1953, the Providence Ladies' HFLA conducted little business. In 1965, the board of directors held its last meeting and contributed the remaining capital to

Jewish charities.[9] As early as 1942, one MLS board member, D. Hays Solis-Cohen, urged stockholders to "make a gift of their shares" to the Federation of Jewish Charities.[10] Although Solis-Cohen's motion was defeated, twelve years later, the MLS was absorbed by the Jewish Family Service.[11] As the number of Jewish families declined in Petaluma, the AHMF curtailed its activities. In 1973, the organization formally ended when it turned over its funds to the San Francisco HFLA. The Boston HFLS ceased its operations during the 1970s by dividing its remaining funds between several charities, including a scholarship fund administered by the Combined Jewish Philanthropies, a Hillel emergency fund, and local homeless shelters.[12]

Transformations within the nation's banking industry combined with changes within America's Jewish community contributed to the demise of these ethnic loan associations. The abysmal Depression record of banks (between 1929 and 1933, nine thousand, or one-third of the nation's banks, folded, involving deposits of nearly seven billion dollars) forced the banking industry to reevaluate its loan practices, including its previous indifference to the small loan market.[13] As a result, banks changed their policies and opened their doors to small borrowers without tangible assets. By 1938, over twelve hundred banks maintained personal loan departments, where loans were made on a comaker basis.[14] And once banks became less stringent about the type of security they required, mid-twentieth-century Jews preferred them to their ethnic institutions. The relationship between increased availability of credit resources and problems faced by Hebrew free loan associations was acknowledged by the executive director of the Los Angeles JLF in 1947:

> The changing concepts of the functions of credit, as well as the greater liberalization of small loan policies, evidenced by the most recent practices of banks and other long established financial institutions, indicates that there is a need to re-examine the present policies of the free loan agencies operating in the United States. Community resources have been extended to include not only more liberal policies in making small loans through established credit and banking organizations, but, in addition, there are now available the resources furnished by Veterans' Agencies under special legislation of the United States government and of many of the States. Whether these changes indicate the necessity for radical change in policy by the free loan agencies is a question which can be answered only

157

upon the re-examination of the history and the existing functions of those types of organizations.[15]

The capital needs of Jewish entrepreneurs—many of whom had built substantial businesses and entered the middle class by the post–World War II period—expanded beyond what philanthropic loan associations could provide.[16] Because banks had greater resources, Jewish entrepreneurs were able to borrow larger sums. Hence, Hebrew free loan and Jewish remedial loan societies may have been victims of their own success: Jewish entrepreneurs outgrew these ethnic institutions precisely because they had accomplished their goal of facilitating business expansion. In his evaluation of the declining importance of Hebrew free loan societies, Michael Freund highlighted their inability to meet Jewish pecuniary needs during the postwar period:

> With no exceptions, free loan societies have not been able to keep up with the growing credit needs of the American small business man. As philanthropic institutions, dependent entirely on charitable contributions and with no earning capacity of their own (since no interest is charged), they have not been able to accumulate sufficient capital to meet the normal credit needs of the small business man the moment he passed the peddler or the hole-in-the-wall candy or grocery stage. . . . Very few free loan institutions are in a position to grant loans up to about $500—and that only to a very small number of borrowers.[17]

While Jewish credit unions had greater resources than philanthropic loan societies, they had difficulty competing with interest rates offered by banks. Furthermore, the residential basis of Jewish credit unions made them particularly vulnerable to forces of geographic dispersion. As Jews increasingly moved out of cities into newly emerging suburbs during the postwar period, their credit union activities were seriously disrupted. When Massachusetts Jews, for example, abandoned the immigrant communities of Dorchester and Chelsea, they usually left their cooperatives behind. Of the twenty-four Jewish credit unions that had existed in Chelsea during the 1920s, only four remained during the 1970s. The rapid growth of banks' personal loan departments loosened American Jews' dependency on their ethnic facilities.

The diminishing popularity of Jewish loan associations suggests that ethnic collectivism is apt to recede when immigrants and their descendants move up the economic ladder, achieve some degree of acculturation, and are able to locate alternative economic options. In her study of Depression-era Chicago, historian Lizabeth Cohen concluded that when the federal government entered the field of mortgage refinancing during the 1930s, Chicago workers preferred "the business practices of more stable, usually larger banks" to their ethnic building and loan associations."[18] And historian Judith Smith concluded that the importance of Italian mutual benefit associations in Providence was undermined "when their economic benefits could no longer compete with alternative forms of life insurance that began to appear in the 1920s and 1930s."[19] Comparing immigrants with contemporary middle-class and well-educated Jews in the Dallas–Fort Worth area, authors Mark Rosentraub and Delbert Taebel found that the latter group exhibited far less interest in ethnic self-help programs and institutions.[20] As groups achieve prosperity, their reliance on collective economic strategies often recedes.

Economic institutions were not the only ethnic organizations to be replaced by modern alternatives. The traditional Jewish burial society, known as the *hevra kadisha,* was ultimately superseded by "the undertaker, or funeral director, a species of middleman made necessary by the complexities of the modern American city." Arranging to transport bodies from hospitals to cemeteries and adhering to complicated municipal regulations related to burial "went beyond the means or the competence of the hevra kadisha's voluntary functionaries."[21]

Despite a decrease in numbers and overall activity since the East European immigrant era, Hebrew free loan societies and Jewish credit unions continue to exist in contemporary America. None of the Jewish remedial loan associations have survived, however. Of the 188 Jewish credit unions that existed in Massachusetts in 1927, 17 were still in operation sixty years later. Since 1982, extant Hebrew free loan societies have banded together under the auspices of the national Association of Hebrew Free Loans (AHFL). The AHFL meets annually in conjuction with the Conference for Jewish Communal Service, publishes a newsletter, and serves as a general clearinghouse for sharing strategies and problems. Although Hebrew free loan societies still exist, they have never regained their collective prewar level of financial importance within the Jewish community. In 1969, the Pittsburgh HFLA was not lending much more than it had thirty years earlier ($83,677 versus $71,155), while the

Providence HFLA loaned less in 1967 than it had in 1939. When correcting for inflation, even the same amount is considerably lower. After taking the New York HFLS over thirty years to catch up to its 1940 level of loan activity, in 1991 it disbursed approximately 8 million dollars.

In order to survive in contemporary America, extant Hebrew free loan societies have designed innovative programs to provide Jewish institutions, home buyers, and college students with interest-free loans. In 1976, four years after it moved its headquarters uptown from Second Avenue to East Forty-Second Street, the New York HFLS assisted seventy-two local organizations, mainly Jewish day schools, with loans aggregating $863,000. In 1992, a New York Jewish day school could borrow amounts to $50,000. Others, such as the Omaha Jewish Free Loan Society, appropriated money to pay for summer camp expenses. In 1979, the Seattle HFLA opened the Victor J. Orloff Branch in Israel while the Cleveland HFLA developed a program in conjunction with the Cleveland Society for the Blind to provide the visually impaired with $5,000 loans in 1985. During the 1980s, the Detroit HFLA created a loan program to stabilize older Jewish neighborhoods. In order to halt the Jewish exodus from Southfield and Oak Park, the Detroit HFLA offered $6,000 loans to Jews who wanted to purchase homes in these areas.[22]

Beginning in the 1950s, student loan programs became particularly popular within Hebrew free loan circles. The Seattle Hebrew Ladies' Free Loan Society contacted the Hillel Foundation at the University of Washington in 1951; and four years later, a $250 revolving student loan fund was in place. The much larger San Francisco HFLA established its student program in 1964, when a donor, Sylvia Waxman, pledged $10,000 for this project. Waxman's generosity, which was partially motivated by her feelings of gratitude toward the Hebrew Free Loan Association for having provided her and her husband with a $200 loan back in 1920 to buy a pharmacy, led her to contribute a total of $50,000 over a four-year period. Within its first ten years, this San Francisco student program granted 625 loans for a total of $325,000. Meanwhile, the New York HFLS did not initiate its college tuition program until the early 1980s. Students from the metropolitan area (but who were enrolled in colleges in any geographical region) were eligible to apply for $2,000 loans made on a ten-month basis with payments beginning thirty days after receiving the funds. While the loans were issued in the students' names, parents were required to endorse the notes. Students from the New York area attending college during the 1990s are eligible for $6,000 loans[23]

Aspiring entrepreneurs are no longer the focus of Hebrew free loan societies; the clientele and goals have changed. Loans, of course, are still extended to individuals who need funds to tide them over a difficult period. Elderly Jews and New Americans, such as Soviet and Iranian immigrants, are beneficiaries of free loans. In addition, professionals have become clients of the associations. For example, Philip Glass, the avant-garde composer, borrowed five hundred dollars from a Hebrew free loan society to press his first album.[24] A recent pamphlet published by the Toronto G'milath Chasodim Association describes the changes that took place during the course of the century:

> In our earlier years, a saddlemaker applied for funds to buy leather stock, an ice and cola dealer to do wagon repairs. In later years, newly arrived refugees applied for funds to bring their families to safety out of war-torn Europe. Today we continue to assist clients with all types of needs. They may be single-parent families or the elderly whose retirement income may be eroded by inflation.[25]

The evolution and subsequent decline of Jewish loan societies points to the dynamic nature of ethnic behavior. Ethnic culture is not a constant that resists change. As contextual theory suggests, immigrants will adapt to emerging social and economic circumstances in a new setting. If a particular cultural element, such as dress or ritual, is discordant with the new circumstances, then it will be altered or abandoned by the vast majority of immigrants and their descendants. For example, adherence to the laws of kashruth (dietary laws) has been dispensed with by most modern Jews. By the same token, if a particular cultural tradition is even more congruent with a new social context than with the previous setting, then that cultural element may take on a new importance. Hanukkah and Passover, for instance, have taken on a special significance in the lives of American Jews because of the correspondence with Christmas and Easter and their emphasis on freedom, an American value.

While culture influenced the East European newcomers to establish a particular type of institution based on the traditional free loan model, contextual factors—large scale immigration, business opportunities, and lack of access to capital—shaped the need for loan

societies in the New World. Ann Swidler's image of culture as a
" 'tool kit' from which actors select differing pieces for constructing
lines of action" is useful here.[26] Specific social and economic conditions influenced East European Jewish immigrants to reach into
their cultural kit and choose tools that would help them to succeed
in the world of entrepreneurship. They selected the Hebrew free
loan society because it supplied immigrant entrepreneurs with capital. Similarly, members of other immigrant groups who were over-
represented in business, such as Asians, also turned to their cultural
traditions and founded loan associations based on models from
their countries of origin. Culture, then, provides ethnics with potentialities, while context determines which of the potentialities are
actually realized.

At the same time, however, ethnic culture and religious tradition
did not limit the parameters of immigrant loan activity. Because their
need for capital was great and Hebrew free loan societies could not
meet all their credit needs, American Jews improvised new tools. In
addition to traditional Hebrew free loan associations, they established credit cooperatives and remedial loan societies, two institutions that had no cultural basis. Unlike Hebrew free loan societies,
credit cooperatives and remedial loan associations charged interest
fees and had no religious roots. Collectively, Jewish loan societies
were an important feature of the cohesive economy that bound Jews
to each other as employees and employers, buyers and sellers, land-
lords and tenants, and lenders and borrowers.

Notes

Chapter 1

1. Eleanor F. Horvitz, "Old Bottles, Rags, Junk! The Story of the Jews of South Providence," *Rhode Island Jewish Historical Notes* 7, no. 2 (November 1976): 239–40.

2. Ivan Light, *Ethnic Enterprise in America: Business and Welfare Among Chinese, Japanese, and Blacks* (Berkeley: University of California Press, 1972); idem, "Asian Enterprise in America: Chinese, Japanese, and Koreans in Small Business," in *Self-Help in Urban America,* ed. Scott Cummings (Port Washington, N.Y.: Kennikat, 1980), 33–57; idem, "Disadvantaged Minorities in Self-Employment," *International Journal of Comparative Sociology,* 10(1979): 31–45; idem, "Ethnicity and Business Enterprise," in *Making It In America,* ed. M. Stolarik and Murray Friedman (Lewisburg, Penn.: Bucknell University Press, 1986), 13–32; Ivan Light, Im-jung Kwuon, and Deng Zhong, "Korean Rotating Credit Associations in Los Angeles," *Amerasia Journal* 16, no. 2 (1990): 35–54; G. Carlos Vélez-Ibañez, *Bonds of Mutual Trust: The Cultural Systems of Rotating Credit Associations Among Urban Mexicans and Chicanos* (New Brunswick, N.J.: Rutgers University Press, 1983); Aubrey W. Bonnett, *Institutional Adaptation of West Indian Immigrants to America: An Analysis of Rotating Credit Associations* (Washington: University Press of America, 1981); Michel S. Laguerre, *American Odyssey: Haitians in New York City,* (Ithaca: Cornell University Press, 1984), 99–102; Shirley Ardener, "The Comparative Study of Rotating Credit Associations," *Journal of the Royal Anthropological Institute* 94(July 1964): 201–29; Maurice Freedman, "The Handling of Money: A Note on the Background to the Economic Sophistication of Overseas Chinese," *Man* 59(1959): 64–65; and Clifford Geertz, "The Rotating Credit Association: A 'Middle Rung' in Development," *Economic Development and Cultural Change* 10, no. 3 (1962): 241–63.

3. Ivan Light and Edna Bonacich, *Immigrant Entrepreneurs: Koreans in Los Angeles, 1965–1982* (Berkeley: University of California Press, 1988), 227–42; Lawrence A. Lovell-Troy, "Clan Structure and Economic Activity: The Case of Greeks in Small Business Enterprise," in *Self-Help in Urban America,* ed. Scott Cummings (Port Washington, N.Y.: Kennikat, 1980), 58–85; Roger Waldinger, *Through the Eye of the Needle: Immigrants and Enterprise in New York's Garment Trades* (New York: New York University Press, 1986), 167–87; Ewa Morawska, "The Sociology and Historiogra-

phy of Immigration," in *Immigration Reconsidered,* ed. Virginia Yans-McLaughlin (New York: Oxford University Press, 1990), 196; I. Light, *Ethnic Enterprise,* 7; and Silvia Pedrazza-Bailey, "Immigration Research: A Conceptual Map," *Social Science History* 14, no. 1 (Spring 1990): 56.

4. Max Weber, *The Protestant Ethic and the Spirit of Capitalism,* trans. Talcott Parsons (New York: Scribner & Sons, 1958). This work was originally published in the form of two articles in 1904 and 1905.

5. Werner Sombart, *The Jews and Modern Capitalism* (Glencoe, Ill.: Free Press, 1951), 192, 205, and 212. Weber vigorously disputed Sombart's hypothesis. Weber argued that Judaism merely inspired the development of pariah capitalism; Puritanism, on the other hand, gave rise to modern industrial capitalism. Pariah capitalism may lead to the accumulation of wealth, but it lacks the potentiality of generating new wealth. It also embodies many irrational characteristics, such as the maintenance of one set of moral standards for dealing with group members and another set for outsiders. In contrast, industrial capitalism has the ability to produce new wealth and promotes the rationalization of economic relationships (Max Weber, *Economy and Society,* ed. Guenther Roth and Claus Wittich [New York: Bedminster, 1968], 611–23).

6. Gerhard Lenski, *The Religious Factor: A Sociologist's Inquiry* (New York: Anchor, 1963, 289, 322.

7. Nathan Glazer and Daniel Patrick Moynihan, *Beyond the Melting Pot: The Negroes, Puerto Ricans, Jews, Italians, and Irish of New York City* (Cambridge: Massachusetts Institute of Technology Press, 1963), 223–26; Andrew Greeley, *Ethnicity in the United States: A Preliminary Reconnaissance* (New York: Wiley, 1974), 97; Barbara Klaczynska, "Why Women Work: A Comparison of Various Groups, Philadelphia, 1910–1930," *Labor History* 17 (Winter 1976): 81–95; and Hasia R. Diner, *Erin's Daughters in America: Irish Immigrant Women in the Nineteenth Century* (Baltimore: Johns Hopkins University Press, 1983), 83.

8. Richard Gambino, *Blood of My Blood: The Dilemma of the Italian–Americans* (Garden City: Anchor Books, 1974), 14.

9. Tamotsu Shibutani and Kian M. Kwan, *Ethnic Stratification: A Comparative Approach* (New York: Macmillan, 1965), 63.

10. *Harvard Encyclopedia of American Ethnic Groups,* 1981 ed., s.v. "Japanese," by Harry L. Kitano; Betty Lee Sung, *Mountain of Gold: The Story of the Chinese in America* (New York: Macmillan, 1967), 124–25. See also William Caudill and George De Vos, "Achievement, Culture, and Personality: The Case of the Japanese Americans," *American Anthropologist,* 58 (1956): 1102–26.

11. Milton Gordon, *Assimilation in American Life: The Role of Race, Religion, and National Origins* (New York: Oxford University Press, 1964), 186. See also Jacob Lestchinsky, "The Position of the Jews in the Economic Life of America," in *Jews in a Gentile World,* ed. Isacque Graeber and S. H. Britt (New York: Macmillan, 1942), 401; Fred Strodtbeck, "Family Interaction, Values, and Achievement," in *The Jews: Social Patterns of an American Group,* ed. Marshall Sklare (Westport, Conn.: Greenwood, 1977), 147–65; Seymour Martin Lipset and Reinhard Bendix, *Social Mobility in Industrial Society* (Berkeley: University of California Press, 1963), 56; Marshall Sklare, *America's Jews* (New York: Random House, 1971), 58; and Edward Shapiro, "American Jews and the Business Mentality," *Judaism* 27 (1978), 214–21. For a cultural analysis of Jewish entrepreneurship in Great Britain, see Harold Pollins, "The Development of Jewish Business in the United Kingdom," in *Ethnic Communi-*

ties in Business, ed. Robin Ward and Richard Jenkins (Cambridge: Cambridge University Press, 1984), 73–88.

12. Nathan Glazer, "The American Jew and the Attainment of Middle-Class Rank: Some Trends and Explanations," in *The Jews: Social Patterns of an American Group,* ed. Marshall Sklare (Westport, Conn.: Greenwood, 1958), 143–44.

13. Scott Cummings, "Collectivism: The Unique Legacy of Immigrant Economic Development," in *Self-Help in Urban America,* ed. Scott Cummings (Port Washington, N.Y.: Kennikat, 1980), 5–29.

14. Calvin Goldscheider and Alan S. Zuckerman, *The Transformation of the Jews* (Chicago: University of Chicago Press, 1984); Leon Jick, *The Americanization of the Synagogue, 1820–1870* (Hanover, N.H.: Brandeis University Press, 1976); Orlando Patterson, "Context and Choice in Ethnic Allegiance: A Theoretical Framework and Caribbean Case Study," in *Ethnicity: Theory and Experience,* ed. Nathan Glazer and Daniel Patrick Moynihan (Cambridge: Harvard University Press, 1975), 304–49; Stanley Lieberson, *A Piece of the Pie: Blacks and White Immigrants Since 1880* (Berkeley: University of California Press, 1980); Stephen Steinberg, *The Ethnic Myth: Race, Ethnicity, and Class in America* (1981; reprint Boston: Beacon, 1989); William L. Yancey, Eugene P. Ericksen, and Richard N. Juliani, "Emergent Ethnicity: A Review and Reformulation," *American Sociological Review* 41 (June 1976): 391–402.

15. Yancey, Ericksen, and Juliani, "Emergent Ethnicity," 400.

16. Lieberson, *Piece of the Pie,* 139–45; C. Vann Woodward, *The Strange Career of Jim Crow* (1974; reprint, New York: Oxford University Press, 1955).

17. Steinberg, *Ethnic Myth,* 135–36. See also Selma Berrol, "Education and Economic Mobility: The Jewish Experience in New York City, 1880–1920," *American Jewish Historical Quarterly,* March 1976, 257–71.

18. William Julius Wilson, *The Truly Disadvantaged: The Inner City, the Underclass, and Public Policy* (Chicago: University of Chicago Press, 1987), 174.

19. Patterson, "Context and Choice," 347.

20. Edna Bonacich and John Modell, *The Economic Basis of Ethnic Solidarity: Small Business in the Japanese American Community* (Berkeley: University of California Press, 1980), 257.

21. William L. Yancey and Eugene P. Ericksen, "Response to Johnston and Yoels," *American Journal of Sociology* 83 (1976): 737–41.

22. Joel Perlmann, *Ethnic Differences: Schooling and Social Structure Among the Irish, Italians, Jews, and Blacks in an American City, 1880–1935* (Cambridge: Cambridge University Press, 1988); Ewa Morawska, *For Bread with Butter: The Life-Worlds of East Central Europeans in Johnstown, Pennsylvania, 1890–1940* (Cambridge: Cambridge University Press, 1985); Bonacich and Modell, *Economic Basis;* John Bodnar, *The Transplanted: A History of Immigrants in Urban America* (Bloomington: Indiana University Press, 1985); and Roger Waldinger, Howard Aldrich, and Robin Ward, *Ethnic Entrepreneurs: Immigrant Business in Industrial Societies* (Newbury Park, Calif.: Sage, 1990).

23. Perlmann, *Ethnic Differences,* 219.

Chapter 2

1. Boris Bogen, *Extent of Jewish Philanthropy in the United States* (Cincinnati: National Conference of Jewish Charities, 1908), 11–12; Harry Linfield, *The Commu-*

nal Organization of the Jews in the United States, 1927 (New York: American Jewish Committee, 1930), 92.

2. Dorchester HFLA Minutes, Beth El Synagogue, Newton, Mass. The Boston HFLS statistic is based on a monthly average for the year 1924 (Boston HFLS, "Twenty-Five Years, 1913–1938," American Jewish Archives, Cincinnati).

3. Linfield, *Communal Organization*, 92–98.

4. This figure accurately corresponds with the results of an earlier New York study. In 1917, 28 percent of 1,127 synagogues operated free loan societies. See *The Jewish Communal Register of New York City, 1917–1918* (New York: Kehillah [Jewish Community] of New York City, 1918); Abraham J. Karp, *Haven and Home: A History of the Jews in America* (New York: Schocken Books, 1985), 239.

5. Morris A. Gutstein, *A Priceless Heritage* (New York: Bloch, 1953), 351–52.

6. William Mitchell, *Mishpokhe: A Study of New York City Jewish Family Clubs* (The Hague: Mouton, 1978), 105–9; "Moses Family Society, Fiftieth Anniversary, 1910–1960," YIVO Institute, New York.

7. Will of Solomon Z. Balinky, June 25, 1932, Private Papers of Amy Meltzer, Cambridge, Mass.

8. *Landmanschaften* are organizations based upon community of origin whose functions included social activities, as well as the provision of benefits, such as burial and medical care.

9. Michael Freund, "The New York Hebrew Free Loan Society and Available Small Loan Facilities in New York City," Paper Prepared for the Bureau of Jewish Social Research, November 1932, Microfilm No. 304.818, Harvard University, Widener Library, p. 34; *Jewish Communal Register*, 732; Bureau of Philanthropic Research, Report of Assistant Director to Board of Trustees, October 17, 1916; Constitution and By-Laws of the United Wilner Benevolent Association, Fifth Revision, January 1919, Jewish Theological Seminary, New York; and Jewish Sisters Mutual Aid Society Records, American Jewish Historical Society, Waltham, Mass.

10. "History of Free Loan Department Hebrew Ladies Relief Association," *Kansas City Jewish Chronicle*, October 19, 1928, p. 8.

11. Frank Shotoro Miyamoto, *Social Solidarity Among the Japanese in Seattle* (Seattle: University of Washington Press, 1939), 75.

12. Exodus 22: 24; Leviticus 25: 35–37; Deuteronomy 15:8 and 23: 20–21. For discussions on interest in Jewish law, see Siegfried Stein, "The Laws on Interest in the Old Testament," *Journal of Theological Studies* 4 (1953): 161–70; idem, "The Development of Jewish Law on Interest from the Biblical Period to the Expulsion of the Jews from England," *Historia Judaica*, 17 (1955): 3–40; Edward Neufeld, "The Prohibitions Against Loans at Interest in Ancient Hebrew Laws," *Hebrew Union College Annual* 26(1955), 359–60; and W. F. Leemans, "The Rate of Interest in Old Babylonian Times," *Revue internationale des droits de l'antiquite* 3(1950): 32, n. 87.

13. Exodus Rabbah, 31:15.

14. See also Sanhedrin 76b, Yebamoth 63a.

15. Abraham Cronbach, "The Gradations of Benevolence," *Hebrew Union College Annual* 16 (1941): 175.

16. *Mishneh Torah* Hilkhot Matnot Aniyim, 10.7. For other comparisons between loans and charity, see *The Fathers According to Rabbi Nathan*, chap. 41; Israel ibn al-Nakawa, *Menorat Hama'or*, chapter 8, ed. H. G. Enelow (New York: Bloch, 1929), vol. 1, p. 83.

17. New York HFLS, Fifth Annual Report, January 1897.

18. *The Poor Man's Bank: The Story of Fifty Years of Loans Without Interest* (New York: New York HFLS, 1942), 1.

19. "Hebrew Free Loan Society," *Jewish Advocate,* May 28, 1925, p. 6.

20. Charitable loans fall under the general Talmudic category of *gemilut hasadim* (deeds of lovingkindness). Originally, *gemilut hasadim* encompassed a wide range of benevolent acts far beyond charity (Sukkah 49b). During the Middle Ages, however, the term *gemilut hasadim* became synonymous with the act of providing the poor with interest-free loans. This change in emphasis may have occurred because of the high concentration of Jews in moneylending (to non-Jews). Consequently, when a Jew loaned money without interest "he was depriving himself of his essential stock in trade" (*Encyclopedia Judaica,* 1971 ed., s.v. "gemilut hasadim," by Louis Isaac Rabinowitz).

21. Emily James, "On the Associated Work of Women in Religion and Philanthropy," in *Woman's Mission,* ed. Angela Georgina Burdett-Coutts (London: Sampson Low, Marston, 1893), 143–44; E. H. Lindo, *A Jewish Calendar for Sixty-Four Years* (London: Thompson, 1838), 102–3; and Salo Baron, *The Jewish Community: Its History and Structure to the American Revolution* (Westport, Conn.: Greenwood, 1942), vol. 2, p. 327.

22. Adolf Kober, *Cologne* (Philadelphia: Jewish Publication Society of America, 1940), 283; New York HFLS, Fifth Annual Report, January 1897; Jacob Shatzky, *Geschichte fun Yidn in Warshe,* vol. 3 (New York: YIVO Institute for Jewish Research, 1953), 179–80.

23. William Glicksman, *Jewish Social Welfare Institutions in Poland* (Philadelphia: Kalish Folkshul, 1976), 65, 71, 74; Isaac Levitats, *The Jewish Community in Russia, 1844–1917* (Jerusalem: Posner & Sons, 1981), 152.

24. Glicksman, *Jewish Social Welfare,* 62–80; Jacob Lestchinsky, "Economic Aspects of Jewish Community Organization in Independent Poland," *Jewish Social Studies* 9 (October 1947): 338; and Samuel D. Kassow, "Community and Identity in the Interwar Shtetl," in *The Jews of Poland Between Two World Wars,* ed. Yisrael Gutman, et al. (Hanover, N.H.: University Press of New England, 1989), 216.

25. Kassow, "Community and Identity," 215.

26. Ibid., 216.

27. Benjamin Nelson, *The Idea of Usury: From Tribal Brotherhood to Universal Otherhood* (Princeton: Princeton University Press, 1949), 19.

28. Jacob Rader Marcus, *The Colonial American Jew, 1492–1776,* vol. 2 (Detroit: Wayne State University Press, 1971), 1037–38.

29. Idem, *American Jewry: Documents, Eighteenth Century* (Cincinnati: Hebrew Union College, 1959), 89–90.

30. Sidney M. Fish, "Communal Leadership in Post-Revolutionary Philadelphia," *Gratz College Annual of Jewish Studies,* 3 (1974): 92.

31. Hyman Grinstein, *The Rise of the Jewish Community in New York, 1654–1860* (Philadelphia: Jewish Publication Society of America, 1947), 108; Stephen Speisman, *The Jews of Toronto: A History to 1937* (Toronto: McClelland & Stewart, 1979), 56; William Toll, *The Making of an Ethnic Middle Class: Portland Jewry over Four Generations* (Albany: State University of New York Press, 1982), 18; Minute Book, Hebrew Beneficient Society of Cincinnati, Ohio, 1860–1863, American Jewish Archives, Cincinnati; and Minute Book, Chevra Gemilath Chesed of the City of Boston, July 22, 1855, February 8, 1858, November 6, 1860, and June 10, 1861, American Jewish Archives, Cincinnati. See also the minutes of the Ladies Hebrew Benevolent

Society of Norfolk, Virginia, 1869–1900, which charged Congregation Ohef Shalom a rate of 7 percent per annum on loans (American Jewish Archives, Cincinnati).

32. Grinstein, *The Rise of the Jewish Community*, 150.

33. *Occident*, 5, no. 10 (January 1848): 43; 5, no. 12 (March 1848): 609; 8, no. 41 (July 1850): 203–4.

34. Ibid., 14, no. 12 (March 1857): 581.

35. Letter from D. N. Morange, Barrag Seligman, and Benjamin J. Hart to Rev. S. M. Isaacs, January 3, 1848, as cited in the *Occident*, 5, no. 11 (February 1848): 553.

36. *Occident*, 5, no. 10 (January 1848): 509. See also 6, no. 10 (January 1849): 474–75.

37. Ibid., 14, no. 8 (November 1856): 2A.

38. Ibid., no. 9 (December 1856): 452–53.

39. Ibid., 25, no. 9 (December 1867): 463.

40. Stephen Mostov, "A 'Jerusalem' on the Ohio: The Social and Economic History of Cincinnati's Jewish Community," Ph.D. diss., Brandeis University, 1981, pp. 121–22.

41. David A. Gerber, "Cutting Out Shylock: Elite Anti-Semitism and the Quest for Moral Order in the Mid-Nineteenth Century American Marketplace," in *Anti-Semitism in American History*, ed. David A. Gerber (Urbana: University of Illinois Press, 1987), 219; Stephen G. Mostov, "Dun and Bradstreet Reports as a Source of Jewish Economic History: Cincinnati, 1840–1875," *American Jewish History* 72(March 1983): 333–53. An exception to this trend is documented by Lyle W. Dorsett in his study of Denver; Jews, he found, were not denied credit ("Equality of Opportunity on the Urban Frontier: Access to Credit in Denver, Colorado Territory, 1858–1876," *Journal of the West* 18, no. 3 (July 1979): 75–81.

42. Lloyd Gartner, "Immigration and the Formation of American Jewry, 1840–1925," in *American Jews: A Reader*, ed. Marshall Sklare (New York: Behrman House, 1983), 5.

43. Mostov, "Jerusalem on the Ohio," 122–23.

44. Arthur A. Goren, "Traditional Institutions Transplanted: The Hevra Kadisha in Europe and America," in *The Jews of North America*, ed. Moses Rischin (Detroit: Wayne State University Press, 1987), 70.

45. I. Light, *Ethnic Enterprise* (see chap. 1, n. 2), 10.

46. Alfred R. Oxenfeldt, *New Firms and Free Enterprise: Pre-War Aspects* (Washington: American Council of Public Affairs, 1943): 139. See also Kurt B. Mayer and Sidney Goldstein, *The First Two Years: Problems of Small Firm Growth and Survival* (Washington: Small Business Administration, 1961), 112.

47. Nathan Goldberg, *Occupational Patterns of American Jewry* (New York: Jewish Teachers' Seminary and People's University Press, 1947), 16; Mitchell Gelfand, "Chutzpah in El Dorado: Social Mobility of Jews in Los Angeles," Ph.D. diss., Carnegie-Mellon University, 1981; Stephen Thernstrom, *The Other Bostonians: Poverty and Progress in the American Metropolis, 1880–1970* (Cambridge: Harvard University Press, 1973), 137; Joel Perlmann, "Beyond New York: The Occupations of Russian Jewish Immigrants in Providence, R.I. and Other Small Jewish Communities, 1900–15," *American Jewish History* 72(1983): 369–94; Judith Smith, *Family Connections: A History of Italian and Jewish Immigrant Lives in Providence, Rhode Island 1900–1940* (Albany: State University of New York Press, 1985), 37; and Morawska, "Sociology and Historiography" (see chap. 1, n. 3), 198.

48. Thomas Kessner, *The Golden Door: Italian and Jewish Immigrant Mobility in New York City, 1880–1915* (New York: Oxford University Press, 1977), 64.

49. Moses Rischin, *The Promised City: New York Jews, 1870–1914* (1962; reprint, Cambridge: Harvard University Press, 1977), 55–56.

50. Smith, *Family Connections*, 35.

51. Goldberg, *Occupational Patterns*, 16; Kessner, *Golden Door*, 63; Rischin, *Promised City*, 67; and Steinberg, *Ethnic Myth*, (see chap. 1, n. 14), 99.

52. *Harvard Encyclopedia of American Ethnic Groups*, 1981 ed., s.v. "Jews," by Arthur Goren.

53. Simon Kuznets, "Immigration of Russian Jews to the United States: Background and Structure," *Perspectives in American History* 9(1975): 108–12.

54. Rischin, *Promised City*, 64.

55. Steinberg, *Ethnic Myth*, 100.

56. Stephen Mostov, "Immigrant Entrepreneurs: Jews in the Shoe Trades in Lynn, 1885–1945," paper prepared for North Shore Jewish Historical Society, Marblehead, Mass., 1982. See also Rischin, *Promised City*, 64, for a brief discussion on Jewish entry into women's wear versus men's clothing.

57. Paul B. Trescott, *Financing American Enterprise* (New York: Harper & Row, 1963); Rolf Nugent, *Consumer Credit and Economic Stability* (New York: Russell Sage Foundation, 1938).

58. John C. Chapman, *Commercial Banks and Consumer Instalment Credit* (New York: National Bureau of Economic Research, 1940), 28.

59. Evan Clark, *Financing the Consumer* (New York: Harper & Brothers, 1930), 5.

60. J. Carroll Moody and Gilbert C. Fite, *The Credit Union Movement: Origins and Development, 1850–1970* (Lincoln: University of Nebraska Press, 1971), 50.

61. Lizabeth Cohen, *Making a New Deal: Industrial Workers in Chicago, 1919–1939* (Cambridge: Cambridge University Press, 1990), 75. See also U.S. Congress, Senate, *Reports on Immigrant Banks*, 61st Cong., 3d sess., 1911, S. Doc. 19; "Opening the Door to the New World," *Jewish Exponent*, July 13, 1984, pp. 85–87; Joseph Giovinco, "Democracy in Banking: The Bank of Italy and California's Italians," *California Historical Quarterly* 47, no. 3 (September 1968): 197.

62. A notable exception was A. P. Giannini's Bank of Italy. Founded in San Francisco in 1904, this institution later became the Bank of America. Giovinco, "Democracy in Banking."

63. Cohen, *Making a New Deal*, 76.

64. Light, *Ethnic Enterprise*, 45–61.

65. Irving Howe with Kenneth Libo, *World of Our Fathers* (New York: Harcourt, Brace, Jovanovich, 1976), 137. See also "To Protect Depositors in East Side Banks," *American Hebrew* 95, no. 16 (August 14, 1914), 407.

66. "The Loan Shark Campaign," *New York Evening Post*, April 11, 1914, reprinted by the Division of Remedial Loans, Russell Sage Foundation, 5–6.

67. John M. Glenn, Lilian Brandt, and F. Emerson Andrews, *Russell Sage Foundation, 1907–1946*, vols. 1 and 2 (New York: Russell Sage Foundation, 1947), 47, 52–54. See Louis N. Robinson and Rolf Nugent, *Regulation of the Small Loan Business* (New York: Russell Sage Foundation, 1936), 57–58 for data on interest rates in other cities.

68. Clark, *Financing the Consumer*, 45–54.

69. Ibid., 91.

70. Mildred John, "Why Workers Borrow: A Study of Four Thousand Credit Union Loans," *Monthly Labor Review* 25(July 1927): 12–16; W. I. King, *The Small Loan Situation in New Jersey in 1929* (Trenton: New Jersey Industrial Lenders' Association, 1929), cited in Clark, *Financing the Consumer,* 180–81.

Chapter 3

1. Throughout the book, borrowers names have been changed to protect their anonymity.

2. HFLA of San Francisco, Financial Report for the Year 1918; Marvin Pitterman, "The Hebrew Free Loan Association, 1938–1950," *Rhode Island Jewish Historical Notes* 8(November 1980), 93–96; Cleveland HFLA, Minutes of the Board of Directors, February 29, 1911; "Annual Meeting of Hebrew Free Loan Association," *Jewish Review and Observer,* January 14, 1910, p. 1; and Marc Lee Raphael, *Jews and Judaism in a Midwestern Community: Columbus, Ohio, 1849–1975* (Columbus: Ohio Historical Society, 1979), 267.

3. New York HFLS, Seventh Annual Report, January 1899.

4. National Conference of Jewish Charities, *Proceeding of the Second National Conference* (Detroit: NCJC, 1902), 61.

5. Charles Bernheimer, *The Russian Jews in the United States* (Philadelphia: Winston, 1905), 97.

6. Pittsburgh HFLA, Fifty-Third Annual Report, 1940.

7. "Hebrew Free Loan Society," *Jewish Advocate,* April 19, 1926, p. 8.

8. "Free Loans That Start Poor Jews in Business," *Providence Sunday Journal,* March 3, 1912, 10.

9. Interview with Bernice Greengard, December 6, 1979, University of Washington Libraries, p. 16.

10. H. J. Glickman to the New York HFLA, October 7, 1946; Abraham Gribetz to Glickman, October 15, 1946, HFLS, New York.

11. See, e.g., San Francisco HFLA, President's Address at Annual Meeting, December 28, 1949.

12. This sample was generated from loan application cards that consist of a total of 1,709 requests from 588 borrowers with surnames that began with letters *A–F* (*G–Z* no longer exist). After deleting requests that were refused and applications that did not indicate a loan's purpose, a sample of 1,038 loans and 453 people remained.

13. San Francisco HFLA, Annual Report, January 1, 1932; and Los Angeles Loan Fund, Monthly Reports, May 1936–May 1937.

14. Los Angeles JLF, Minutes of the Board of Directors, April 6, 1936.

15. Viviana A. Zelizer, "The Social Meaning of Money: 'Special Monies'," *American Journal of Sociology* 95, no. 2 (September 1989), 358–59.

16. BAC of the Los Angeles JLF, Minutes, December 1940–November 1942.

17. Lenore Davidoff and Catherine Hall, *Family Fortunes: Men and Women of the English Middle Class 1780–1850* (London: Hutchinson, 1987), 272–315; Sidney Stahl Weinberg, *The World of Our Mothers* (New York: Schocken Books, 1988), 134–37 and 284, n. 42; Charlotte Baum, "What Made Yetta Work? The Economic Role of Eastern European Jewish Women in the Family," *Response* 7, no. 2 (1973): 32–38; and Smith, *Family Connections* (see chap. 2, n. 47), 44–52.

18. The average annual rate of inflation between 1913 and 1945 was 2.5 percent; one hundred dollars in 1913 was equivalent to approximately twelve hundred dollars in 1990. Industrial Commission on Immigration, *Reports*, vol. 15 (Washington: GPO, 1901); New York HFLS, Ninth Annual Report, January 1901 and Twenty-Seventh Annual Report, 1919. Oliver B. Pollack, "The Jewish Free Loan Societies of Omaha, Nebraska, 1911–1987," *Memories of the Jewish Midwest* 3(1987), 7; *The Chicago Jewish Community Blue Book* (Chicago: Sentinel, [ca. 1918]), 16; Boston HFLS, Fourth Annual Report, 1916; San Francisco HFLA, President's Message, January 10, 1929; and Los Angeles HFLA, Minutes of the Board of Directors, May 19, 1942.

19. Freund, "New York HFLS" (see chap. 2, n. 9), 37–39.

20. Ibid., 4.

21. Pollack, "Jewish Free Loan Societies," 7; see also San Francisco HFLA, Annual Report, January 16, 1916.

22. New York HFLS, Fortieth Annual Report, February 29, 1932.

23. Executive Secretary of the Detroit HFLA to Lillian Ledeen, November 12, 1936, Out-of-Town File. JFLA, Los Angeles.

24. San Francisco HFLA, Annual Reports for 1935 and of December 28, 1949; and "Free Loan Society Blessing to Many," *Cleveland News*, May 28, 1931, p. 8.

25. David Solomon (pseud.) to Morris Balter, August 16, 1937; Emil Steinbach and Sidney Teller to Alfred M. Cohen, June 1, 1936, HFLA, Pittsburgh; and Pittsburgh HFLA, Fifty-Third Annual Report, 1940.

26. "Free Loan Society Blessing to Many," *Cleveland News*, May 28, 1931, p. 8; Rehabilitation Loan Fund, Minutes, December 11, 1934, Western Jewish History Center, Berkeley.

27. Pittsburgh HFLA, Minutes of the Annual Meeting, January 18, 1931. See also San Francisco HFLA, President's Message, January 2, 1931. For similar statements see the annual reports dated May 14, 1933 and March 18, 1934.

28. San Francisco HFLA, Annual Report, April 5, 1937; and Chester E. Elsinger, "A Brief History of the Lafayette Orthodox Hebrew Free Loan Association, 1907–1960," *Indiana Jewish Historical Society Publication* no. 9 (1977): 6.

29. Leon Kasman to Herman Kretzker, September 13, 1940, Out-of-Town File; JFLA, Los Angeles. Mark H. Elovitz, *A Century of Jewish Life in Dixie: The Birmingham Experience* (University: University of Alabama Press, 1974), 112; and Elsinger, "Brief History," 6.

30. Lloyd P. Gartner, "The Midpassage of American Jewry, 1929–1945," paper presented at the fifth annual Rabbi Louis Feinberg Memorial Lecture in Judaic Studies, University of Cincinnati, 1982, p. 4. See also Ronald H. Bayor, *Neighbors in Conflict: The Irish, Germans, Jews, and Italians of New York City, 1929–1941*, 2d ed. (Urbana: University of Illinois Press, 1988); Thomas Kessner, "Jobs, Ghettoes, and the Urban Economy, 1880–1935," *American Jewish History* 71, no. 2 (December 1981), 218–38.

31. "Report of the Executive Secretary of the Pittsburgh Hebrew Free Loan Association for the Period Ending November 1, 1941," Pittsburgh HFLA; Oliver B. Pollack, "Communal Self-Help and Capital Formation: Omaha's Jewish Loan Associations, 1911–1979," *American Jewish History* 78, no. 1 (September 1988), 33; and New York HFLS, Forty-Sixth Annual Report, June 1938.

32. "Report of the President of the Hebrew Free Loan Association of San Francisco to the Federation of Jewish Charities," October 26, 1951, San Francisco HFLA office.

33. Minutes of the Meeting of the BAC, December 4 and 17, 1940, January 31, February 14, June 20, July 19, August 1 and 15, and September 26, 1941.

34. Minutes of the meeting of the BAC, December 4 and 17, 1940, February 14 and March 14, 1941, and July 10, 1942.

35. Minutes of the Meeting of the BAC, January 9, June 20, July 18, August 1, September 26, October 10, and November 19, and December 6, 1941.

36. Los Angeles JFLA, Annual Reports for 1948, 1953, and 1959.

37. Los Angeles JLF, Report of the Executive Secretary Delivered at the Annual Meeting, November 18, 1941.

38. Los Angeles JFLA, Annual Report for 1955.

39. San Francisco HFLA, Report to the President and Members of the Federation of Jewish Charities, October 31, 1947.

40. San Francisco HFLA, Annual Report, October 31, 1946; Los Angeles HFLA, Minutes of the Board of Directors, June 6, 1944 and March 5, 1946.

Chapter 4

1. "Free Loans That Start Jews" (see chap. 3, n. 8), 10.

2. Memorandum from H. L. Lurie to HFLS, May 2, 1933, Out-of-Town File, JFLA, Los Angeles.

3. New York HFLS, Seventh Annual Report, January 1899 and Twenty-Seventh Annual Report, January 1919. See also Pitterman, "HFLA, 1938–50," 92–93.

4. Letter from William G. Weiss to Max S., January 8, 1936, Out-of-Town File, JFLA, Los Angeles.

5. National Conference of Jewish Charities, *Proceedings of the Eighth Biennial Session* (Memphis: NCJC, 1914), 9; Los Angeles HFLA, Minutes of the Board of Directors, August 16, 1927; Robert Lesser to Edward S. Sheinberg, April 25, 1950; Edward S. Sheinberg to Endorsers, April 26, 1950, and Edward S. Sheinberg to HFLA, December 6, 1950—all in the Out-of-Town File, JFLA, Los Angeles.

6. San Francisco HFLA, Annual Report, January 16, 1916; Pittsburgh HFLA, Minutes of the Board of Directors, June 10, 1942; NCJC *Proceedings* (1914), 15; Rhoda Glick, "A Study of Loans Made by the Hebrew Free Loan Association and Guaranteed by the Jewish Family Welfare Association from 1926 Through 1935," master's thesis, University of Pittsburgh, 1938, p. 65; Charles Richmond Henderson, *Modern Methods of Charity* (London: Macmillan, 1904), 680; and Freund, "New York HFLS" (see chap. 2, n. 9), 39–42.

7. *Jewish Charities* 5(August 1914): 21; Records of the United Hebrew Charities, 1890–1899, Philadelphia Jewish Archives Center, Philadelphia; and NCJC *Proceedings*, 1902, 62 (see chap. 3, n. 4).

8. NCJC, (1902), 63.

9. San Francisco HFLA, Annual report for 1934; A. R. Glick to Lillian Ledeen, January 23, 1936, Out-of-Town File, JFLA, Los Angeles; Los Angeles HFLA, Minutes of the Board of Directors, January 9, 1934; and Cleveland HFLS, Annual Report, January 11, 1932.

10. Elsinger, "Brief History" (see chap. 3, n. 28), 5; San Francisco HFLA, Annual Report, January 1, 1932; and Los Angeles JLF, Annual Report for 1930.

11. H. L. Lurie to HFLS, May 2, 1933, Out-of-Town File, JFLA, Los Angeles; M. Freund to Sidney Teller, March 6, 1934, HFLA, Pittsburgh.

12. See, e.g., A. R. Glick to Lillian Ledeen, January 23, 1936, Out-of-Town File, JFLA, Los Angeles; Elsinger, "Brief History," 5; Freund, "New York HFLS," J; and New York HFLS, Minutes of the Board of Directors, January 18, 1933.

13. San Francisco HFLA, Report to the Federation of Jewish Charities, April 5, 1937; Boston HFLS, Minutes of the Annual Meeting, February 23, 1932.

14. New York HFLS, Sixteenth Annual Report, January 26, 1908; Cleveland HFLA, Minutes of the Board of Directors, March 26, 1907; and Gemilath Chesed HFLA of Providence, Constitution and By-Laws, 1928.

15. Los Angeles HFLA, Minutes of the Board of Directors, April 9, 1932; Cleveland HFLA, Minutes of the Board of Directors, March 2, 1931, April 18, 1932, April 24, 1933, and December 10, 1934.

16. E. Margolin to William Thornton, September 21, 1927, Out-of-Town File, JFLA, Los Angeles; Los Angeles HFLA, Minutes of the Board of Directors, November 1, 1927, August 18, and September 22, 1931, and July 2, and October 22, 1935.

17. New York HFLS, Twenty-Fifth Annual Report, February 11, 1917.

18. New York HFLS, Twenty-Seventh Annual Report, February 16, 1919 and Thirty-Second Annual Report, February 10, 1924; New York HFLS, Minutes of the Board of Directors, March 26, 1928.

19. New York HFLS, Forty-Seventh Annual Report, October 30, 1939.

20. New York HFLS, Forty-Eighth Annual Report, June 27, 1940.

21. San Francisco HFLA, President's Address at Annual Meeting, December 28, 1949.

22. Jacob Schiff to Leopold Zinsler, February 1, 1897, JTS/Schiff Microfilm, Reel 690, Frame 196; Jacob Schiff to Julius Dukas, December 11, 1913, December 16, 1915, and January 10, 1917, JTS/Schiff Microfilm, Reel 690, frames 201–203, American Jewish Archives, Cincinnati; New York HFLS, Sixth Annual Report, January 1898; from Jacob Schiff to Clara Frances Wolff, February 15, 1915, Jacob Schiff Papers, Box 447, American Jewish Archives, Cincinnati; New York HFLS, Fifth Annual Report, January 1897; and Julius Dukas to Jacob Schiff, March 4, 1918, Jacob Schiff Papers, Box 465, American Jewish Archives, Cincinnati.

23. Cyrus Adler, *Jacob Schiff: His Life and Letters*, vol. 1 (Garden City: Doubleday, 1928), 365–66; NCJC, *Proceedings* (1914), 19; and New York HFLS, Twenty-Second Annual Report, January 25, 1914.

24. "Hebrew Free Loan Society," *American Hebrew*, January 26, 1900, p. 379.

25. Jacob Schiff to Leopold Zinsler, cited in Adler, *Jacob Schiff*, vol. 1, p. 394.

26. Louis Marshall to Julius Dukas, January 20, 1913, Louis Marshall Papers, Box 1582, American Jewish Archives, Cincinnati.

27. "Aid, Rather than Alms, Goal of Hebrew Free Loan Association," *Jewish Transcript*, December 22, 1983, p. 16; San Francisco HFLA, President's Message, January 2, 1931; Los Angeles HFLA, Minutes of the Board of Directors, May 12, 1931 and March 3, 1936; Los Angeles JLF, 1930 Annual Report; Elsinger, "Brief History," 3; Pittsburgh HFLA, Minutes of the Annual Meeting, January 18, 1931; and Boston HFLS, Minutes of the Annual Meeting, February 23, 1932.

28. "This Bank Lends from the Heart," *Newark Sunday News*, November 26, 1950, p. 66.

29. Los Angeles HFLA, Minutes of the Board of Directors, July 4, 1916;

December 11, 1928, and February 26, 1929; Pollack, "Jewish Free Loan Societies" (see chap. 3, n. 18), 10; and San Francisco HFLA, President's Address at Annual Meeting, December 28, 1949.

30. Los Angeles HFLA, Minutes of the Board of Directors, November 21, 1937; Rose Schwartz, Interview by Shelly Tenenbaum, April 3, 1984, New York; "The Hebrew Free Loan Association," *American Hebrew* May 10, 1907, p. 10 and February 5, 1909, p. 375; "Hebrew Free Loan Society," *American Hebrew*, January 26, 1900, p. 378.

31. New York HFLS to Jacob Schiff, April 14, 1914, Hebrew FLS, New York; New York HFLS, Thirteenth Annual Report, January 22, 1922; Freund, "New York HFLS," 24–25; Gemilath Chesed HFLA of Providence, Financial Report for 1927; San Francisco HFLA, Annual Report, December 19, 1926; and Elsinger, "Brief History," 3.

32. Los Angeles HFLA, Minutes of the Board of Directors, December 17, 1929, January 28, February 11, April 8, 22, and 29, and May 13 and May 20, 1930, and October 20, 1931; New York HFLS, Twelfth Annual Report, January 1904; New York HFLS, Thirty-Third Annual Report, February 8, 1925; Cleveland HFLA, Minutes of the Board of Directors, January 28, 1907; and Los Angeles HFLA, Minutes of the Board of Directors, May 19, 1942 and February 11, 1947; and New York HFLS, Minutes of the Board of Directors, December 7, 1936 and January 28, 1937.

33. While women's loan societies began in modern times, Jewish women have a long history as private creditors that dates back to medieval Europe. According to one estimate, about half of all European Jews who loaned money at interest to Christians were women. See William Chester Jordan, "Jews on Top: Women and the Availability of Consumption Loans in Northern France in the Mid-Thirteenth Century," *Journal of Jewish Studies* 29, no. 1 (Spring 1978): 39–56.

34. Grinstein, *Rise of the Jewish Community* (see chap. 2, n. 31), 152. See also Beth Wenger, "Jewish Women and Voluntarism: Beyond the Myth of Enabler," *American Jewish History* 79, no. 1 (Autumn 1989): 16–36.

35. *Chicago Jewish Community Blue Book* (see chap. 3, n. 18), 16; and NCJC, *Proceedings* (1902), 62.

36. Bernheimer, *Russian Jews* (see chap. 3, n. 5), 97.

37. NCJC, *Proceedings* (1914), 257.

38. Minnie Low to David Bressler, February 1, 1915, and Bressler to Low, February 4, 1915, National Association of Jewish Social Workers Papers, American Jewish Historical Society, Waltham, Mass.

39. Low to Bressler, February 16, 1915, National Association of Jewish Social Workers Papers, American Jewish Historical Society, Waltham, Mass.

40. "Hebrew Ladies' Free Loan Society Merger with JFCS," *Jewish Transcript*, December 20, 1973, p. 3; Grace Rubin, "History of the Seattle Hebrew Ladies' Free Loan Society," University of Washington Library, 1965.

41. Eleanor F. Horvitz, "The Jewish Woman Liberated: A History of the Ladies' Hebrew Free Loan Association," *Rhode Island Jewish Historical Notes* 7(November 1978): 501–13.

42. Montreal HFLA, Seventh Annual Report, May 1, 1918.

43. "Aid, Rather Than Alms," 16.

44. Martin Light, "A Brief History of the Lafayette Orthodox Hebrew Free Loan Association, Part 2: 1960–1980," *Indiana Jewish Historical Society Publication* 18(1984): 50–54.

45. New York HFLS, Application Cards, 1892–1906; Cleveland HFLS, Minutes of the Board of Directors, September 27, 1938; and Los Angeles HFLA, Minutes of the Board of Directors, June 9, 1931.

46. Boston HFLS, Minutes, October 6 and 13, 1912; New York HFLS, Minutes of the Board of Directors, December 7, 1936 and January 28, 1937; and David Alexander, "History of the Jews of Toledo," *Reform Advocate*, June 20, 1908, p. 17.

47. N. S. Fineburg to William G. Weiss, June 26, 1942, HFLS, New York.

48. Ibid.

49. San Francisco HFLA, President's Address at Annual Meeting, December 28, 1949.

50. New York HFLS, Tenth Annual Report, January 1902; NCJC, *Proceedings* (1914), 15; Abraham Gribetz to William G. Weiss, June 22, 1942, HFLS, New York.

51. Joseph B. Goldberg to William G. Weiss, December 1, 1950, Out-of-Town File, JFLA, Los Angeles; Los Angeles JFLA, Annual Reports, 1954 and 1955; and Jack J. Frishman to Board Members of the Pittsburgh HFLA, February 1929, HFLA, Pittsburgh.

52. Cleveland HFLA, Minutes of the Annual Meeting, January 14, 1935; Cleveland HFLA, Minutes of the Board of Directors, February 13 and March 26, 1939; and Cleveland HFLA, Report of the Ways and Means Committee, April 7, 1959.

53. William G. Weiss to New York HFLS, February 4, 1957, and Abraham Gribetz to William G. Weiss, February 14, 1957, HFLS, New York.

Chapter 5

1. NCJC, *Proceedings* (1914), 12 (see chap. 4, n. 5).

2. Frank Dekker Watson, *The Charity Organization Movement in the United States: A Study in American Philanthropy* (New York: Macmillan, 1922), 53, 188.

3. Ibid., 525.

4. Ibid., 271.

5. Ibid., 266; see also Robert H. Bremner, *American Philanthropy* (Chicago: University of Chicago Press, 1960).

6. Glenn, Brandt, and Emerson, *Russell Sage Foundation* (see chap. 2, n. 66), vol. 1, 136.

7. Robinson and Nugent, *Regulation* (see chap. 2, n. 66), 84, 147.

8. Clark, *Financing the Consumer* (see chap. 2, n. 59), 102, 106.

9. Provident Loan Society of New York, Seventeenth Annual Report for 1911, p. 89; Freund, "New York HFLS" (see chap. 2, n. 9), 45; and *The Provident Loan Society of New York, 1894–1944: Fifty Years of Remedial Lending* (New York: Provident Loan Society of New York, 1944), 27.

10. H. Joseph Hyman, "The Indianapolis Jewish Community Credit Union," *Jewish Social Service Quarterly* 7, no. 3 (March 1931), 13.

11. Maurice J. Karpf, *Jewish Community Organization in the United States* (New York: Arno, 1971), 68. I assume that Karpf used the term *remedial loans* to mean philanthropic loans with interest, but he never defined the term.

12. NCJC, *Proceedings* (1914), 15.

13. New York HFLS, Fifth Annual Report, January 1897.

14. Ibid.

15. NCJC, *Proceedings* (1914), 13.

16. "History of the Jewish Aid Association," 1939, Saint Louis Jewish Federation Office.

17. Ibid.

18. NCJC, *Proceedings* (1914), 14; NCJC, *Proceedings* (1902), 50 (see chap. 3, n. 4).

19. Annual Report of the HFLA of San Francisco, October 29, 1943.

20. San Francisco HFLA, Annual Report, December 28, 1949.

21. Freund, "New York HFLS," K; New York HFLS, (Forty-Ninth) Annual Report for 1940.

22. For a discussion of the dynamic character of ethnicity, see Yancey, Ericksen, and Juliani, "Emergent Ethnicity" (see chap. 1, n. 14), 391–401.

23. Unfortunately, no records remain from the Free Loan Society of Philadelphia. According to a brief written account dated 1922, the organization was plagued by political infighting and secessions. See P. Tannenbaum, "History of the Free Loan Association," November 5, 1922, Philadelphia Jewish Archives Center.

24. Edwin Wolf II, "The German–Jewish Influence in Philadelphia's Jewish Charities," in *Jewish Life in Philadelphia, 1830–1940,* ed. Murray Friedman (Philadelphia: Institute for the Study of Human Issues Publications, 1983), 142; *Universal Jewish Encyclopedia,* 1969 ed., s.v. "Mastbaum, Jules E."

25. FLA, Minutes of the Third Annual Meeting of Stockholders, December 12, 1923.

26. FLA, Minutes of the Board of Directors, March 31, 1922 and October 13, 1927; FLA, Minutes of the Seventh Annual Meeting of Stockholders, December 14, 1927.

27. William Hirsch to Samuel Gerson, July 29, 1938; Saint Louis Jewish Federation Office, p. 3.

28. William Hirsch, "Remedial Loans to the Needy," *Jewish Social Service Quarterly,* June 1936, p. 371.

29. Terry K. Fisher, "Lending as Philanthropy: The Philadelphia Jewish Experience, 1847–1954," Ph.D. diss., Bryn Mawr College, 1987, pp. 135–36.

30. FLA, Minutes of the Twenty-Second Regular Meeting of the Board of Directors, March 18, 1926.

31. MLS, Minutes of the Eighth Annual Meeting of Stockholders, December 20, 1928.

32. Ibid.

33. FLA, Minutes of the Seventh Annual Meeting of Stockholders, December 14, 1927.

34. MLS, Annual Report, November 11, 1936.

35. FLA, Minutes of the Fourth Annual Meeting of Stockholders, December 18, 1924.

36. FLA, Minutes of the Seventh Annual Meeting of Stockholders, December 14, 1927.

37. MLS, Minutes of the Twenty-Fourth Annual Board Meeting, February 28, 1945.

38. William Hirsch, "Discussion of Rolf Nugent's 'Credit Facilities for Marginal Jewish Groups'," in *Proceedings of the National Conference of Jewish Social Service* (Atlantic City, 1934), 47.

39. MLS, Minutes of the Eighth Annual Meeting of Stockholders, December 20, 1928; MLS, Annual Report, November 11, 1936.

40. MLS, Minutes of the Twenty-First Annual Board Meeting, February 24, 1942.

41. MLS, Minutes of the Fiftieth Regular Meeting of the Board of Directors, January 31, 1936.

42. William Hirsch to Samuel Gerson, July 29, 1938; Saint Louis Jewish Federation Office, p. 7.

43. MLS, Minutes of the Twenty-First Annual Board Meeting, February 24, 1942.

44. MLS, Minutes of the Fifty-Ninth Regular Meeting of the Board of Directors, May 1, 1942. By this point, even Albert Greenfield had not been attending meetings for a long time, and the board declared his seat vacant.

45. "Discussion of Adolph Held's 'Community Provision for Reconstruction Through Credit'," *Jewish Social Service Quarterly* 9, no. 1 (December 1932), 127; MLS, Minutes of the Nineteenth Annual Board Meeting, January 26, 1940.

46. MLS, Minutes of the Thirty-Third Regular Meeting of the Board of Directors, March 8, 1929.

47. MLS, Minutes of the Thirty-Third Regular Meeting of the Board of Directors, March 8, 1929.

48. MLS, Minutes of the Thirty-Seventh Regular Meeting of the Board of Directors, November 20, 1930.

49. MLS, Minutes of the Forty-Eighth Meeting of the Board of Directors, May 10, 1935.

50. MLS, Minutes of the Thirty-Seventh Regular Meeting of the Board of Directors, November 20, 1930; MLS, Minutes of the Forty-Eighth Meeting of the Board of Directors, May 10, 1935. In 1935, half of all the Saint Louis Jewish Aid Association's loans were for business purposes. See Jewish Aid Association, Annual Report for 1935.

51. MLS, Minutes of the Thirtieth Regular Meeting of the Board of Directors, March 6, 1928.

52. Ibid.

53. MLS, Annual Report, November 11, 1936.

54. MLS, Minutes of an Executive Committee Meeting, April 7, 1939.

55. MLS, Minutes of the Fifty-Seventh Regular Meeting of the Board of Directors, May 4, 1939.

56. MLS, Minutes of the Eighth Annual Meeting of Stockholders, December 20, 1928.

57. MLS, Minutes of the Twenty-Second Annual Board of Directors Meeting, June 16, 1943.

58. MLS, Minutes of the Regular Meeting of the Board of Directors, October 4, 1932.

59. MLS, Memorandum re Jennie and Leon G., August 9, 1932.

60. MLS, Minutes of the Fortieth Regular Meeting of the Board of Directors, January 15, 1932.

61. MLS, Minutes of the Fortieth Regular Meeting of the Board of Directors, November 20, 1930.

62. MLS, Minutes of the Thirtieth Regular Meeting of the Board of Directors, March 6, 1928.

63. MLS, Minutes of the Forty-Second Regular Meeting of the Board of Directors, June 24, 1932.

64. MLS, Minutes of the Thirty-Sixth Regular Meeting of the Board of Directors, April 17, 1930.

65. William Hirsch to Samuel Gerson, July 29, 1938, Saint Louis Jewish Federation Office.

66. FLA, Minutes of the Fifth Annual Meeting of Stockholders, February 24, 1926.

67. Ibid.

68. MLS, Minutes of the Thirty-Ninth Regular Meeting of the Board of Directors, May 8, 1931.

69. MLS, Loan Application, March 3, 1942.

70. MLS, Minutes of the Fifty-Third Regular Meeting of the Board of Directors, October 8, 1937.

71. MLS, Minutes of the Thirty-Ninth Regular Meeting of the Board of Directors, May 8, 1931.

72. MLS, Minutes of the Forty-Seventh Regular Meeting of the Board of Directors, November 15, 1934.

73. MLS, Minutes of the Fifty-Eighth Regular Meeting of the Board of Directors, March 31, 1941.

74. MLS, Minutes of the Twentieth Annual Board Meeting, January 29, 1941.

75. JLHA, Minute Book, July 31, 1923.

76. JLHA, Articles of Incorporation, August 7, 1923.

77. Stanley Lieberson, *Ethnic Patterns in American Cities* (New York: Free Press, 1963), 211; Marshall Sklare, "Jews, Ethnics, and the American City," *Commentary* 53, no. 4 (April 1972): 70–77; and Cohen, *Making a New Deal* (see chap. 2, n. 61), 76, and 391, n. 59. For a general discussion of ethnic home ownership, see Bodnar, *The Transplanted* (see chap. 1, n. 22), 180–83.

78. JLHA, Minute Book, January 6, 1925.

79. JLHA, Minute Book, October 6 and December 14, 1926.

80. JLHA, Minute Book, February 9, 1926.

81. JLHA, Minute Book, December 14, 1926.

82. JLHA, Minute Book, February 2 and June 8, 1926, and April 24, 1928.

83. JLHA, Annual Report for 1926, January 3, 1927; JLHA, Annual Report for November 1, 1931–October 31, 1932; JLHA, Minutes of the Annual Meeting, November 11, 1934; JHLA, Balance Sheets, October 31, 1936, and October 30, 1937.

84. JLHA, Minutes of the Board of Directors, January 28, 1930; Jewish Loan Fund, Annual Report for November 1, 1930 to October 31, 1931; and Memo entitled "To the Budget Committee of the Los Angeles Community Chest the Jewish Loan Fund Presents the Following Request for the Year 1932," ca. July 1931.

85. JLF, Annual Report for November 1, 1931–October 31, 1932.

86. Herman J. Levine and Benjamin Miller, *The American Jewish Farmer in Changing Times* (New York: Jewish Agricultural Society, 1966), 83–84; "Leading the Way," *B'nai Brith Magazine* 51, no. 7 (April 1937): 228.

87. Samuel Joseph, *History of the Baron De Hirsch Fund* (Philadelphia: Jewish Publication Society, 1935), 122.

88. "Leading the Way," 228; Levine and Miller, *American Jewish Farmer*, 84.

89. Gabriel Davidson to I. Irving Lipsitch, January 4, 1920, Box 79/B, Jewish Agricultural Society File, Western Jewish History Center. The JAIAS, founded in 1900, had the following three goals: to encourage agriculture among American Jews, support the development of cooperative enterprises, and remove industries from large urban areas. Granting loans to individuals who were involved in these pursuits was an important organizational strategy. In 1920, for example, farmers received loans from the JAIAS amounting to $417,000 (Joseph, *History of the Baron*, 158).

90. M. E. Jaffa to Lucious Solomons, December 22, 1919, Box 79/B, Jewish Agricultural Society File, Western Jewish History Center.

91. I. Irving Lipsitch to Morgan A. Gunst, June 3, 1922, Abraham Haas Memorial Fund Collection, Western Jewish History Center.

92. Fannie K. Haas and Children to the Federation of Jewish Charities, August 16, 1922, Abraham Haas Memorial Fund Collection, Western Jewish History Center.

93. *American Hebrew* 10, no. 9 (April 14, 1882): 97.

94. "Publicity," n.d. AHMF.

95. Bernice Scharlach, "Abe Haas: Portrait of a Proud Businessman," *Western States Jewish Historical Quarterly* 12, no. 1 (October 1979): 3–24.

96. AHMF, Report to the Board of Directors of the Federation of Jewish Charities for the Year Ending December 31, 1926.

97. Ibid.

98. I. Irving Lipsitch to William Weiss, January 11, 1923, Abraham Haas Memorial Fund Collection, Western Jewish History Center.

99. Ibid.

100. William Weiss to I. Irving Lipsitch, January 12, 1923, Abraham Haas Memorial Fund Collection, Western Jewish History Center.

101. Ibid.

102. Daniel Koshland and I. Irving Lipsitch to Morgan A. Gunst, September 17, 1924, Abraham Haas Memorial Fund Collection, Western Jewish History Center.

103. Myer J. Heppner, "A Survey of the Petaluma Jewish Community with Special Reference to Borrowers of the Abraham Haas Memorial Fund," submitted to Daniel Koshland on August 21, 1929, Western Jewish History Center, p. 11.

104. Ibid., 13.

105. Ibid., 5.

106. Ibid., 18.

107. Ibid.

108. Ibid., 16–17.

109. Idem., "A Survey of the Borrowers of the Abraham Haas Memorial Fund," Part 2, submitted to Daniel Koshland on August 27, 1929, Western Jewish History Center, pp. 3–4.

110. Ibid., 5.

111. Ibid., 6.

112. Zelda Bronstein and Kenneth Kann, "Basha Singerman, Comrade of Petaluma," *California Historical Quarterly* 56, no. 1 (Spring 1977): 20. Basha Singerman is a pseudonym.

113. AHMF, Minutes, March 22, 1934.

114. "Leading the Way," 237.

115. Ibid., 1.

116. Bronstein and Kann, "Basha Singerman," 20.

117. Ibid., 32.

118. Kenneth Kann, "Reconstructing the History of a Community," *International Journal of Oral History* 2, no. 1 (February 1981): 6–8; "Radicals and Chickens: The Jews of Petaluma," *Jewish Radical* 7, no. 2 (February 1975): 11.

119. Levine and Miller, *American Jewish Farmer,* 85; San Francisco HFLA, Ninetieth Anniversary Gala Dinner Dance Brochure, June 5, 1988, p. 10.

Chapter 6

1. Moody and Fite, *Credit Union Movement* (see chap. 2, n. 60), 26–30.

2. The following discussion on European credit cooperatives is based on several published works: Henry W. Wolff, *People's Banks: A Record of Social and Economic Progress* (London: King, 1919); Myron T. Herrick, *Rural Credits; Land and Cooperative* (New York: Appleton, 1914); and Moody and Fite, *Credit Union Movement.*

3. Moody and Fite, *Credit Union Movement,* 7.

4. Ibid., 12–13.

5. Leon Harris, *Merchant Princes: An Intimate History of Jewish Families Who Built Great Department Stores* (New York: Harper & Row, 1977), 23; Saul Engelbourg, "Edward A. Filene: Merchant, Civic Leader, and Jew," *American Jewish Historical Quarterly* 66, no. 1 (September 1976): 113–14.

6. M. Cezar, *Credit Unions* [in Yiddish] New York: Russell Sage Foundation, 1916), 51–52; Robinson and Nugent, *Regulation* (see chap. 2, n. 66), 152–53; and Freund, "New York HFLS" (see chap. 2, n. 9), 50, 57.

7. Milton Gordon, *Assimilation in American Life: The Role of Race, Religion, and National Origins* (New York: Oxford University Press, 1964), 51–54.

8. MCUA, "Massachusetts Credit Unions," ca. 1917. Filene Collection, Pamphlets and Clippings, 1903–33, CUNA Archives, Madison, Wisc., p. 2.

9. MCUA, Minutes of the Special Finance Committee, October 6, 1917; MCUA, "Massachusetts Credit Unions," 3. Filene Collection, Pamphlets and Clippings, 1903–33, CUNA Archives, Madison, Wisc.

10. Lillian Schoedler, Memorandum re Filene's March 1919 contribution to the Federated Jewish Charities, n.d., Filene Collection, Personal and Biographical Matters, Jewish Matters File, CUNA Archives, Madison, Wisc.

11. Edward A. Filene, Memorandum, November 7, 1932, Filene Collection, Personal and Biographical Matters, Jewish Matters File, CUNA Archives, Madison, Wisc.

12. Edward A. Filene, "The Spread of Credit Unions," *Survey Graphic,* November 1930, 135.

13. Memorandum from Josephine A. Bruorton to Edward A. Filene, March 2, 1917, Filene Papers, 1917 Correspondence File, CUNA Archives, Madison, Wisc.

14. MCU, Minutes of the Executive Session of the Board of Directors, April 24, 1914, CUNA Archives, Madison, Wisc.

15. William J. Stanton, "Massachusetts Credit Union Situation," November 12, 1915; Uncatalogued Stanton Material, CUNA Archives, Madison, Wisc.

16. Alphonse Desjardins to Arthur H. Ham, May 29, 1918, Desjardins Collec-

tion, 1918 Correspondence File, CUNA Archives, Madison, Wisc. Two decades earlier, Desjardins wrote to William Henry Wolff, author of several books on people's
banks, that he planned to introduce credit cooperatives in Canada in order to protect
citizens from "that Jew money lender" (Desjardins to Wolff, June 6, 1898, Desjardins
Collection, 1898 Correspondence File, CUNA Archives, Madison, Wisc.

17. "Credit Unions Will Raise $50,000 Fund," *Boston Post,* May 10, 1916, p.
11.

18. MCUA, "Massachusetts Credit Unions," 4.

19. Rabbi Harry Levi, "The Work of the Massachusetts Credit Union," May
5, 1916, published by the Massachusetts Credit Union, Massachusetts Maintenance
Society File, CUNA Archives, Madison, Wisc., p. 5.

20. "Boston Jews and the Credit Union Movement," *Jewish Advocate,* July 25,
1928, pt. 2, p. 4.

21. "New York Jews and Credit Unions," *Jewish Advocate,* September 13,
1928, p. 8.

22. Filene Marginalia on Memorandum from Roy Bergengren to Filene,
April 13, 1933, Filene Collection, 1933 Correspondence File, CUNA Archives, Madison, Wisc.

23. Moody and Fite, *Credit Union Movement,* 236.

24. Elsie Terry Blanc, *Co-operative Movement in Russia* (New York: Macmillan,
1924), 47; *Encyclopedia Judaica,* 1971 ed., s.v. "Jewish Colonization Association," by
Ann Ussishkin.

25. Moses Shohet, *She'elot U'Teshuvot Ohel Moshe* (Jerusalem: Zion, 1933),
46–49.

26. Freund, "New York HFLS," 50.

27. *Jewish Communal Register* (see chap. 2, n. 4), 728–29.

28. Freund, "New York HFLS," 50–53.

29. Morris Silverman, Hartford Jews, 1659–1970 (Hartford: Connecticut Historical Society, 1910), 34; Robert R. Cherlin to Shelly Tenenbaum, September 26,
1984, in my possession.

30. Freund, "New York HFLS," 57.

31. Massachusetts Commissioner of Banks, *Annual Report on Credit Unions,*
1927.

32. John, "Why Workers Borrow" (see chap. 2, n. 69), 8.

33. MCU, Minutes of the Board of Directors, May 6 and 12, June 5, October
7, November 24, and December 27, 1914.

34. MCU, Minutes of the Board of Directors, August 5, 1914.

35. Moody and Fite, *Credit Union Movement,* 39, 48, 145–46; Massachusetts
Commissioner of Banks, *Annual Report on Credit Unions,* 1927; and Joseph Snider,
Credit Unions in Massachusetts (Cambridge: Harvard University Press, 1939), 54.

36. Roy F. Bergengren, *Credit Union: A Cooperative Banking Book* (New York:
Beekman Hill, 1931), 193.

37. Bergengren to Filene, January 6, 1933, Filene Collection, 1933 Correspondence File, CUNA Archives, Madison, Wisc.; Bergengren, *Credit Union,* 193–
95; idem, *Cooperative Banking: A Credit Union Book* (New York: Macmillan, 1923), 84;
and Bergengren to Earl D. Miller, May 8, 1935, Bergengren Collection, 1935 Correspondence File, CUNA Archives, Madison, Wisc.

38. See Moody and Fite, *Credit Union Movement,* 119.

39. Bergengren, *Cooperative Banking,* 126–32; idem, *Credit Union,* 229–34;

Bergengren to Filene, December 4, 1929, Filene Collection, 1929 Correspondence File, CUNA Archives, Madison, Wisc.; and Bergengren to Filene, January 30, 1931, Filene Collection, 1931 Correspondence File, CUNA Archives, Madison, Wisc. For a detailed discussion of the importance of common bonds, see Jerry Burns, "Origin of the term *Common Bond* in Credit Union Usage," prepared for the CUNA, Madison, Wisc. 1979.

40. Bergengren, *Cooperative Banking*, 137–38.

41. Idem, "Report for Mr. Filene, September 16–October 14, 1922," Filene Collection, 1922 Correspondence File, CUNA Archives, Madison, Wisc.

42. Bergengren to Leon Henderson, April 12, 1928, Filene Collection, 1928 Correspondence File, CUNA Archives, Madison, Wisc.; John M. Glenn to Filene, May 3, 1928, Filene Collection, 1928 Correspondence File, CUNA Archives, Madison, Wisc.; and Bergengren to Filene, May 10, 1928, Filene Collection, 1928 Correspondence file, CUNA Archives, Madison, Wisc.

43. Bergengren to Filene, April 30, 1930, Filene Collection, 1930 Correspondence file, CUNA Archives, Madison, Wisc.

44. Francis E. Wilcox, *A Statistical Study of Credit Unions in New York* (Chicago: University of Chicago Press, 1940), 20–21.

45. *New York State Credit Union League Monthly Bulletin*, May–June 1931, p. 1.

46. Roy Bergengren to Agnes Gartland, July 22, 1952, Bergengren Collection, 1952 Correspondence File, CUNA Archives, Madison, Wisc.

47. "Discussion of Adolph Held's" (see chap. 5, n. 45), 128.

48. Ibid.

49. Ibid., 15.

50. Roy F. Bergengren, *Crusade* (New York: Exposition, 1952), 55; Memorandum from Bergengren to Filene entitled "Summary of Organization Work 1923 up to and Including October 18, 1923," Filene Collection, 1923 Correspondence File, CUNA Archives, Madison, Wisc.

51. Other spellings that appear in the text are *axias* and *oxies*.

52. Clark, *Financing the Consumer* (see chap. 2, n. 59), 109; and Herman Frank, "Economic Organizations of the Jewish Middle-Class in the United States" [in Yiddish], *YIVO Bleter* 15, nos. 1–2 (January–February 1940): 107.

53. Freund, "New York HFLS," 59; Clark, *Financing the Consumer*, 109. See also Herman Frank, "Economic Self-Help Through Credit Unions" [in Yiddish], *Daily Food News and Food Magazine*, September 16, 1936, p. 8.

54. Hyman Kurnitsky, interview by Emma Cohen of the Jewish Historical Society of Greater Hartford, October 29, 1980.

55. Rolf Nugent, *Consumer Credit and Economic Stability* (New York: Russell Sage Foundation, 1939), 403–4.

56. Snider, *Credit Unions in Massachusetts*, 29.

57. Freund, "New York HFLS," 61. See also Adolph Held, "Community Provision for Reconstruction through Credit," *Jewish Social Service Quarterly* 9, no. 1 (December 1932): 124–25.

58. "Oxies—Symbol of a Fading Era," *Courier* 4, no. 1 (January 1976): 7.

59. Rolf Nugent, "Credit Facilities for Marginal Jewish Groups," *Proceedings of the National Conference of Jewish Social Service* (Atlantic City, N.J., NCJSS, 1934).

60. *New York State Credit Union League Monthly Bulletin*, August–September 1931, p. 1; Freund, "New York HFLS," 61.

61. "Oxies—Symbol of a Fading Era," *Courier*, January 1976, p. 7.

62. Ibid., 12.

63. Snider, *Credit Unions in Massachusetts*, 32, 50; Hyman Kurnitsky, interview by Shelly Tenenbaum, May 10, 1984, Hartford, Conn.; and " 'Oxies', a Link with the Past," *New York Times*, June 29, 1980, sec. 23, p. 1.

64. Snider, *Credit Unions in Massachusetts*, 28–29.

65. E. W. Kemmerer, "Agricultural Credit in the United States," *American Economic Review* 2 (December 1912): 868.

66. "The Jews Ahead," *Indianapolis News*, December 14, 1912, p. 6.

67. "Cooperative Credit Unions," *Cooperation*, April 1914, p. 120; Gabriel Davidson, "The Jew in Agriculture in the United States," *American Jewish Yearbook*, 1935–36:108.

68. Arthur H. Ham and Louis G. Robinson, *A Credit Union Primer* (New York: Russell Sage Foundation, 1914).

69. JAIAS, Annual Reports, 1911, 1912, and 1913, CUNA Archives, Madison, Wisc.

70. Herman Frank, "Di Yiddishe Credit-Cooperatziya in America" [in Yiddish], *Virtschaft un Lebn* 2, no. 3 (June 1929): 51.

71. "Solving the Problem of Financing the Farmer," *New York Times*, December 8, 1912, pt. 6, p. 5; and Joseph, *History of the Baron*, 146.

72. For a discussion of how loans provided by the Jewish Agricultural Society placed Jewish homesteaders at an advantage compared with their native-born American neighbors, see Janet E. Schulte, "Proving Up and Moving Up: Jewish Homesteading Activity in North Dakota," *Great Plains Quarterly* 10(Fall 1990): 234, 241.

73. JAIAS, Annual Report, 1914, CUNA Archives, Madison, Wisc.

74. Joseph, *History of the Baron*, 153. See also Gabriel Davidson, *Our Jewish Farmer: The Story of the Jewish Agricultural Society* (New York: Fischer, 1943), 47–48; and George M. Price, "The Russian Jews in America," in *The Jewish Experience in America*, ed. Abraham J. Karp, vol. 4 (New York: Ktav, 1969).

75. Frank, "Di Yiddishe Credit-Cooperatziya," 55 (translation mine).

76. Nugent, "Credit Facilities," 45.

77. Pollack, "Communal Self-Help" (see chap. 3, n. 31), 22.

78. Snider, *Credit Unions in Massachusetts*, 44–45, 50. Before reorganizing as the Skandia Bank and Trust Company in 1929, the Skandia Credit Union, one of the largest credit unions in Massachusetts, catered to the real estate needs of Worcester's Swedish community. See Roy F. Bergengren to Filene, January 4, 1930, Filene Collection, 1930 Correspondence File, CUNA Archives, Madison, Wisc.

79. Hyman, "Indianapolis Jewish Community" (see chap. 5, n. 10), 13.

80. Hyman, "Indianapolis Jewish Community," 15.

81. Ibid.

82. Ibid.

83. Eli N. Evans, "An Interview with Morris B. Abram," *American Jewish History* 73(September 1983): 15–16.

84. Frank, "Economic Organizations," 112.

85. Bergengren, *Cooperative Banking*, 133; MCU, Minutes of the Board of Directors, November 30, 1914; and Frank, "Economic Organizations," 107, 109–10.

86. Marie Chesler to Shelly Tenenbaum, January 19, 1984, in my possession.

87. Selig Adler and Thomas E. Connally, *From Ararat to Suburbia: The History of the Jewish Community of Buffalo* (Philadelphia: Jewish Publication Society, 1960), 253.

88. Ibid., 191.

89. Ibid., 254.

90. Massachusetts Commissioner of Banks, "Annual Report on Credit Unions" 1927; Frank, "Di Yiddishe Credit-Cooperatziya," 53.

91. NCJC, *Proceedings* (1914), 17 (see chap. 4, n. 5).

92. Judah J. Shapiro, *The Friendly Society: A History of the Workmen's Circle* (New York: Media Judaica, 1970), 49.

93. Pollack, "Communal Self-Help," 23.

94. The discussion of Jewish credit unions in Omaha relies on Pollack, "Communal Self-Help."

95. *Jewish Press*, September 14, 1939; p. C-8, cited in Pollack, "Communal Self-Help," 26.

96. Pollack, "Communal Self-Help," 35.

97. Ibid., 32.

98. John, "Why Workers Borrow," 8.

99. Freund, "New York HFLS," 58.

100. Meyer Finkel interview by Shelly Tenenbaum, February 3, 1984.

101. Freund, "New York HFLS," 58.

102. *Jewish Charities* 5, no. 1 (August 1914): 19; see also Freund, "New York HFLS," 58.

103. Evelyn Nakano Glenn, *Issei, Nisei, War Bride; Three Generations of Japanese American Women in Domestic Service* (Philadelphia: Temple University Press, 1986), 39.

104. "Saugus Credit Union Seized," *Boston Globe*, February 15, 1991, p. 69; "Grove Bank Acquires Blue Hill Federal," *Jewish Advocate*, December 20, 1991, p. 19.

105. Henry Bikofsky to Edward Odell, May 16, 1969, Washington Credit Union Office; Freyda P. Koplow to Washington Credit Union, May 20, 1969, Washington Credit Union Office.

106. Frank, "Di Yiddishe Credit-Cooperatziya," 54.

Chapter 7

1. William G. Weiss to Herman Kretzer, October 7, 1942, Out-of-Town File, Los Angeles JFLA; Kretzer to Weiss, October 5, 1942, Out-of-Town File, Los Angeles JFLA.

2. MLS, Minutes of the Twenty-Second Annual Board of Directors' Meeting, June 16, 1943; Memorandum from Hertha Magnus to Hyman Kaplan, AHMF, October 25, 1944, Abraham Haas Memorial Fund Collection, Western Jewish History Center; Massachusetts Commissioner of Banks, "Annual Report on Credit Unions," 1927.

3. Harry H. Fein to Herman Kretzer, August 20, 1940, Out-of-Town File, Los Angeles JFLA; Harry H. Fein to Hannah Shapiro, March 6, 1944, Out-of-Town File, Los Angeles JFLA; Ida B. Colten to Herman Kretzer, October 14, 1942, Out-of-Town File, Los Angeles JFLA; Hyman Kaplan, "Digest of Significant Finds and Recommendations from 'Report of the Hebrew Free Loan Society of Detroit' by Harold Silver, January 1944," June 3, 1949, Federation of Jewish Charities of San Francisco Collection, Box 76, Western Jewish History Center; New York HFLS, "Seventy-Five Years of Service," 1967; Emil Steinbach, "Suggestions for Post-War

and Increased Loan Planning," November 29, 1943, Pittsburgh HFLA; Pitterman, "HFLA, 1938–50" (see chap. 3, n. 2), 92; and Cleveland HFLA, Minutes of the Board of Directors Meeting, October 2, 1945.

4. Los Angeles HFLA, Minutes of the Board of Directors, November 7, 1944; Los Angeles JLF, Minutes of the Board of Directors, November 14, 1945; William G. Weiss to Herman Kretzer, October 7, 1942, Out-of-Town File, Los Angeles JFLA; Harry H. Fein to Hannah Shapiro, March 6, 1944, Out-of-Town File, Los Angeles JFLA; MLS, Minutes of the Twenty-First Annual Meeting, February 24, 1942; and Pitterman, "HFLA, 1938–50," 101.

5. Pollack, "Communal Self-Help" (see chap. 3, n. 31), 32.

6. Rubin, "History of the Seattle" (see chap. 4, n. 40), 6.

7. Edward Dobrin to Mrs. E. E. Lescher, October 12, 1963, Seattle Hebrew Ladies' Free Loan Collection, University of Washington Library.

8. "Hebrew Ladies' Free Loan Society Merger with JFCS," *Jewish Transcript*, December 20, 1973, p. 3.

9. Hyman Kaplan, "Memorandum Regarding 'A Study of the Woman's Loan Association of Chicago,' by Esther Beckenstein for the Jewish Charities of Chicago, March, 1943," June 3, 1949, Federation of Jewish Charities of San Francisco Collection, Box 76, Western Jewish History Center; Horvitz, "Jewish Woman Liberated" (see chap. 4, n. 41), 509–12.

10. MLS, Minutes of the Sixtieth Regular Meeting of the Board of Directors, October 2, 1942; MLS, Minutes of a Special Meeting of the Executive Committee, July 8, 1942.

11. Robert Tabak, "The Mastbaum Loan System: 1920–1954, Low Interest Loans in Philadelphia," 1980, MLS Collection, Philadelphia Jewish Archives Center.

12. Records of the Boston HFLS, American Jewish Historical Society, Waltham, Mass.; Justin Wyner, phone interview by Shelly Tenenbaum, July 17, 1991.

13. Trescott, *Financing American Enterprise* (see chap. 2, n. 57), 205.

14. Chapman, *Commercial Banks* (see chap. 2, n. 58), 28.

15. Joseph B. Goldberg to the HFLS of Manhattan, January 16, 1947, New York HFLA Office. In his study of Jewish family clubs, William Mitchell also found that loan requests had diminished by the 1940s because of the availability of loans from commercial banks. (*Mishpokhe* [see chap. 2, n. 6], 106).

16. For a discussion of Jewish economic transformations, see Goldscheider and Zuckerman, *Transformation* (see chap. 1, n. 14); Walter Zenner, *Minorities in the Middle: A Cross-Cultural Analysis* (Albany: State University of New York Press, 1991).

17. "Excerpt from Letter by Michael Freund in 1945 on Free Loans," in H. L. Lurie to Hyman Kaplan, April 13, 1949, Federation of Jewish Charities of San Francisco Collection, Western Jewish History Center.

18. Cohen, *Making a New Deal* (see chap. 2, n. 61), 276.

19. Smith, *Family Connections* (see chap. 2, n. 47), 160.

20. Mark Rosentraub and Delbert Taebel, "Jewish Enterprise in Transition: From Collective Self-Help to Orthodox Capitalism" in *Self-Help in Urban America,* ed. Scott Cummings (Port Washington, N.Y.: Kennikat, 1980): 191–214.

21. Goren, "Traditional Institutions" (see chap. 2, n. 44), 71–72.

22. New York HFLS, "Five Years and Eighty-Five: The Story of the Hebrew Free Loan Society of New York," ca. 1977; "The Hebrew Free Loan Society: A Century Without a Profit, and Darned Proud of It," *Jewish World*, July 24–30, 1992, pp. 14–15; Oliver B. Pollack, "The Jewish Free Loan Societies of Omaha, Nebraska,

1911–1987," *Memories of the Jewish Midwest* 3(1987): 9; "Aid, Rather Than Alms" (see chap. 4, n. 27), 16; Memorandum from Arthur J. Stern to Jerome C. Frankel re HFLA–Storer Center of the Cleveland Society for the Blind, March 12, 1985, San Francisco HFLA Office; and "Detroit's Neighborhood Preservation Project," *AHFL News,* January 1988, pp. 3–4.

23. Seattle Hebrew Ladies' Free Loan Society, Minutes of the Meeting of the Board of Directors, January 16, 1951; Rubin, "History of the Seattle," 5; San Francisco HFLA, Newsletter, September–October 1986, p. 2; "Hebrew Free Loan Association Fights 'War on Poverty'," *San Francisco Jewish Bulletin,* September 6, 1974, p. 10; "For Free: Hebrew Society Loans and Grants Available to Needy," *Jewish World,* January 13, 1984, p. 24; and "The Hebrew Free Loan Society" (see chap. 7, n. 22).

24. Robert Coe, "Philip Glass Breaks Through," *New York Times Magazine,* October 25, 1981, p. 68.

25. "Toronto Jewish Assistance Services, G'milath Chasodim Association," ca. 1986.

26. Ann Swidler, "Culture in Action: Symbols and Strategies," *American Sociological Review* 51(April 1986): 273–86.

References

Adler, Cyrus. *Jacob Schiff: His Life and Letters.* 2 vols. Garden City: Doubleday, 1928.

Adler, Selig, and Thomas E. Connolly. *From Ararat to Suburbia: The History of the Jewish Community of Buffalo.* Philadelphia: Jewish Publication Society of America, 1960.

"Aid, Rather Than Alms Goal of Hebrew Free Loan Association." *Jewish Transcript.* December 22, 1983, p. 16.

Alexander, David. "History of the Jews of Toledo." *Reform Advocate.* June 20, 1908, p. 17.

"Annual Meeting of Hebrew Free Loan Association." *Jewish Review and Observer.* January 14, 1910, p. 1.

Ardener, Shirley. "The Comparative Study of Rotating Credit Associations." *Journal of the Royal Anthropological Institute.* 94(July 1964): 201–9.

Baron, Salo. *The Jewish Community: Its History and Structure to the American Revolution.* 3 vols. Westport, Conn.: Greenwood, 1942.

Baum, Charlotte. "What Made Yetta Work? The Economic Role of East European Jewish Women in the Family." *Response* 76(1973): 32–38.

Bayor, Ronald H. *Neighbors in Conflict: The Irish, Germans, Jews, and Italians of New York City, 1929–1941.* 2d ed. Urbana: University of Illinois Press, 1988.

Bergengren, Roy. *Cooperative Banking: A Credit Union Book.* New York: Macmillan, 1923.

———. *Credit Union: A Cooperative Banking Book.* New York: Beekman Hill, 1931.

———. *Crusade.* New York: Exposition, 1952.

Bernheimer, Charles, ed. *The Russian Jew in the United States.* Philadelphia: Winston, 1905.

Berrol, Selma. "Education and Economic Mobility: The Jewish Experience in New York City, 1880–1920," *American Jewish Historical Quarterly.* March 1976, pp. 257–71.

Blanc, Elsie Terry. *Co-operative Movement in Russia.* New York: Macmillan, 1924.

Bodnar, John. *The Transplanted: A History of Immigrants in Urban America.* Bloomington: Indiana University Press, 1985.

Bogen, Boris. *Extent of Jewish Philanthropy in the United States*. Cincinnati: National Conference of Jewish Charities, 1908.

Bonacich, Edna, and John Modell. *The Economic Basis of Ethnic Solidarity: Small Business in the Japanese American Community*. Berkeley: University of California Press, 1980.

Bonnett, Aubrey W. *Institutional Adaptation of West Indian Immigrants to America: An Analysis of Rotating Credit Associations*. Washington: University Press of America, 1981.

"Boston Jews and the Credit Union Movement." *Jewish Advocate*. July 25, 1928, Pt. 2, p. 4.

Bremner, Robert H. *American Philanthropy*. Chicago: University of Chicago Press, 1960.

Bronstein, Zelda, and Kenneth Kann. "Basha Singerman, Comrade of Petaluma." *California Historical Quarterly*. 56(Spring 1977): 20–33.

Burns, Jerry. "Origin of the Term *Common Bond* in Credit Union Usage." Paper prepared for Credit Union National Association, Madison, 1979.

Caudill, William, and George De Vos. "Achievement, Culture, and Personality: The Case of the Japanese Americans." *American Anthropologist* 58(1956): 1102–26.

Cezar, M. *Credit Unions* [in Yiddish]. New York: Russell Sage Foundation, 1916.

Chapman, John M. *Commercial Banks and Consumer Instalment Credit*. New York: National Bureau of Economic Research, 1940.

The Chicago Jewish Community Blue Book. Chicago: Sentinel Company, [ca. 1918].

Clark, Evan. *Financing the Consumer*. New York: Harper & Brothers, 1930.

Coe, Robert. "Philip Glass Breaks Through." *New York Times Magazine*, October 25, 1981, pp. 68ff.

Cohen, Lizabeth. *Making A New Deal: Industrial Workers in Chicago, 1919–39*. Cambridge: Cambridge University Press, 1990.

"Cooperative Credit Unions." *Cooperation*, April 1914, p. 120.

"Credit Unions Will Raise $50,000 Fund." *Boston Post*, May 10, 1916, p. 11.

Cronbach, Abraham. "The Gradations of Benevolence." *Hebrew Union College Annual* 16(1941): 163–86.

Davidoff, Lenore, and Catherine Hall. *Family Fortunes: Men and Women of the English Middle-Class 1780–1850*. London: Hutchinson, 1987.

Davidson, Gabriel. "The Jew in Agriculture in the United States." *American Jewish Yearbook* 1935–36: 99–134.

————. *Our Jewish Farmer: The Story of the Jewish Agricultural Society*. New York: Fischer, 1943.

"Detroit's Neighborhood Preservation Project." *AHFL News*, January 1988, pp. 3–4.

Diner, Hasia R. *Erin's Daughters in America: Irish Immigrant Women in the Nineteenth Century*. Baltimore: Johns Hopkins University Press, 1983.

"Discussion of Adolph Held's 'Community Provision for Reconstruction Through Credit'," *Jewish Social Service Quarterly* 1(December 1932): 125–29.

Dorsett, Lyle W. "Equality of Opportunity on the Urban Frontier: Access to Credit in Denver, Colorado Territory, 1858–1877," *Journal of the West* 18(July 1979): 75–81.

Elovitz, Mark H. *A Century of Jewish Life in Dixie: The Birmingham Experience*. University: University of Alabama Press, 1974.

Elsinger, Chester E. "A Brief History of the Lafayette Orthodox Hebrew Free Loan Association, 1907–1960." *Indiana Jewish Historical Society Publication* 9(1977): 1–26.

Encyclopedia Judaica. 1971 ed. S.v. "gemilut hasadim," by Louis Isaac Rabinowitz.

———, 1971 ed. S.v. "Jewish Colonization Association," by Ann Ussishkin.

Engelbourg, Saul. "Edward A. Filene: Merchant, Civic Leader, and Jew," *American Jewish Historical Quarterly* 66(September 1976): 106–22.

Evans, Eli N. "An Interview with Morris B. Abram." *American Jewish History* 73(September 1983): 7–19.

The Fathers According to Rabbi Nathan. Ed. Judah Goldin. New Haven: Yale University Press, 1955.

Filene, Edward A. "The Spread of Credit Unions." *Survey Graphic,* November 1930, pp. 132–35, 176, 180–81.

Fish, Sidney M. "Communal Leadership in Post-Revolutionary Philadelphia." *Gratz College Annual of Jewish Studies* 3(1974): 83–94.

Fisher, Terry K. "Lending as Philanthropy: The Philadelphia Jewish Experience, 1847–1954." Ph.D. diss., Bryn Mawr College, 1987.

"For Free: Hebrew Society Loans and Grants Available to Needy." *Jewish World,* January 13–19, 1984, p. 24.

Frank, Herman. "Economic Organizations of the Jewish Middle-Class in the United States" [in Yiddish]. *YIVO Bleter* 15(January–February 1940): 103–123.

———. "Economic Self-Help Through Credit Unions" [in Yiddish]. *Daily Food News and Food Magazine,* September 16, 1936, pp. 7–8.

———. "Di Yiddishe Credit-Cooperatziya in America" [in Yiddish]. *Virtschaft un Lebn* 2(June 1929): 48–56.

Freedman, Maurice. "The Handling of Money: A Note on the Background to the Economic Sophistication of Overseas Chinese." *Man* 59(1959): 64–65.

"Free Loan Society Blessing to Many." *Cleveland News,* May 28, 1931, p. 8.

"Free Loans That Start Poor Jews in Business." *Providence Sunday Journal,* March 3, 1912, sect. 5, p. 10.

Freund, Michael. "The New York Hebrew Free Loan Society and Other Available Small Loan Facilities in New York City." Paper prepared for the Bureau of Jewish Social Research, November 1932. Microfilm No. 304.818. Harvard University, Widener Library.

Gambino, Richard. *Blood of My Blood: The Dilemma of the Italian–Americans.* Garden City: Anchor Books, 1974.

Gartner, Lloyd. "Immigration and the Formation of American Jewry, 1840–1925." In *American Jews: A Reader,* ed. Marshall Sklare. New York: Behrman House, 1983.

———. "The Midpassage of American Jewry, 1929–1945." Paper presented at the Feinberg Memorial Lecture in Judaic Studies, University of Cincinnati, 1982.

Geertz, Clifford. "The Rotating Credit Association: A 'Middle Rung' in Development." *Economic Development and Cultural Change* 10(April 1962): 241–263.

Gelfand, Mitchell. "Chutzpah in El Dorado: Social Mobility of Jews in Los Angeles." Ph.D. diss., Carnegie–Mellon University, 1981.

Gerber, David A. "Cutting Out Shylock: Elite Anti-Semitism and the Quest for Moral Order in the Mid–Nineteenth Century American Marketplace." In *Anti-Semitism in American History,* ed. David Gerber. Urbana: University of Illinois Press, 1987.

Giovinco, Joseph. "Democracy in Banking: The Bank of Italy and California's Italians." *California Historical Society Quarterly* 47, no. 3 (September 1968): 195–218.

Glazer, Nathan. "The American Jew and the Attainment of Middle-Class Rank:

Some Trends and Explanations." In *The Jews: Social Patterns of an American Ethnic Group*, ed. Marshall Sklare. Westport, Conn.: Greenwood, 1958.

Glazer, Nathan, and Daniel Patrick Moynihan. *Beyond the Melting Pot: The Negroes, Puerto Ricans, Jews, Italians, and Irish of New York City*. Cambridge: Massachusetts Institute of Technology Press, 1963.

Glenn, Evelyn Nakano. *Issei, Nisei, War Bride: Three Generations of Japanese American Women in Domestic Service*. Philadelphia: Temple University Press, 1986.

Glenn, John M., Lilian Brandt, and F. Emerson Andrews. *Russell Sage Foundation, 1907–1946*. 2 vols. New York: Russell Sage Foundation, 1947.

Glick, Rhoda. "A Study of Loans Made by the Hebrew Free Loan Association and Guaranteed by the Jewish Family Welfare Association from 1926 Through 1935." Master's thesis, University of Pittsburgh, 1938.

Glicksman, William. *Jewish Social Welfare Institutions in Poland*. Philadelphia: Kalish Folkshul, 1976.

Goldberg, Nathan. "Occupational Patterns of American Jewry." *Jewish Review* 3(April 1945): 3–24.

Goldscheider, Calvin, and Alan S. Zuckerman. *The Transformation of the Jews*. Chicago: University of Chicago Press, 1984.

Gordon, Milton. *Assimilation in American Life: The Role of Race, Religion, and National Origins*. New York: Oxford University Press, 1964.

Goren, Arthur A. "Traditional Institutions Transplanted: The Hevra Kadisha in Europe and America." In *The Jews of North America*, ed. Moses Rischin. Detroit: Wayne State University Press, 1987.

Greeley, Andrew. *Ethnicity in the United States: A Preliminary Reconnaissance*. New York: Wiley, 1974.

Grinstein, Hyman. *The Rise of the Jewish Community of New York, 1654–1860*. Philadelphia: Jewish Publication Society of America, 1947.

"Grove Bank Acquires Blue Hill Federal." *Jewish Advocate*, December 20–26, 1991, p. 19.

Gutstein, Morris A. *A Priceless Heritage*. New York: Bloch, 1953.

Ham, Arthur, and Louis G. Robinson. *A Credit Union Primer*. New York: Russell Sage Foundation, 1919.

Harris, Leon. *Merchant Princes: An Intimate History of the Jewish Families Who Built Great Department Stores*. New York: Harper & Row, 1979.

Harvard Encyclopedia of American Ethnic Groups. 1981 ed. S.v. "Japanese," by Harry H. L. Kitano.

———, 1981 ed. S.v. "Jews," by Arthur Goren.

"The Hebrew Free Loan Society: A Century without a Profit, and Darned Proud of It." *Jewish World*, July 24–30, 1992, pp. 14–15.

"Hebrew Free Loan Society," Part I. *Jewish Advocate*, April 19, 1926, p. 8.

"Hebrew Free Loan Society," Part II. *Jewish Advocate*, May 28, 1925, p. 6.

"Hebrew Free Loan Society Fights War on Poverty." *San Francisco Jewish Bulletin*, September 6, 1974, p. 10.

"Hebrew Ladies' Free Loan Merger with JFCS." *Jewish Transcript*, December 20, 1973, p. 3.

Held, Adolph. "Community Provision for Reconstruction Through Credit." *Jewish Social Service Quarterly* 9(December 1932): 123–25.

Henderson, Charles Richmond. *Dependent, Defective, and Delinquent Classes*. Boston: Heath, 1893.

Heppner, Myron J. "A Survey of the Borrowers of the Abraham Haas Memorial Fund." Part 2. Paper prepared for the Abraham Haas Memorial Fund, San Francisco, 1929.

———. "A Survey of the Petaluma Jewish Community with Special Reference to Borrowers of the Abraham Haas Memorial Fund." Paper prepared for the Abraham Haas Memorial Fund, San Francisco, 1929.

Herrick, Myron T. *Rural Credits: Land and Cooperative.* New York: D. Appleton, 1914.

Hirsch, William. "Discussion of Rolf Nugent's 'Credit Facilities for Marginal Groups'," *Proceedings of the National Conference of Jewish Social Service* 1934: 46–47.

———. "Remedial Loans to the Needy." *Jewish Social Service Quarterly,* June 1936, pp. 370–375.

"History of Free Loan Department Hebrew Ladies Relief Association." *Kansas City Jewish Chronicle,* October 19, 1928, p. 8.

Horvitz, Eleanor F. "The Jewish Woman Liberated: A History of the Ladies' Hebrew Free Loan Association." *Rhode Island Jewish Historical Notes* 7(November 1978): 501–13.

———. "Old Bottles, Rags, Junk! The Story of the Jews of South Providence." *Rhode Island Jewish Historical Notes* 7(November 1976): 189–257.

Howe, Irving, with Kenneth Libo. *World Of Our Fathers.* New York: Harcourt, Brace, Jovanovich, 1966.

Hyman, H. Joseph. "The Indianapolis Jewish Community Credit Union." *Jewish Social Service Quarterly* 7(March 1931): 13–15.

Industrial Commission on Immigration. *Reports.* Vol. 5. Washington: GPO, 1901.

James, Emily. "On the Associated Work of Women in Religion and Philanthropy." In *Woman's Mission,* ed. Angela Georgina Burdett-Coutts. London: Sampson Low, Marston, 1893.

The Jewish Communal Register of New York City, 1917–1918. New York: Kehillah (Jewish Community) of New York City, 1918.

"The Jews Ahead." *Indianapolis News,* December 14, 1912, p. 6.

Jick, Leon. *The Americanization of the Synagogue, 1820–1870.* Hanover, N.H.: Brandeis University Press, 1976.

John, Mildred. "Why Workers Borrow: A Study of Four Thousand Credit Union Loans." *Monthly Labor Review* 25(July 1927): 6–16.

Jordan, William Chester. "Jews on Top: Women and the Availability of Consumption Loans in Northern France in the Mid-Thirteenth Century. *Journal of Jewish Studies* 29(Spring 1978): 39–56.

Joseph, Samuel. *History of the Baron de Hirsch Fund.* Philadelphia: Jewish Publication Society of America, 1935.

Kann, Kenneth. "Reconstructing the History of a Community." *International Journal of Oral History* 2(February 1981): 6–8.

Karp, Abraham J. *Haven and Home: A History of the Jews in America.* New York: Schocken Books, 1985.

Karpf, Maurice. *Jewish Community Organization in the United States.* New York: Bloch, 1938.

Kassow, Samuel D. "Community and Identity in the Interwar Shtetl." In *The Jews of Poland Between Two World Wars,* ed. Yisrael Gutman, Ezra Mendelsohn, Yehuda Reinharz, and Chone Shmeruk. Hanover, N.H.: University Press of New England, 1989.

Kemmerer, E. W. "Agricultural Credit in the United States." *American Economic Review* 2(December 1912): 852–72.

Kessner, Thomas. *The Golden Door: Italian and Jewish Immigrant Mobility in New York City, 1880–1915.* New York: Oxford University Press, 1977.

———. "Jobs, Ghettoes, and the Urban Economy, 1880–1935." *American Jewish History* 71(December 1981): 218–38.

Klaczynska, Barbara. "Why Women Work: A Comparison of Various Groups, Philadelphia, 1910–1930." *Labor History* 17(Winter 1976): 81–95.

Kober, Adolf. *Cologne.* Philadelphia: Jewish Publication Society of America, 1940.

Kuznets, Simon. "Immigration of Russian Jews to the United States: Background and Structure." *Perspectives in American History* 9(1975): 35–126.

Laguerre, Michel S. *American Odyssey: Haitians in New York City.* Ithaca: Cornell University Press, 1984.

"Leading the Way," *B'nai B'rith Magazine,* April 1937, p. 22.

Leemans, W. F. "The Rate of Interest in Old Babylonian Times." *Revue internationale des Droits de l'antiquite* 3(1950): 7–34.

Lenski, Gerhard. *The Religious Factor: A Sociologist's Inquiry.* New York: Anchor, 1963.

Lestchinsky, Jacob. "Economic Aspects of Jewish Community Organization in Independent Poland." *Jewish Social Studies* 9(October 1947): 319–338.

———. "The Position of the Jews in the Economic Life of America." In *Jews in a Gentile World,* ed. Isacque Graeber and S. H. Britt. New York: Macmillan, 1942.

Levine, Herman J. and Benjamin Miller. *The American Jewish Farmer in Changing Times.* New York: Jewish Agricultural Society, 1966.

Levitats, Isaac. *The Jewish Community in Russia, 1772–1844.* New York: Columbia University Press, 1943.

Lieberson, Stanley. *A Piece of the Pie: Blacks and White Immigrants Since 1880.* Berkeley: University of California Press, 1980.

———. *Ethnic Patterns in American Cities.* New York: Free Press, 1963.

Light, Ivan. "Asian Enterprise in America: Chinese, Japanese, and Koreans in Small Business." In *Self-Help in Urban America,* ed. Scott Cummings. Port Washington, N.Y.: Kennikat, 1980.

———. "Disadvantaged Minorities in Self-Employment." *International Journal of Comparative Sociology* 20(1979): 31–45.

———. *Ethnic Enterprise in America: Business and Welfare Among Chinese, Japanese, and Blacks.* Berkeley: University of California Press, 1972.

———. "Ethnicity and Business Enterprise." In *Making It In America: The Role of Ethnicity in Business Enterprise, Education, and Work Choices,* ed. M. Stolarik, and Murray Friedman. Lewisburg, Penn.: Bucknell University Press, 1986.

Light, Ivan, and Edna Bonacich. *Immigrant Entrepreneurs: Koreans in Los Angeles, 1965–1982.* Berkeley: University of California Press, 1988.

Light, Ivan, Im Jung Kwuon, and Deng Zhong. "Korean Rotating Credit Associations in Los Angeles." *Amerasia Journal* 16(1990): 35–54.

Light, Martin. "A Brief History of the Lafayette Orthodox Hebrew Free Loan Association, Part 2: 1960–1980." *Indiana Jewish Historical Society Publications* 18(1984): 43–57.

Lindo, E. H. *A Jewish Calendar for Sixty-Four Years.* London: L. Thompson, 1838.

Linfield, Harry. *The Communal Organization of the Jews in the United States, 1927.* New York: American Jewish Committee, 1930.

Lipset, Seymour Martin, and Reinhard Bendix. *Social Mobility in Industrial Society.* Berkeley: University of California Press, 1963.

References

"The Loan Shark Campaign." *New York Evening Post,* April 11, 1914. Reprint by the Division of Remedial Loans, Russell Sage Foundation.

Lovell-Troy, Lawrence A. "Clan Structure and Economic Activity: The Case of Greeks in Small Business Enterprise." In *Self-Help in Urban America,* ed. Scott Cummings. Port Washington, N.Y.: Kennikat, 1980.

Maimonides, Moses. *Mishneh Torah.* Ed. Zvi H. Preisler. Jerusalem: Ketuvim, 1985.

Marcus, Jacob Rader. *American Jewry: Documents, Eighteenth Century.* Cincinnati: Hebrew Union College, 1959.

———. *The Colonial American Jew, 1492–1776.* 3 vols. Detroit: Wayne State University Press, 1970.

Mayer, Kurt B., and Sidney Goldstein. *The First Two Years: Problems of Small Firm Growth and Survival.* Washington: Small Business Administration, 1961.

Mitchell, William. *Mishpokhe: A Study of New York City Jewish Family Clubs.* The Hague: Mouton, 1978.

Miyamoto, Shotaro Frank. *Social Solidarity Among the Japanese in Seattle.* University of Washington Publications in the Social Sciences, vol. 11, no. 2. Seattle: University of Washington Press, 1939.

Moody, J. Carroll, and Gilbert C. Fite. *The Credit Union Movement: Origins and Development 1850–1970.* Lincoln: University of Nebraska Press, 1971.

Morawska, Ewa. *For Bread with Butter: The Life-Worlds of East Central Europeans in Johnstown, Pennsylvania, 1890–1940.* Cambridge: Cambridge University Press, 1985.

———. "The Sociology and Historiography of Immigration." In *Immigration Reconsidered: History, Sociology, and Politics,* ed. Virginia Yans-McLaughlin. New York: Oxford University Press, 1990.

Mostov, Stephen G. "Dun and Bradstreet Reports as a Source of Jewish Economic History: Cincinnati, 1840–1875." *American Jewish History* 72(March 1983): 333–53.

———. "Immigrant Entrepreneurs: Jews in the Shoe Trades in Lynn, 1885–1945." Paper prepared for the North Shore Jewish Historical Society, Marblehead, Mass., 1982.

———. "A 'Jerusalem' on the Ohio: The Social and Economic History of Cincinnati's Jewish Community." Ph.D. diss., Brandeis University, 1981.

al-Nakawa, Israel ibn. *Menorat Hama'or.* chapt. 8. Ed. H. G. Enelow. New York: Bloch, 1929.

National Conference of Jewish Charities. *Proceedings of the Eighth Biennial Session.* Memphis, NCJC, 1914.

———. *Proceedings of the Second National Conference.* Detroit, NCJC, 1902.

Nelson, Benjamin. *The Idea of Usury: From Tribal Brotherhood to Universal Otherhood.* Princeton: Princeton University Press, 1949.

Neufeld, Edward. "The Prohibitions Against Loans at Interest in Ancient Hebrew Laws." *Hebrew Union College Annual* 26(1955): 355–412.

"New York Jews and Credit Unions." *Jewish Advocate,* September 13, 1928, p. 8.

Nugent, Rolf. *Consumer Credit and Economic Stability.* New York: Russell Sage Foundation, 1938.

———. "Credit Facilities for Marginal Jewish Groups." In *Proceedings of the National Conference of Jewish Social Service.* Atlantic City, N.Y.: NCJSS, 1934.

"Opening the Door to the New World." *Jewish Exponent,* July 13, 1984, pp. 85, 87, 119.

Oxenfeldt, Alfred R. *New Firms and Free Enterprise: Pre-War and Post-War Aspects.* Washington: American Council of Public Affairs, 1943.

References

" 'Oxies', a Link with the Past," *New York Times*, June 29, 1980, sec. 23, pt. 1, pp. 1, 19.

"Oxies—Symbol of a Fading Era." *Courier*, January 1976, p. 12.

Patterson, Orlando. "Context and Choice in Ethnic Allegiance: A Theoretical Framework and Caribbean Case Study." In *Ethnicity: Theory and Experience*, ed. Nathan Glazer and Daniel Patrick Moynihan. Cambridge: Harvard University Press, 1975.

Pedrazza-Bailey, Silvia. "Immigration History: A Conceptual Map." *Social Science History* 14(Spring 1990): 43–67.

Perlmann, Joel. "Beyond New York: The Occupations of Russian Jewish Immigrants in Providence, Rhode Island and Other Small Jewish Communities, 1900–1915." *American Jewish History* 72(1983): 369–94.

———. *Ethnic Differences: Schooling and Social Structure Among the Irish, Italians, Jews, and Blacks in an American City, 1880–1935*. Cambridge: Cambridge University Press, 1988.

Pitterman, Marvin. "The Hebrew Free Loan Association, 1938–1950." *Rhode Island Jewish Historical Notes* 81(November 1980): 91–108.

Pollack, Oliver B. "Communal Self-Help and Capital Formation: Omaha's Jewish Loan Associations, 1911–1979." *American Jewish History* 78(September 1988): 20–35.

———. "The Jewish Free Loan Societies of Omaha, Nebraska, 1911–1987." *Memories of the Jewish Midwest* 3(1987): 1–14.

Pollins, Harold. "The Development of Jewish Business in the United Kingdom." In *Ethnic Communities in Business: Strategies for Economic Survival*, Robin Ward and Richard Jenkins. Cambridge: Cambridge University Press, 1984.

The Poor Man's Bank: The Story of Fifty Years of Loans Without Interest. New York: New York HFLS, 1942.

Price, George M. "The Russian Jews in America." In *The Jewish Experience in America*, vol. 4, ed. Abraham Karp. New York: Ktav, 1969.

The Provident Loan Society of New York: Fifty Years of Remedial Lending. New York: Provident Loan Society of New York, 1944.

"Radicals and Chickens: The Jews of Petaluma." *The Jewish Radical* 7(February 1976): 9–11.

Raphael, Marc Lee. *Jews and Judaism in a Midwestern Community: Columbus, Ohio, 1840–1975*. Columbus: Ohio Historical Society, 1979.

Rischin, Moses. *The Promised City: New York's Jews, 1870–1914*. Cambridge: Harvard University Press, 1977.

Robinson, Louis N., and Rolf Nugent. *Regulation of the Small Loan Business*. New York: Russell Sage Foundation, 1935.

Rosentraub, Mark, and Delbert Taebel. "Jewish Enterprise in Transition: From Collective Self-Help to Orthodox Capitalism." In *Self-Help in Urban America*, ed. Scott Cummings. Port Washington, N.Y.: Kennikat, 1980.

Rubin, Grace. "History of the Seattle Hebrew Ladies' Free Loan Society." University of Washington, 1965.

"Saugus Credit Union Seized." *Boston Globe*, February 15, 1991, p. 69.

Scharlach, Bernice. "Abe Haas: Portrait of a Proud Businessman." *Western States Jewish Historical Quarterly* 12(October 1979): 3–24.

Schulte, Janet E. " 'Proving Up and Moving Up': Jews in Homesteading Activity in North Dakota, 1900–1920," *Great Plains Quarterly* 10(Fall 1990): 228–44.

Shapiro, Edward. "American Jews and the Business Mentality." *Judaism* 27(1978): 214–21.

Shapiro, Judah J. *The Friendly Society: A History of the Workmen's Circle.* New York: Media Judaica, 1970.

Shatzky, Jacob. *Geschichte fun Yidn in Warshe* [in Yiddish]. New York: YIVO Institute for Jewish Research, 1953.

Shibutani, Tamotsu, and Kian M. Kwan. *Ethnic Stratification: A Comparative Approach.* New York: Macmillan, 1965.

Shohet, Moses. *She'elot U'Teshuvot Ohel Moshe.* Jerusalem: Zion, 1933.

Silverman, Morris. *Hartford Jews, 1659–1970.* Hartford: Connecticut Historical Society, 1970.

Singer, Ruth K. "To the Editor," *American Jewish History* 74(March 1984): 345–47.

Sklare, Marshall. *America's Jews.* New York: Random House, 1971.

———. "Jews, Ethnics, and the American City." *Commentary* 53, no. 4 (April 1972): 70–77.

Smith, Judith. *Family Connections: A History of Italian and Jewish Immigrant Lives in Providence, Rhode Island, 1900–1940.* Albany: State University of New York Press, 1985.

Snider, Joseph. *Credit Unions in Massachusetts.* Cambridge: Harvard University Press, 1939.

"Solving the Problem of Financing the Farmer." *New York Times,* December 8, 1912, sec. 6, p. 5.

Sombart, Werner. *The Jews and Modern Capitalism.* Glencoe, Ill.: Free Press, 1951.

Speisman, Joseph. *The Jews of Toronto: A History to 1937.* Toronto: McClelland & Stewart, 1979.

Stein, Siegfried. "The Development of the Jewish Law on Interest from the Biblical Period to the Expulsion of the Jews from England." *Historia Judaica* 17(1955): 3–40.

———. "The Laws on Interest in the Old Testament." *Journal of Theological Studies* 4(1953): 161–70.

Steinberg, Stephen. *The Ethnic Myth: Race, Ethnicity, and Class in America.* New York: Atheneum, 1981.

Strodtbeck, Fred. "Family Interaction, Values, and Achievement." In *The Jews: Social Patterns of an American Group,* ed. Marshall Sklare. Westport, Conn.: Greenwood, 1977.

Sung, Betty Lee. *Mountain of Gold: The Story of the Chinese in America.* New York: Macmillan, 1967.

Swidler, Ann. "Culture Versus Action: Symbols and Strategies." *American Sociological Review* 51(April 1986): 273–86.

Tabak, Robert. "The Mastbaum Loan System: 1920–1954, Low Interest Loans in Philadelphia." Philadelphia Jewish Archives Center, 1980.

Tannenbaum, P. "History of the Free Loan Association." Paper prepared for the Philadelphia Jewish Archives Center, 1922.

Thernstrom, Stephan. *The Other Bostonians: Poverty and Progress in the American Metropolis, 1880–1970.* Cambridge: Harvard University Press, 1973.

"This Bank Lends from the Heart." *Newark Sunday News,* November 26, 1950, p. 66.

Toll, William. *The Making of an Ethnic Middle Class: Portland Jewry Over Four Generations.* Albany: State University of New York Press, 1982.

The Torah: The Five Books of Moses. Philadelphia: Jewish Publication Society of America, 1962.

Trescott, Paul B. *Financing American Enterprise.* New York: Harper & Row, 1963.

The Universal Jewish Encyclopedia. 1969 ed. S.v. "Mastbaum, Jules E."

U.S. Congress Senate. *Reports on Immigrant Banks.* 61st Cong., 3d sess., 1911, S. Doc. 19.

Vélez-Ibañez, G. Carlos. *Bonds of Mutual Trust: The Cultural Systems of Rotating Credit Associations Among Urban Mexicans and Chicanos.* New Brunswick: Rutgers University Press, 1983.

Waldinger, Roger. *Through the Eye of the Needle: Immigrants and Enterprise in New York's Garment Trades.* New York: New York University Press, 1986.

Waldinger, Roger, Howard Aldrich, and Robin Ward. *Ethnic Entrepreneurs: Immigrant Business in Industrial Societies,* Newbury Park: Sage, 1990.

Watson, Frank Dekker. *The Charity Organization Movement in the United States: A Study in American Philanthropy.* New York: Macmillan, 1922.

Weber, Max. *Economy and Society.* Ed. Guenther Roth and Claus Wittich. New York: Bedminster, 1968.

———. *The Protestant Ethic and the Spirit of Capitalism.* Trans. Talcott Parsons. New York: Scribner's & Sons, 1958.

Weinberg, Sidney Stahl. *The World of Our Mothers.* New York: Schocken Books, 1988.

Wenger, Beth. "Jewish Women and Voluntarism: Beyond the Myth of Enabler." *American Jewish History* 79(Autumn 1989): 16–36.

Wilcox, Frances E. *A Statistical Study of Credit Unions in New York.* Chicago: University of Chicago Press, 1940.

Wilson, William Julius. *The Truly Disadvantaged: The Inner City, the Underclass, and Public Policy.* Chicago: University of Chicago Press, 1987.

Wolf, Edwin II. "The German–Jewish Influence in Philadelphia's Jewish Charities." In *Jewish Life in Philadelphia, 1830–1940,* ed. Murray Friedman. Philadelphia: Institute for the Study of Human Issues Publications, 1983.

Wolff, Henry W. *People's Banks: A Record of Social and Economic Progress.* London: King, 1919.

Woodward, C. Vann. *The Strange Career of Jim Crow.* 1955. Reprint. New York: Oxford University Press, 1974.

Yancey, William L., Eugene P. Ericksen, and Richard N. Juliani. "Emergent Ethnicity: A Review and Reformulation." *American Sociological Review* 41(June 1976): 391–402.

Yancey, William L., and Eugene P. Ericksen. "Response to Johnston and Yoels." *American Journal of Sociology* 83(1977): 737–41.

Zelizer, Viviana A. "The Social Meaning of Money: 'Special Monies'," *American Journal of Sociology* 95(September 1989): 342–77.

Zenner, Walter. *Minorities in the Middle: A Cross-Cultural Analysis.* Albany: State University of New York Press, 1991.

Index

197